D0891813

LANCASTRIAN KINGS

AND

LOLLARD KNIGHTS

LANCASTRIAN KINGS
AND
LOLLARD KNIGHTS

K. B. McFARLANE

Late Fellow of Magdalen College
Oxford

OXFORD
AT THE CLARENDON PRESS
1972

Oxford University Press, Ely House, London W. 1

GLASGOW NEW YORK TORONTO MELBOURNE WELLINGTON
CAPE TOWN IBADAN NAIROBI DAR ES SALAAM LUSAKA ADDIS ABABA
DELHI BOMBAY CALCUTTA MADRAS KARACHI LAHORE DACCA
KUALA LUMPUR SINGAPORE HONG KONG TOKYO

© OXFORD UNIVERSITY PRESS 1972

DA
255
.M3

PRINTED IN GREAT BRITAIN
AT THE UNIVERSITY PRESS, OXFORD
BY VIVIAN RIDLER
PRINTER TO THE UNIVERSITY

Contents

PART ONE. LANCASTRIAN KINGS

PART TWO. LOLLARD KNIGHTS

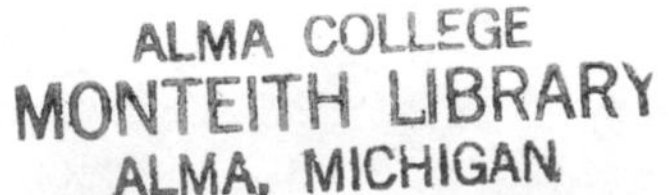

ALMA COLLEGE
MONTEITH LIBRARY
ALMA, MICHIGAN

PART ONE

LANCASTRIAN KINGS

Editor's Note

THE lectures on Henry IV were given to undergraduates in the Honours School of Modern History in Oxford. Mr. McFarlane first lectured on the reign of Henry IV in Trinity Term 1936, but in Michaelmas Term 1940 he extended his discussion to include Henry's career before 1399 and thereafter the scope of the lectures was not greatly changed. The lectures of 1940 were, however, completely rewritten in 1947 and it was on this text that McFarlane lectured, with minor modifications, in 1950 and 1953. It was never his intention that these lectures should be printed and to do so seventeen years after their last delivery requires some justification. There is no doubt that those who heard these lectures valued them both as an intelligible introduction to a neglected and baffling period and as a vivid presentation of the character and world of the first Lancastrian king. Since 1953 many of the problems with which the lectures deal have been the subject of research and publications, not least by McFarlane's own pupils, yet there is still no single work which deals with the career of Henry of Bolingbroke first as magnate and then as king and which approaches the problems of his reign in the light of his personality.[1]

In preparing the lectures for publication I have had to take some liberties with the text as it was delivered. Although McFarlane wrote —and rewrote—his lectures in full, the text was not wholly suitable for publication as it stood. Some ephemeral comments have been removed and some alterations of syntax and punctuation have been necessary in order to transfer the spoken word to the printed page. Two more important changes have also been made. First, some passages from the earlier series of lectures have been inserted into the text of 1947 where they added material it seemed desirable to preserve. Second, the text has been recast from eight lectures into six chapters. None of these alterations has seriously changed the character of the lectures, although what is now read will not be exactly what any generation of undergraduates actually heard. Mr. McFarlane, of course, left no references to his text and since these were introductory lectures at undergraduate level, to have added extensive footnotes would have

[1] J. L. Kirby's *Henry IV of England* (London, 1970), was published when these lectures were in the press.

been otiose. I have endeavoured to supply references with two considerations in mind: first that readers should be able to verify statements with the minimum of trouble; second, that undergraduates in particular should be made aware of the points on which subsequent research has elaborated or, in a few cases, modified, McFarlane's conclusions. Where McFarlane cited or drew on still unpublished material I have used the transcripts among his papers.

The single lecture on Henry V was delivered to the Oxford branch of the Workers' Educational Association in November 1954. It followed his lecture on Henry IV, based on the undergraduate series, which he had delivered in the previous year as part of a course on 'Notable Kings and Queens'. Although couched in a slightly different vein to the undergraduate lectures, it forms a natural complement to the study of Henry IV. The text is printed almost exactly as delivered and the manuscript sources quoted are from Mr. McFarlane's transcripts.

G. L. HARRISS

CHAPTER I

Henry of Bolingbroke

THE life of Henry of Bolingbroke falls into two sharply divided parts, separated by what it is usual, but unreasonable, to call the 'revolution' of 1399. From 1387 onwards he was closely involved in the political events of his time, and his acts as king can only be understood fully in the light of his scheming youth. I shall therefore be mixing biography with history, dealing with both the reign and the man, approaching the reign through the man. My subject is the life rather than the times, the whole life rather than just the reign, of him who is known variously as Henry of Bolingbroke, Henry of Lancaster, Henry, Earl of Derby, Henry, Duke of Hereford, and Henry IV, King of England.

To my mind at any rate the life and personality of Henry of Bolingbroke offer a series of fascinating problems, mostly unsolved and some probably insoluble. For most people he is only a rather dreary, if ambitious, fumbler, who was carried to the throne by a popular upheaval to which he contributed little, and whose short and sordid reign formed an interlude between that of the brilliant and erratic Richard and that of the still more brilliant and versatile conqueror of France. That is the impression to which one of the two great historians who have dealt with this period has lent all the weight of his influence. Before advancing further it would be as well to consider briefly the answers given by earlier historians to the problems of Henry's character and aims.

The historian to whose powerful influence I have just referred was Shakespeare. Thanks to the work of Dr. Tillyard and to that of Professor Dover Wilson,[1] we are no longer in any danger of

[1] E. M. W. Tillyard, *Shakespeare's History Plays* (London, 1944, paperback edn. 1962). J. Dover Wilson edited *Richard II* (1939), *1 Henry IV* and *2 Henry IV* (1946), and *Henry V* (1947) for the Cambridge University Press. See also G. Bullough, *Narrative and Dramatic Sources of Shakespeare*, vols. iii and iv (1960, 1962).

underestimating the dramatist's share in the interpretation of medieval English history. I use the word interpretation advisedly. The medieval chroniclers described events but they had little or no grasp of historical development and their criterion of selection was not a strictly historical one. Their Tudor successors, from Polydore Vergil onwards, had on the other hand a view of late medieval English history as a whole. They went to the two centuries before 1485 to prove a theory and they imposed an interpretation upon what they found. That is what we mean by calling them historians rather than chroniclers. Shakespeare was by far the greatest of them. He accepted much from Hall and Holinshed but he brought to his work a power which they lacked and one essential to a great historian; whereas Hall's kings and statesmen are scarcely even two-dimensional, some at least of Shakespeare's are alive. His reading of characters and events has immensely influenced all subsequent historians. His plays were for centuries what they were for the great Duke of Marlborough 'the only History of England I ever read'.

The fact that Shakespeare ignored Henry of Bolingbroke was therefore fatal for the latter's reputation. In the three historical plays which cover the period of his life, though two of them are devoted to his reign and what is more are named after him, he is a minor and therefore to all intents a pasteboard character, essential only to the action. So little did he fire Shakespeare's imaginative genius that there is not even any attempt to give a unity to his conduct and personality in his successive appearances. In *Richard II* he is the instrument of the king's downfall, but that downfall is clearly seen to be due to the frailties of Richard's youth rather than to a clash of character between him and his supplanter. Henry of Derby is just any man of action and ambition taking advantage of a rival's faults. In the two parts of *Henry IV* we do not encounter the same man; but he is not the hero—and not even the villain—of the plays which bear his name. He is merely a royal platitude, a lay-figure representing the majesty and cares of kingship which he superbly voices in the background, while the prince and Hotspur and Falstaff hold the stage. The prince is the hero and we are being prepared for the time when he shall ascend the throne and heal the diseases of the body politic in a war of conquest. Only once does Shakespeare offer us a glimpse of what might have happened had he focused his dramatic interest upon the king—in the scene between the dying Henry and his heir. Had Shakespeare written a play *about* Henry IV, it would have been the tragedy of a more complex Macbeth, and as such it would not have wanted historical accuracy: Henry *was* a more complex Macbeth. But since the Tudors were the heirs of Lancaster, to have traced their origins too obviously to a bloodthirsty usurper would have been unwise; Shakespeare preferred to ignore the tragedy of Bolingbroke.

This obscurity to which the Tudors condemned Henry has enveloped him nearly to our own times—obscurity rather than neglect. For no one could complain of neglect who had been the subject of a monograph of four volumes by Dr. J. H. Wylie. *The History of England under Henry the Fourth* is not, however, a biography. It is an attempt to do for those fourteen years at the opening of the fifteenth century what Froude and Macaulay had done for later times. It is a product, though a late product, of the classic age of English history-writing, and even as such it cannot be called a success. Not that it is not immensely valuable; its painstaking, almost morbid, collection of detail smooths the path of Wylie's successors, but it is not history, and scarcely more than the materials for history without even the virtue of completeness. It is a mine of information but the reader stumbles in confusion among the pit-props. Above all no portrait of the king emerges. Dr. Wylie lacks the quality in which the great Victorians abounded. However inaccurate they were, however devoid of insight into the structure and dynamic of the societies with which they dealt, they were at least interested in living men. While it is a part of the historian's business to analyse the great impersonal forces at work in society, he must take account of the human instruments, those who held power, through which those forces had in part to find expression. There is a tendency nowadays for medievalists to neglect both the forces and the instruments and to take refuge in a sterile antiquarianism. Of that school Wylie is a notable example. He had, as we should say, no sense of values; he collected all facts, great and small—like a medieval chronicler—without relating them to each other. He had no theme; his book lacks purpose and Henry IV himself remains mysterious.

There is, however, one exception to this tale of missed opportunities. Henry IV is one of the heroes—indeed *the* hero—of the third volume of Stubbs's *Constitutional History of England.* Stubbs rescued him from obscurity and made him the protagonist of a 'great constitutional experiment'. It will be necessary, therefore, to consider what sort of character and career Stubbs set up against the traditional or Shakespearian ones. Now although Stubbs was the contemporary of the great Victorians he did not write their kind of history. He was the father of the modern school of institutional historians, concerned primarily with the development of the institution of monarchy rather than with the kings who held temporary sway. Unlike many of his followers, however, Stubbs was too shrewd a man or perhaps too much a product of the Victorian school to neglect wholly the men who worked the institution. He avoided, that is to say, the great pitfall of constitutional history. Stubbs persuaded himself that among the kings of the fourteenth and fifteenth centuries Henry IV alone stood for the principle of what he called 'constitutionalism' in opposition to the absolutist tendencies which ultimately enjoyed a partial triumph under the houses of York and Tudor. He believed that the house of Lancaster had stood for this principle in the person of Earl Thomas against Edward II and that the tradition was handed down in the family and among its supporters under Edward III and Richard II to win a victory in the 'revolution' of 1399. He believed that after the disappearance of Henry IV it was kept alive by his half-brother Bishop Beaufort who contended for it, generally with success, until his death in 1447. I have no intention of criticizing this theory in general now beyond saying that I believe it to be wholly wrong. But it is important to see how Stubbs fitted together the facts of Bolingbroke's career to make his share in it convincing—or at least not obviously incredible. It demanded the rejection at many points of the traditional reading and the substitution of a highly flattering portrait of a king who had the misfortune to live before his time. It is fair to add that

Stubbs's rewriting of later medieval history in terms of Lancastrian constitutionalism and Yorkist absolutism never completely carried the day, but his ascendancy was rightly so great that it has never been submitted to the searching criticism it deserves. Nor has it been replaced by anything better; it has rather been eroded at many points and great fragments of it still survive at the foot of the cliff untouched—one such boulder is the New Monarchy of the Yorkists. Stubbs's interpretation of Henry IV's character has aroused so little interest that it has been allowed to crumble in neglect, but it is even now undemolished; yet it is in a way one of his most remarkable achievements.

Stubbs begins cautiously: 'There is scarcely one in the whole line of our kings of whose personality it is so difficult to get a definite idea.'[1] He finds the explanation of this in the controversial atmosphere in which the struggle of York and Lancaster inevitably shrouded it. He then proceeds to draw a sharp line between Henry as subject and Henry as king and to suggest that at the great crisis of his life in 1399 'he underwent some deep change of character. As Henry of Derby he is the adventurous, chivalrous crusader; prompt, energetic, laborious; the man of impulse rather than of judgement; led sometimes by his uncle Gloucester, sometimes by his father; yet independent in action, averse to bloodshed, strong in constitutional beliefs. As king we find him suspicious, cold-blooded and politic, undecided in action, cautious and jealous in private and public relations, and if not personally cruel, willing to sanction and profit by the cruelty of others.' Stubbs thought, however, that this deep change did not run right through Henry's composition. It was not a complete metamorphosis, Jekyll into Hyde; though deep it was less radical. It is a little difficult to grasp the distinction but it is none the less clear that one existed in Stubbs's mind and it is important to emphasize it; criticism can come later. For 'throughout his career [Henry] is consistently devout, pure in life, temperate and careful to avoid offence, faithful to the church and clergy, unwavering in orthodoxy . . . Throughout his career, too, he is consistent in political faith: the house of Lancaster had risen by advocating

[1] W. Stubbs, *Constitutional History of England*, 4th edn. (Oxford, 1890), iii. 7

constitutional principles and on constitutional principles they governed.'[1] And so on for two more pages in which a very persuasive attempt is made to reconcile the deep changes with the underlying consistency. Unsatisfactory though much of this may be, especially the constitutionalism, it is far more penetrating and written with much greater sympathetic understanding than any other portrait that we have. What is more, it goes deep even if it does not reach the heart of the problem of Bolingbroke's character. It touches, as no other analysis does, on the contradictions that need explaining and calls attention to the changes that undoubtedly occurred in Henry's later years.

There is no full contemporary description of Henry's person or his character by those who knew him. Capgrave's brief collection of anecdotes contains only one or two points which may prove instructive. For instance we learn from him that Henry as king had a love of casuistry, the science of Christian morals;[2] that he delighted to dispute hypothetical questions in ethics with the learned of his court may be a valuable clue when used in its right place. The chroniclers, rendered wary by revolution and in any case growing lazy at their task, tell us little. We are driven to seek the truths about his personality *through* his actions, with occasional assistance from more direct sources. The character, that is to say, must be largely imagined from behaviour; but even our knowledge of Henry's behaviour is incomplete—for the years before 1399 for example and, owing to an unexplained disappearance of Council records, during the critical period between 1407 and 1410. There are, however, some half-dozen aspects worth further study, aspects of his career and policy likely to reveal Henry under a brighter light than others, and if the study of each aspect in turn fails to dispel the mystery there is at least some hope that collectively they will be more successful.

The first topic I wish to consider is Bolingbroke's youth. He was about thirty-three years of age when he usurped the throne, that is, very nearly the same age as Richard himself; in all he only

[1] Stubbs, op. cit. iii. 8.

[2] John Capgrave, *Liber de Illustribus Henricis*, trans. F. C. Hingeston (R.S. 1858), p. 116.

lived for less than forty-seven. It is dangerous to concentrate on those last fourteen years, important though they are. It is more important to remember that he was not brought up as a future king; though a royal prince he was of a cadet line with small chance of becoming heir-presumptive. His life had therefore to be planned and perhaps lived as a subject not as a ruler, and for some dozen years Henry played a prominent part in politics without arousing any suspicion that he aimed at or even coveted the crown. Thirty-three was a mature age in the late fourteenth century; it was long enough for a man, especially a magnate and member of the royal family, to show the stuff he was made of. It is, after all, the age at which Richard II died. As we have seen, Stubbs thought the evidence considerable enough to bear a superstructure of ponderous judgements. There was one sentence that I did not quote earlier, but it might be taken as the text of my next three lectures: 'If with Gloucester and Arundel [Henry] is an appellant in 1388, it is against the unconstitutional position of the favourites; if against Gloucester and Arundel in 1397 he takes part with John of Gaunt and Richard, it is because he believes his old allies to have crossed the line which separates legal opposition from treason and conspiracy.'[1] We must ask: how far is it possible to read Bolingbroke's early political career on those lines? It is high time that this period was scrutinized. Yet Mr. Steel in his *Richard II* has very little to say about the man who was to supplant his hero on the throne. There is even less in Armitage Smith's life of *John of Gaunt*. But there is one source, hardly as yet tapped, which can be made to yield much that is fresh and valuable, namely the household accounts of Henry as Earl of Derby which are preserved among the archives of the duchy of Lancaster. Only those for his foreign expeditions have been printed and studied *in extenso*.[2] The rest tell us a great deal—mostly of only minor importance—about his clothes, pastimes, and his personal expenses generally, but they also help to determine his movements and to reveal his political connections, his

[1] Loc. cit.

[2] *Expeditions to Prussia and the Holy Land made by Henry, Earl of Derby*, ed. L Toulmin Smith (Camden Soc. 2nd ser., 1894).

visitors, and his correspondents. They enable one to construct a clearer picture than was previously possible of the great baron, the head of a widespread territorial affinity and the member of a class which was still almost international in its relationships. They show him surrounded from early youth by those who remained his ministers and confidants when he became king. From their very nature these accounts cannot answer the most important questions, but they fill out the picture at its barest corner; the years before the 'revolution'.[1]

Upon the second subject, the 'revolution' itself, much work has been done.[2] Since Stubbs wrote, the events of 1399 have been reinterpreted almost completely and enough has been brought to light to suggest that the reinterpretation reveals as never before the workings of the usurper's mind at the great turning-point of his career. It is not very far-fetched to suppose that at such a crisis Henry was unable entirely to conceal his motives; it is obviously the point upon which concentration is necessary.

Then thirdly, how far do Henry's methods of government bear out Stubbs's assertion about constitutional principles? A good deal of fresh material has been brought to light since Stubbs's day, comprising a few new chronicles, notably that of Thomas Walsingham from 1406 onwards, but chiefly conciliar documents. The warrants of the Council and the great offices of state still remain for the most part in manuscript. The results of a preliminary survey were published in 1913 by Baldwin in his book *The King's Council*, but this short reign occupies but a small place in his wider scheme. From these conciliar minutes

[1] P.R.O., *Records of the Duchy of Lancaster, Lists and Indexes*, vol. xiv, pp. 1–2. Hereafter cited as DL. Mr. McFarlane made transcripts of these, which have been used for the citations below. Extracts were also published by J. H. Wylie, *History of England under Henry IV* (London, 1884), iv, app. A.

[2] See principally, M. V. Clarke and V. H. Galbraith, 'The Deposition of Richard II', *Bulletin of the John Rylands Library*, xiv (1930), 125–81 (reprinted in *Fourteenth Century Studies* [Oxford, 1937], pp. 53–98); G. Lapsley, 'The Parliamentary Title of Henry IV', *E.H.R.* xlix (1934), 423–49, 577–606 (reprinted in *Crown, Community and Parliament* [Oxford, 1951], pp. 273–340); B. Wilkinson, 'The Deposition of Richard II and the Accession of Henry IV', *E.H.R.* liv (1939), 215–39, and *Constitutional History of Medieval England* (1952), ii, chap. 9; A. Steel, *Richard II* (Cambridge, 1941).

and memoranda it is possible to follow the day-to-day working of government, who were the king's inner circle of advisers, and what policies were discussed. Any serious attempt to understand the significance of the reign must start from them and I shall make frequent use of them. From them it is easy to pass to a consideration of Henry's treatment of the problems with which he was confronted, the problems of internal order, finance, and foreign policy. That leaves two aspects of somewhat unequal importance, namely the king's dealings with Parliament and his relations with his eldest son.

* * *

At the beginning of 1399 the exiled Bolingbroke, waiting in Paris, could look back on a full and varied career. At thirty-two years of age, he was already something of a European celebrity, a widower with a large family of young children, an experienced campaigner, an unrivalled jouster, and a politician with twelve years of first-hand knowledge of the tortuous manœuvres of Richard II's court and council. He was also the lord of considerable estates by the courtesy of England, that is to say by life tenure in the right of his dead wife, and heir to much more, the enormous principality of Lancaster. Who was he and how had he come by his wide experience?

Henry was born at his father's castle of Bolingbroke on the edge of the Lincolnshire fens in either 1366 or 1367. The commonly accepted date is 3 April 1367, but a better case can be made out for 4 April 1366. I do not propose to waste time dealing with the evidence on this point, but there can be little doubt that he was born within the year of which those days are the first and last, and that is good enough for anyone but an astrologer. It almost seems as if Henry himself did not know.[1] He was the fourth but only surviving son of John of Gaunt by his first wife, Blanche of Lancaster, sole heiress of the first ducal house of that name. When Henry usurped the throne he laid claim to it in the first instance by blood; it is therefore essential to bear in mind an accurate picture of his place in the tree of the royal family.

[1] The most recent discussion of the date of Henry's birth is in *The Complete Peerage*, vii. 417 n.a. Cf. J. H. Wylie, op. cit. iv. 330–1 (app. DD).

His father, born at Ghent in 1340, was the third son of Edward III to survive childhood. Gaunt's eldest brother, the Black Prince, had an only child in Richard II; the second son, Lionel, Duke of Clarence, died in 1368 leaving an only child, Philippa, Countess of March. Two lines, though each was a single thread (Philippa, however, had four children), therefore stood between him and the throne of England. His father was a claimant to that of Castile, but since this was by right of his second wife, Constance, his eldest son did not inherit that claim.

But although the prospect of a throne was distant, Bolingbroke, as the eldest son of Gaunt and the only son of the Duchess Blanche, was heir to the finest inheritance under the English crown. The duchy of Lancaster incorporated the lands of the ancient earldoms of Lancaster, Leicester, Derby, Lincoln, and Salisbury. There were only seven counties in England in which the duke had no manors or lands. He had over thirty castles and his revenues were such that in a single year, between 2 February 1394 and 2 February 1395, John of Gaunt was able to spend over £15,000. Gaunt's landed income was about £12,000 p.a. and in most years he was in receipt of revenue from other sources. In 1394–5, for example, he received large sums from the royal Exchequer and from his pension under the Spanish treaty.[1] Until Richard, Duke of York, in the next century became heir to the houses of Clarence, March, Ulster, and Cambridge, there was nothing except the Black Prince's landed income of some £8,600 p.a. to compare even remotely in wealth and territorial influence with the vast duchy which Edward III conferred on his beloved third son.

It was not, however, until he became king that Henry entered on the Lancastrian inheritance. For his father lived until 1399

[1] The certificate of account of the receiver-general of the duchy for 2 Feb. 1394–2 Feb. 1395 is printed in S. Armitage Smith, *John of Gaunt* (London, 1904), pp. 447–50. The auditors' *valors*, for 1393–4 and 1394–5, a summary of which is printed in R. Somerville, *History of the Duchy of Lancaster* (London, 1953), i. 92, gives the gross value of the estates. Under the Treaty of Spain of 1388 the Duke of Lancaster was to receive a capital payment of £100,000 and an annual pension of £6,600 (P. E. Russell, *The English Intervention in Spain and Portugal* [Oxford, 1955], p. 506). The receiver-general's certificate shows that almost the whole of this sum was paid in two instalments for the year 1394–5.

and crown and patrimony came to Bolingbroke together at the 'revolution'. His childhood and upbringing were those usual to his class and need not detain us long. He is first heard of on 30 September 1372 sharing a household with his two young sisters, Philippa, the future Queen of Portugal, and Elizabeth, afterwards in succession Countess of Pembroke and Huntingdon. Their treasurer, Sir John Cheyne, received £200 p.a. for the expenses of their establishment.[1] The sisters had a governess who was the young and beautiful wife of one of their father's retainers. Their mother Blanche had died in September 1369 and two years later their father married Constance, daughter and heiress of Peter I of Castile and Leon. It was a marriage of policy only and at about the same time the duke formed a less regular, but as it happened more permanent, connection with his daughters' governess. Dame Katherine Swinford was the daughter of a Flemish soldier, Sir Pain Roet, who had entered the service of Edward III; his other daughter Philippa was the wife of the poet Chaucer. Sir Hugh Swinford, the husband, died in Gascony in 1372. His widow, the governess, continued, however, to give birth to children, six of them in the course of the next ten years. Many years later in 1396 when the Duchess Constance too had died, the mistress of a quarter of a century married Gaunt as his third wife. Her four surviving children were legitimized in 1397 to form the family of Beaufort. The family life of the house of Lancaster must have been somewhat free and easy. It is perhaps not surprising that one of Bolingbroke's sisters, Elizabeth, went to the bad.

In December 1374 Henry was given a 'governor' of his own, Thomas Burton, one of his father's retainers and a servant of his maternal grandfather, the warlike Duke Henry.[2] The next we hear of him is his addition to the household of the future Richard II. Richard was recognized as Prince of Wales in November 1376 at the request of the Good Parliament and on 1 January 1377 his household was suitably augmented to dignify his new position.[3]

[1] *John of Gaunt's Register, 1371–1376*, ed. S. Armitage Smith (Camden Soc., 1911), i. 127 (no. 299).

[2] Ibid. 251 (no. 679).

[3] T. F. Tout, *Chapters in Medieval Administrative History* (Manchester, 1933), iv. 189–91.

The two princes were admitted together to the order of the Garter and knighted on St. George's Day 1377 and at the same time Henry was granted by his father the courtesy title of Earl of Derby.[1] When, on 21 June, Richard succeeded his grandfather on the throne, his eleven-year-old cousin bore the sword before him at his coronation.[2] In the following year, when John of Gaunt went to France, Henry was put in nominal charge of the Lancastrian lands with the title of 'Warden of the regality of the palatine county of Lancaster' until his return. The administration was in fact in the charge of the duke's councillors and officials; but the heir was already being given a share of responsibility.[3] What, alas, we do not know is how he and his royal playmate got on together. Henry seems to have continued to spend his time at court until 1381.

A year before that, however, the first event of real importance in his life had occurred with his marriage to Mary Bohun, younger of the two daughters and co-heiresses of Humphrey, Earl of Hereford, Essex, and Northampton. Her elder sister Eleanor had already married Edward III's youngest son, Thomas of Woodstock (born January, 1355). As co-heiresses they divided their inheritance equally—a fertile source of possible dispute and one which did indeed eventually play its part in estranging the bridegrooms whom these two marriages at first brought together. The betrothal took place in July 1380 and the marriage followed probably before the end of the year at the bride's home at Rochford in Essex. The king lent ten minstrels and the Earl of Cambridge four.[4] Mary Bohun was only ten or at the most eleven years old at the date of her wedding, and it was not intended that the married children should at first live together. Fourteen was at this time regarded as the earliest age at which a

[1] G. F. Beltz, *Memorials of the Order of the Garter* (London, 1841), p. 11, cites a letter of Privy Seal ordering two hoods of white-cloth lined with blue on 4 Apr. 1377 for the two new knights of the Garter, Richard and Henry. Cf. *The Anonimalle Chronicle*, ed. V. H. Galbraith (London, 1927), p. 106.

[2] *Anon. Chron.*, p. 114. *Complete Peerage*, vii. 413, 417.

[3] R. Somerville, *History of the Duchy of Lancaster*, i. 120.

[4] *John of Gaunt's Register, 1379–1383*, ed. E. C. Lodge and R. Somerville (Camden Soc. 3rd ser., 1937), i. 180, 222 (no. 868).

girl might become a wife, and Mary remained for the present under her mother's roof while Henry returned to his own household.[1] However, they must have met occasionally, for on 16 April 1382 the Countess of Derby gave birth to her first child, a son who not unnaturally failed to live; his father was sixteen, his mother thirteen.[2] We have no record of any more children for a time, but in 1386 the young couple set up house together at Monmouth and it was there that the future Henry V was born on 16 September 1387.[3] He was followed by a child each year except one until in 1394 Mary Bohun died in childbirth at the age of twenty-five, the mother of at least seven sons and daughters of whom six survived. The weakness of the Lancastrian royal stock is sufficiently explained by the treatment to which its ancestress was subjected. Active and hard living though they were, none of Henry IV's children were particularly strong, and most of them died prematurely. Three of his sons were without legitimate offspring; only one of his grandchildren had issue and even that one, Henry VI, is only the putative father of Edward, Prince of Wales. However, in 1394 the future of the Lancastrian dynasty seemed assured; eighty years later it was extinct.

It is perhaps unnecessary to look very far to find a reason why Bolingbroke and Richard II, though they were thrown together as boys, failed to become friends. Playmates do not always love one another even when they are cousins, and the youthful companions of infant kings have a particularly delicate task to avoid offence. Richard and Henry had little in common and it was the subject who had the greater share of the qualities that make a popular king. It would not therefore be difficult to guess the stages of their estrangement, but as a matter of fact there is some evidence for this.

The last known occasion when they were together as boys was in June 1381 at the time of the Peasants' Revolt. On 13 June the

[1] John of Gaunt assigned to Joan, Countess of Hereford, an annuity of 100 marks for the keep of Mary until she should reach the age of fourteen. *Register, 1379–83*, i. 210 (no. 646), 220 (no. 679), ii. 309 (no. 996). Mary came of age in 1384.

[2] J. H. Wylie, op. cit. iii. 325.

[3] J. H. Wylie and W. T. Waugh, *The Reign of Henry V* (Cambridge, 1929), iii. 427 (app. B).

rebels broke into the City of London while the king, the court, and the ministers shut themselves up in the Tower. Next day the king went to Mile End to try to persuade the men of Essex, encamped there, to go home. He was accompanied by the courtiers, the princess-mother, and a strong band of armed men, but the unpopular ministers, the Chancellor Sudbury, the Treasurer Hales, and with them Bolingbroke, were left behind in the ill-defended Tower. Now some contemporaries believed that Richard—or rather the courtiers of the princess's circle—deliberately abandoned the ministers to the vengeance of the mob. We cannot say that it is more than possible. The court was ready to be thought friendly towards the peasants, even though the latter were demanding the destruction of the baronial class, and certainly succeeded in persuading the rebels themselves that the king was with them. It is necessary to remember this in estimating the degree of suspiciousness about their leaving Derby behind. He was the son and heir of the chief object of the peasants' hatred, the Duke of Lancaster. The latter, on hearing of the revolt while in the north, hurried across the Scottish border. His duchess was chased in a panic up the midlands to Pontefract, only to have the gates shut in her face, and on the night before the meeting at Mile End the rebels had celebrated their entry into the capital by pillaging and destroying the duke's palace of the Savoy, the richest mansion in England. It does therefore seem rather strange that the heir of Lancaster was left behind in the Tower and that the drawbridge was not up. During the king's absence the mob entered the building unresisted, brought out those who were taking refuge there, including the wretched Archbishop of Canterbury, and executed them on Tower Hill. Derby too was seized and nearly suffered the same fate, but was saved by the intervention of one John Ferrour, whose motives are unknown. He was a disabled soldier and pensioner of the Black Prince, who may have been a member of the royal household. Derby remembered him with gratitude and repaid him liberally when he became king.[1] What happened next is not clear, but Richard

[1] J. E. Tyler, *Memoirs of the Life and Character of Henry V* (London, 1838), i. 7. *Cal. Pat. Rolls, 1399–1401*, pp. 86, 423.

did not return to the Tower and when Henry is next heard of in the autumn he was with his father in Yorkshire. This episode can hardly have failed to make a deep impression on a boy of fifteen and it supplies some reason for the coldness which developed between Derby and the court.

Another reason is hinted at in the earliest of the household accounts of Derby which has survived, that for the accounting year Michaelmas 1381 to Michaelmas 1382 (if there had been earlier ones still they would have been destroyed in the Savoy). Probably at the time when he made his son an earl, Lancaster had granted Henry for his support, among other revenues, the manor of Passenham, Northamptonshire. It was near Stony Stratford, whose inhabitants were the tenants of Aubrey de Vere, one of the inner circle of the king's household officers, at that date acting Chamberlain. His nephew Robert, Earl of Oxford, was soon to become Richard's chief friend and hated favourite. From entries in Derby's accounts it appears that at some time in 1381, possibly during the Peasants' Revolt, the men of Stony Stratford invaded Passenham and attacked its inhabitants. A similar attack took place on 29 May 1382 when Passenham was defended by sixty bowmen specially dispatched by Derby from Leicester for that purpose. The battle of Passenham makes a number of appearances in the accounts. Finally Hugh Waterton, the young earl's receiver and man-of-business—he was one day to be a member of Henry IV's council —was sent for by the king 'about the discord between the tenants of my lord of Derby in Passenham and the tenants of Aubrey de Vere in Stony Stratford'. Waterton told Richard 'that a false suggestion had been made to the king' in the matter. The interview seems to have been unavailing and Derby never obtained justice against de Vere from the partial Richard.[1] Here then we

[1] DL 28/1/1, Mich. 1381–2, fo. 8v: 'Et in expensis Willelmi provisoris domini euntis de Leycestria usque Stonystratford ad scrutandum malefactores qui fuerant contra tenentes domino [*sic*] de Passenham existent' extra per iii dies quolibet die vid. xviiid. Et xxix die Maii dominus misit ad Stonystratford lx valettos cum arcubus ad capiendum predictos malefactores et datum erat eis ad iantaculum xxvis. viiid. loquere cum Waterton.'
fo. 9 'In expensis Hugonis de Waterton euntis de Leycestria ad Banneburi iiiito die Junii ad reportandum equum qui furatus fuit apud Passenham cui circa vc

have the existence of a definite grievance against the courtier-group and against the defects of royal justice. This should be remembered when a reason is sought for Derby's action in taking up arms to stop Robert de Vere when he marched to aid Richard in the autumn of 1387.

Before dealing with that first political crisis of his career it is necessary to give a few details of Derby's education and to try to picture what sort of man he was when he came of age in the very year of the Appellants' rising. In the autumn of 1386 when Richard's minister Suffolk was impeached, Derby was still a minor; he was nevertheless summoned to the Lords and probably took his seat, though there is no evidence that he played any part in the proceedings.[1]

Hugh Waterton's accounts for 1381–2 are our only really solid evidence for this period. The main series now preserved in the archives of the duchy of Lancaster begins on 1 March 1391 and is continuous until the end of the century. Apart from a Wardrobe account of 1387–8, nothing else survives from the 1380s. Waterton's account is short and leaves much unmentioned. We learn from it nothing, for example, of Derby's education, whereas Henry's later accounts have by contrast many details about the education of his sons. From other sources we know that as king Henry wrote English and French readily, that he knew at least some Latin tags, that he was a patron of poets and that he was

armigerorum et valettorum de Coventria et de patria advenierant quibus fecit nomine domini unum iantaculum xxxviii s. vi d. loquere cum Waterton. In expensis Hugonis de Waterton euntis de Leycestria usque ad Passenham xi° die Junii pro curia tenenda ibidem et ad faciendum tenentes domini et vicinos suos de Stonystratford concordare pro verberacione tenentium domini. Et stetit extra curiam per iii dies quolibet die xii d. iii s.'

fo. 9ᵛ: 'Et in expensis Hugonis de Waterton euntis de Leycestria ad Londoniam et de Londonia ad Yesthamstede ad Regem per preceptum domini mei Lancastrie ad narrandum regi de discordia inter tenentes domini mei Derbie de Passenham et tenentes domini Aubray le Veer de Stonystretford quia suggestio non vera facta fuit domino nostro Regi, et dictus Hugo stetit extra ibidem et in negotio domini apud London per x dies, quolibet die xiid. x s.' (McFarlane's transcript.) For Hugh Waterton's career in Henry's service see the summary in R. Somerville, *Duchy of Lancaster*, i. 385.

[1] *Report on the Dignity of a Peer*, iv. 722. Derby had first been summoned to Parliament in Oct. 1385. Ibid. 718.

a skilled musician. About all this Waterton's account is silent. It tells us, however, other things; that Gaunt had made over to his sons the three manors of Soham in Cambridgeshire, Daventry, and Passenham in Northamptonshire, and an annuity of 250 marks from the duchy lands in Norfolk. These brought in an income of just over £350 p.a.[1] Like most members of the fourteenth-century governing class, Derby lived a strange, roaming, unsettled life; both as baron and king he never ceased to perambulate the country. The account for the financial year Michaelmas 1381–Michaelmas 1382 finds him at Pontefract in Yorkshire. He comes south to spend Christmas at Leicester. In January he is in Westminster and on the 14th attends the coronation of Anne of Bohemia. The rest of the winter is passed at Hertford with a visit to Windsor for a chapter of the Garter on St. George's Day. From the beginning of May until the following Michaelmas he is continuously on the move with Leicester as a base but with two progresses to Yorkshire, another to Lincoln, and a fourth to Kenilworth. That is a typical year.

These accounts also bear witness to the scale of his living. He showed a certain extravagance in his dress. There are the numerous suits of velvet and cloth of gold, embroidered all over with his favourite devices, above all the forget-me-not, splendid furs and the costly jewels. On the other hand he seems to have been much less of a gambler than were many of his fellow nobles, among whom his uncle, the Black Prince, was probably the most reckless; Henry's rare losses may be symptomatic of his cautious temper.[2] There was nothing moderate, however, in his indulgence in the fashionable and dangerous sport of jousting. During the year 1381–2 he had taken part in two tournaments, one in London at the time of the queen's coronation, the other on May Day at Hertford.[3] Although only sixteen, he was already laying the

[1] In this year his receipts from the three manors totalled £191. 13*s*. 4*d*. and from Gaunt's Norfolk manors £146. 13*s*. 4*d*. The account records a total receipt of £426. 9*s*. 11¾*d*. DL 28/1/1, fo. 1. See *Register, 1379–83*, i. 228 (no. 706) for the grant of Soham to him. Derby was in receipt of 250 marks p.a. from his father before 1380. Ibid. i. 68 (no. 206); ii. 418 (no. 308a).

[2] See the extracts printed by Wylie, *Henry IV*, iv, app. A.

[3] DL 28/1/1, fos. 4, 6. Besides his outfit for the coronation, including his mantle of St. George, the accounts record the purchase of a quantity of silver gilt and copper gilt 'spangles' of roses for the jousts.

foundation of that skill as a jouster which was to bring him so much fame and popularity. It was in 1386 that he emerged the victorious favourite in a series of jousts held in the capital. The citizens of London were passionately interested in the tournament and Derby was enormously popular with them in consequence. It was this popularity which was to undo him when too openly demonstrated in 1398, but which was to carry him in triumph to the throne a year later. By the spring of 1390 his reputation as a jouster was firmly established on a larger stage after a prolonged tournament held in the marches outside Calais, commanding the discerning praise of Froissart—who was no mean connoisseur. Of his affability, his courtesy, his vigour not only of body but of mind, all are agreed. But he was far from being merely the 'strenuissimus Comes Derbiae' of one writer. He had other qualities than those of mere physical skill and personal charm. He is said to have been a keen musician: his accounts show that he maintained, as did most of his well-to-do contemporaries, a small troup of minstrels, and at the height of the political crisis of 1387–8 he was purchasing a recorder for his own use.[1] He followed his father in patronage of poets like Chaucer and Gower; he regularly, as Earl of Derby, employed the same painters and jewellers as the court. He was also a man of some formal education: the first King of England of whom we possess letters written in his own hand; and these are in both French and English. Marginal notes from his pen are frequently met with in the state papers of his reign; once the words 'necessitas non habet legem' pay tribute to the elegance of his scholarship and to his political realism.[2] Scholarship attracted him; he was learned and had a retentive memory for what he read. One dictum of his is recorded; during his exile he attended a debate and lectures at the University of Paris, then at the height of its fame and influence, where he is said to have remarked that while they had in England clerks more subtle, yet those in Paris had the true and sound theology.[3]

[1] DL 28/1/2, Mich. 1387–8, fo. 15v: 'Et pro i fistula nomine Recordor empta Londoniis pro domino iiis. iiii d.'

[2] For this signet letter, dated from Bristol on 23 October 1403, see *Catalogue of the Museum of the Public Record Office* (London, 1948), p. 34.

[3] J. H. Wylie, *Henry IV*, iv. 138.

When he became king he tried to induce the bluestocking and early feminist Christine de Pisan to reside in his court, but she refused. He valued books. On a short visit to the monastery of Bardney in Lincolnshire in August 1406 he spent a whole morning in the library.[1] Not surprisingly his sons, long before 1399, had been well grounded in their books, possibly, according to tradition, up to university level; three of them were certainly to become notable bibliophiles. Henry, in fact, was that comparatively rare combination, the man of action who was also an intellectual. In this heredity triumphed. For he was not only the grandson of the victor of Crécy, but also of his namesake Henry, first Duke of Lancaster, both one of Edward III's most distinguished captains in France and the author of a book of mystical devotion.

Before 1390 his household staff was on the whole modest: a couple of knights, a couple of esquires, a receiver, a wardrober, an armourer, a number of grooms, clerks, and pages and, of course, a chaplain. You cannot run a very large establishment on £350 a year. When we next have a view of his income we find him spending just under £2,000 in the nine months from March to December 1391.[2] On coming of age he had taken possession of his wife's inheritance and had begun to live on a scale more befitting his rank.

[1] Ibid. ii. 460; iv. 136, 139.

[2] DL 28/3/3. The account is described as running from 1 Mar. 1391 to 1 Jan 1392, but also as comprising a period of 277 days. Probably, therefore, 31 Mar. was intended. The total receipt is given as £3,315. 10*s*. 7½*d*.; total expenditure as £1,949. 7*s*. 5½*d*. Of this receipt no less than £1,574. 9*s*. 11*d*. was arrears; his Welsh lands provided £1,060 and he drew £311. 8*s*. 4*d*. from the royal Exchequer. Soham and Daventry continued to be his most valuable single properties.

CHAPTER II

Appellant and Crusader 1387–1397

ON approaching the crisis of 1386–8 it is necessary to recall Stubbs's dictum that Derby joined the Appellants because he was 'against the unconstitutional position of the favourites' just as ten years later he deserted them because he believed 'his old allies to have crossed the line which separates legal opposition from treason and conspiracy'. Stubbs boldly asserts his faith in the strength of Derby's constitutional beliefs, in his political consistency, above all in his consistency in siding with Gloucester against Richard in 1387–8 and against Gloucester with Richard in 1397. In considering this interpretation it should be made clear from the start that there is not the slightest *direct* evidence that Derby acted from constitutional principle; the only basis on which it is possible to maintain Stubbs's thesis is a circumstantial one. As expressed by Stubbs this constitutional principle is that of the mean of a balance of power between king and lords. Richard, says Stubbs, overstepped the limits in 1387; Gloucester overstepped them in 1397; Derby with unusual—not to say precocious—awareness of the strait and narrow way impartially assisted in reducing each in turn to conformity. It has only to be pondered over to begin to look slightly absurd. If, therefore, it is possible to explain Derby's actions on a theory in itself less unlikely, there is every reason for stating it and some for preferring it. There is certainly no need for Stubbs's view to account for Derby's behaviour. That he acted from a mixture of prejudice, self-interest, and miscalculation is just as probable. I would maintain that in politics Henry was not a man of constitutional principle at all but an opportunist and a *politique*, that his choice of sides was made from a compound of personal preference and calculation, and that to read consistency into it is only a waste of time. Had he in speech or writing taken his stand on principle alone it would be necessary to agree with Stubbs, but so far as we know he did not.

The first indication that Derby was likely to throw in his lot with the opposition is a statement by Walsingham, not necessarily accurate, that he was among those who in the spring of 1387 were obnoxious to the king and the court. It was not until the autumn that he openly joined his brother-in-law and uncle Thomas of Woodstock, now Duke of Gloucester, and the group of lords soon to be known as the Appellants.[1] Reasons for the estrangement of Derby and Richard have already been suggested; his father likewise had personal reasons for hostility to the court. The truth is that the relations between the Lancastrian faction and the inner circle of Richard's friends had never been really cordial. From the first the grounds for co-operation had been convenience and it had always been an uneasy alliance. With Richard II's personal intervention in government, which grew steadily after 1383, wilder counsels began to prevail at court. The king, it is true, succeeded in winning over to his side a number of Lancastrian retainers, the most notable of whom were Michael de la Pole, Sir Richard Adderbury, and Sir William Beauchamp. There were constant quarrels between the king and his uncle of Lancaster and more than once the Princess of Wales prevented an open breach only with difficulty. Her death in the summer of 1385 removed one of the few influences in favour of moderation, though it is fair to say that Gaunt was extremely long-suffering in face of frequent provocation. The estrangement between the courtiers and the Lancastrians came to a head in the autumn of 1385 when Richard rejected Gaunt's advice on his Scottish expedition. Following the king's refusal to listen to the duke's demand for an invasion of France this made co-operation impossible. It led to the duke's disappearance from the English scene for the next three years, since Richard, in order to get rid of him, encouraged and materially assisted him to attempt the conquest of the Castilian throne.

There was certainly nothing constitutional about these differences. Gaunt's motives were both personal and political, but

[1] *Chronicon Angliae*, ed. E. M. Thompson (R.S., 1874), pp. 378, 383.

he never questioned Richard's right to govern as he pleased. Derby could have learned nothing about constitutional opposition from his father whose notions of government were as autocratic as those of Edward III. Politically, however, his departure left Richard face to face with critics who had none of Gaunt's attachment to the rights of monarchy. The Lancastrian 'interest' had been for years the largest single family group in English politics; by occupying a central position it had checked any tendency to a clear-cut division between the court on the one hand and a united aristocracy on the other. So long as it maintained its alliance with the courtiers there was little chance of trouble. Had Richard had the sense to realize that, the humiliations of 1386–8 would have been spared him. After Gaunt's return he had learnt that lesson well enough to keep his uncle on his side for the rest of the latter's life.

Lancaster's departure left the way open for the remnant of his supporters under the youthful and hot-headed leadership of his son to join up with Gloucester and the Arundels in the years of crisis that now opened. The large force with which the duke set sail for Spain—about 8,000 fighting-men—must have drained his resources heavily and limited his son's capacity to raise an army in England in his absence.[1] Gaunt was seen off by Derby from Plymouth on 8 July 1386. It was not until 19 November 1389 that he landed again in England at the same port. As before, the administration of his estates was committed nominally to his son.[2]

Trouble had begun without any warning in the 'Wonderful' Parliament of 1 October 1386. During the previous summer there had been a panic caused by the mustering of a French army at Sluys for an invasion of England. It was in reaction from this panic that an attack was launched on the ministers as soon as the estates met. The lead was taken by Thomas of Woodstock, newly raised in the previous year to the duchy of Gloucester, and by Thomas Arundel, Bishop of Ely and brother of the earl. Richard's resistance was overcome by a reference to the fate of his great-

[1] Russell, *The English Intervention in Spain and Portugal*, pp. 417–18.

[2] Armitage Smith, *John of Gaunt*, pp. 310–11; Somerville, *Duchy of Lancaster* i. 120.

grandfather, Edward II, and his Chancellor, Michael de la Pole, was impeached, found guilty and sentenced to forfeiture and imprisonment. Parliament ended on 28 November leaving Richard saddled with a Continual Council without which he was not to govern. This was appointed on 20 November and was to hold office for a year. It is important to notice that it contained only two of the five future Appellants, Gloucester and Arundel; but Bishop Arundel, as Chancellor, was also included. Gloucester and the Arundels were the nucleus of the coming association.

Richard soon retired to Windsor, leaving the Council permanently resident at Westminster, and for the next eleven months toured the country, trying to raise his supporters, preparing to recover his authority by force and elaborating a new theory of the prerogative. It is this last which introduced—but on the king's side—a constitutional element into what had been hitherto, and for the Appellants largely remained, a political quarrel. The attack on the ministers in 1386 had been primarily a criticism of their conduct of affairs, of corruption and inefficiency. That in 1387 it developed into a constitutional conflict was largely due to the fact that Richard chose to take his stand on the prerogative. The king's impetuousness gave a quarrel over policies and personalities the character of a constitutional crisis. The opposition was far less ready than the king to clothe its programme in high-sounding general principles and merely swept aside the king's theories of kingship by a resort to force. In 'appealing' his advisers and the judges whom he had coerced into supporting his conception of the prerogative, the lords enunciated no theory of constitutionalism, although such action implicitly repudiated Richard's exalted notions of monarchy. Their threats of deposition and coercion were as barefaced as their ambitions. The malcontents of 1386, of whom Gloucester was the recognized leader, were an opposition of have-nots. They drew popular support from the fear of French invasion and their best argument was that of damaged national prestige. The behaviour of the Appellants (their choice of an 'appeal' rather than the process of impeachment for example) throughout the period of crisis, and for that matter afterwards, makes it difficult if not absolutely impossible to treat their constitutionalism as even skin-deep.[1] They hated the favourites, they wanted revenge and a share of the fruits of office so far denied them. At least one of them even had hopes of the crown itself. No one but Stubbs has felt inclined to respect the genuineness of their few and half-hearted constitutional professions. The best argument in their favour is that they acted in self-defence. It was pretty clear from Richard's questions to the judges in August 1387 at Nottingham that he intended violence, and it was then that the rumour circulated that Derby was one of those most obnoxious to the king and court.

Unfortunately we do not know why. From the time of his father's embarkation in July 1386 until his appearance at a council of war with the four other Appellants at Huntingdon on 12 December 1387, his attitude towards the political crisis is undiscoverable; even his movements are uncertain. Although Gaunt had left him in nominal charge of his affairs, the few records of the duchy council show no sign that the titular guardian was consulted; presided over by a group of tried officials, among them the duke's chamberlain, Sir Robert Swillington and his chief steward, Sir Thomas Hungerford, the council continued to meet in London and to receive frequent communications from Spain.[2] It is difficult therefore to maintain that the considerable private army with which Derby joined the Appellants was drawn from the already reduced manpower of the Lancastrian affinity. It is more likely to have come principally from his own circle based upon the estates which he then owned, since by 1387 he was in possession of his wife's inheritance. In the share-out of the Bohun inheritance, a third had been reserved as the widow's dower, a third

[1] Since these lectures were written, the nature of parliamentary appeals of treason and the reasons why this procedure was adopted have been intensively debated in the following works: T. F. T. Plucknett, 'State Trials under Richard II', *T.R.H.S.*, 5th ser. 2 (1952); 'Impeachment and Attainder', ibid., 5th ser. 3 (1953); B. Wilkinson, *Constitutional History of Medieval England* (London, 1952), ii, chap. viii; J. G. Bellamy, 'Appeal and Impeachment in the Good Parliament', *B.I.H.R.* 39 (1966); A. Rogers, 'Parliamentary Appeals of Treason in the Reign of Richard II', *American Journal of Legal History*, 8 (1964); R. H. Jones, *The Royal Policy of Richard II* (Oxford, 1968), chap. v.

[2] *John of Gaunt's Register, 1379–1383*, ii. 405–10.

centred on Pleshy in Essex had gone to Thomas of Gloucester, and a third had come to Henry. Of his share the most important part was the marcher lordship of Brecon, but it included manors in several southern and western counties. The effect of the division is seen in the respective Bohun titles which the brothers-in-law assumed. Gloucester calls himself, besides Duke of Gloucester and Earl of Buckingham, Earl of Essex; Henry is described in his formal documents as Earl of Derby, Hereford, and Northampton, Lord of Brecon. As the joint inheritors of the great Bohun 'connection' there was much to draw Thomas and Henry together, especially in the absence of the latter's father. There is really little need to look further for a motive, especially when it was, as we know, reinforced by a quarrel with the elder de Vere and the experience of Richard's coldness if not active hostility. It would have been unlike the knightly, adventurous, and inexperienced Derby to keep out of a fight, and if he had to choose a side there was every reason to choose that of Gloucester. I doubt if there was more in it than that.

Once committed, it was characteristic of Derby to take an active share in what was to be done. But before even a beginning could be made a difference of opinion arose among the Appellants themselves which threatened to render all their plans ineffectual. If we are to understand the next decade of English politics it is essential to remember that the Appellants were a coalition. The division which became obvious in 1397 between Gloucester, Arundel, and Warwick on the one hand and Derby and Nottingham on the other existed from the first. It was not until late in 1387 that the latter two joined the original three, and their background was different. Neither Derby nor Nottingham was old enough to have been summoned to Parliament before 1386 and neither played any known part in it. They were novices learning the ropes. Both belonged to the Lancastrian faction and not, as did the three older Appellants, to the embittered older generation of the nobility. Thomas Mowbray, Earl Marshal and Earl of Nottingham, was born in the same year as Derby, and as Richard's kinsman and coeval had likewise spent his youth at court. At one time he had indeed bade fair to become the king's chief favourite, but his nose had been put out of joint by the success of Robert de Vere.[1] He was an ambitious, unintelligent, restless, and fundamentally weak character. In 1384 he became a brother-in-law of the Arundels by his marriage with their sister. Hatred of the de Veres and kinship with one of the elder Appellants, as in the case of Derby, provided the explanation of his attendance at the council of war at Huntingdon.

Of the three older associates, Thomas of Woodstock was nearly thirty-three in December 1387 and had sat in Parliament since 1376. From the beginning of Richard II's reign he had taken a prominent, though not spectacularly successful, part in the wars against France and Scotland both by land and sea. A rough, ruthless, and self-confident man he had been a prominent enemy of the court from the first, and had brutally threatened his nephew the king in 1386 with the fate of Edward II. His closest associate, Richard, Earl of Arundel, was if anything coarser and more ruthless. His life is punctuated with violent quarrels. Born in 1346, he had succeeded his father at the age of thirty and had been a councillor since Richard II's accession. His war service, mainly at sea, showed him to be brilliant but unreliable; yet he was a brave, proud man and a savage hater. He too had married a Bohun, an aunt of Mary and the Duchess of Gloucester.[2] The third of the older Appellants, Thomas Beauchamp, Earl of Warwick, was a year Arundel's senior, had seen some service in France with John of Gaunt and on Richard's minority Councils. He was an indolent, weak man, fond of living peacefully on his estates and of building, and it is a little surprising that he joined the Appellants at all. He seems to have been easily led by Gloucester and Arundel. The latter's brother Thomas, the future Primate, probably provided more than his share of the brains to the seniors. Although he had been provided to the see of Ely in his twenty-first year as long ago as 1373, he had not been heard of until 1386. His political capacity became evident later. His cloth prevented him from being a party to the appeal.

[1] *Historia Anglicana*, ed. H. T. Riley (R.S., 1864), p. 156.

[2] He married (in 1359) Elizabeth Bohun, daughter of William, Earl of Northampton. She died 3 April 1385. *Complete Peerage*, i. 244.

Of these two groups among the Appellants, one was irreconcilable, the other only temporarily alienated. The two younger Appellants with less experience and less sympathy with the opposition's ultimate aims could be satisfied once the de Veres and de la Pole had gone. The three elder malcontents could not. They were against the king himself. In 1387 Derby and Nottingham were in the nature of untried reinforcements secured by their brothers-in-law at the second stage of the struggle, called in when it was seen by their elders that Richard was not going to submit tamely to conciliar control and that an armed clash was inevitable. It does not appear that the infatuated and angry king made any attempt to prevent them from making common cause with his enemies, but that was one of the lessons that 1387–8 taught him. Later on he was to distinguish the elements of coalition and drive a wedge between them. In 1387, however, he was immature and pliant in the hands of the de Veres, a frightened Earl of Suffolk, and the extremists of the household. All through the summer of 1387 the court was feverishly planning to overthrow its critics by force, and counter-measures were obviously necessary. Therefore the two younger earls, backed by the lands of the houses of Bohun and Mowbray and at least the prestige of that of Lancaster, were valued accessions to the strength of the opposition. Outside the royal estates in Cheshire and North Wales very little sympathy was felt by the landed class for the king's cause, and the combined force of the five earls was large enough to deal with the resources of men and material which the Crown could command. Yet Richard risked a throw. To the last he does not seem to have realized what he was up against.

On 10 November 1387 he returned to Westminster to outface his critics, and when that failed to quell them dispatched de Vere to bring up a royal army. It was then that the three senior Appellants raised their followers and encamped at Waltham Cross; they were not yet joined by their two young kinsmen. Derby seems to have been at Kenilworth with his wife and infant son.[1] When the first 'appeal' of the king's ministers took place in

[1] I have not been able to find the evidence for this. From DL 28/1/2 it would appear that Henry's household was at Stony Stratford at this time.

Westminster Hall on 17 November it was made in the names of Gloucester, Arundel, and Warwick alone.[1] It was only when it became necessary to take the field against de Vere's army advancing from Cheshire that the meeting of the five Appellants at Huntingdon at last took place on 12 December. Though it was a council of war, there was an immediate division of opinion and a radical one at that. Richard was residing defenceless in London, the citizens having refused to come to his aid. Arundel therefore proposed that they should march at once to capture and depose him; they could deal with de Vere later; with Richard in their hands the game would be won. Derby and Nottingham were opposed to this plan. Their quarrel was primarily with de Vere; they were not prepared to renounce their allegiance to the king, but only to rid him of the hated favourites. In deference to their wishes Arundel's proposal was dropped, to be revived when the threat from Cheshire had been disposed of. It was therefore decided to intercept the rescuing royalist army by a march to Northampton. They were only just in time for the Duke of Ireland—de Vere's novel title—was already close. He had information of their movements and now attempted to slip past them to the south by taking the road through Oxfordshire.[2] On the evening of 19 December he was encamped near Stow-on-the-Wold. The Appellants were, however, on his track and managed to get between him and Oxford. Next morning there was some sort of skirmish at Burford where the royalists succeeded in brushing Arundel aside only to find Derby holding Radcot Bridge and blocking the remaining route to the lower Thames. The other Appellants were close behind, Ireland's troops proved unreliable, a thick mist made it impossible to see what forces Derby had with him, and after only a brief fight the disorderly Cheshire army had been routed and Ireland was a fugitive from the field. Crossing the Thames at Bablockhythe, he managed to reach Queenborough in Kent and to get away to the Continent. The victorious Appellants lost little time in returning via Oxford

[1] *Polychronicon Ranulphi Higden*, ed. J. R. Lumby (R.S., 1886), ix. 104–8.

[2] J. N. L. Myres, 'The Campaign of Radcot Bridge in December 1387', *E.H.R.* 42 (1927), 20–33.

and Notley to the capital. On 26 December they encamped at Clerkenwell Fields and the Londoners opened their gates in welcome.[1] Richard, after hearing of his friend's flight and the collapse of all his hopes, had spent a miserable Christmas in the Tower, deserted by most of the courtiers. There he powerlessly awaited the arrival of his enemies. The city was against him and the ways of escape were blocked. What followed is obscure but immensely important. On 27 or 28 December the Appellants, after taking elaborate precautions against treachery, entered the Tower with five hundred picked and armed followers and closed the gates behind them. Then the curtain falls until the re-appointment of a Council and the issue of writs for a Parliament in Richard's name on 1 January 1388. There passed a series of meetings and negotiations of which the outside world heard little, of which no minutes or official record have survived, and only a crop of hints and rumours exist to feed our curiosity. There must have been several who knew what happened on those critical days but for various reasons they maintained silence.

A chronicle written at Whalley Abbey in Lancashire and only discovered in modern times preserves an account which tallies with the evidence from other sources already known and is so inherently probable that it has won immediate and general acceptance. According to this the Appellants decided at once to depose the king as Arundel had proposed before Radcot Bridge, so that for three days Richard ceased to reign; but when Thomas of Gloucester was put forward for the vacant throne, either by himself or by Arundel, Derby at once pointed out that the line of Lancaster was senior in blood to that of Gloucester and had first claim. Nothing apparently was said about Philippa, Countess of March, whose right derived from Edward III's second son, Lionel, Duke of Clarence. Fearing the effect of dissension, the lords thereupon decided to retain (or rather to restore) Richard, but to govern jointly in his name.[2]

[1] *Polychronicon*, ix. 113; *Chronicon Henrici Knighton*, ed. J. R. Lumby (R.S., 1895), ii. 254.

[2] M. V. Clarke and V. H. Galbraith, 'The Deposition of Richard II' in *Fourteenth Century Studies*, pp. 91–5.

In judging the probability of this story, there are one or two considerations which it is necessary to bear in mind. First, that Lancaster was believed in 1377 to have given circulation to the lie that the house of Lancaster sprang from an elder brother of Edward I, Edmund—in reality Edward's junior—who had been passed over because he was a cripple. Henry Bolingbroke was to revive this story in 1399. Secondly, that in 1386 at the height of the parliamentary crisis over the impeachment of Suffolk, Richard had only been induced to acquiesce when reminded by Gloucester and Thomas Arundel of the events of 1327. The documents concerning Edward II's deposition were then circulating freely and had been re-examined in Parliament. The removal of Richard was therefore in the air long before his reckless behaviour in 1387 further weakened his hold over the loyalty of the greater baronage. The Whalley story also explains several otherwise meaningless phrases in Gloucester's deathbed confession which was made at Calais in 1397, probably under duress. It fits in with hints dropped by other writers—Favent for example—who, however good their information, were naturally chary of describing anything so treasonable as the temporary deposition of a king who ten years later was taking exhaustive revenge on all involved in those events. Such hints are consistent only with the account preserved at remote Whalley and written down even there not until Richard had ceased to reign. If we accept this story, much becomes clear. We see that a danger of serious cleavage threatened to develop among Richard's principal opponents just at the moment of victory, and that although it was quickly papered over the fact remained that Derby's intervention had cheated the Duke of Gloucester of the throne. The personal ambition of Gloucester nearly destroyed the unity of the Appellants at the outset of their task, and the threatened but averted crisis was a sign-post for the future. That Richard even at the time realized the possibilities of the situation is suggested by the fact that when the lords prepared to withdraw from their first interview with him, he succeeded in inducing Derby and Nottingham (or according to one chronicler, Derby only) to stay behind to supper with him. But it was too soon to drive a wedge between the elder and younger Appellants; for Derby chose this occasion to conduct the king to the window that he might see the crowd without the walls roaring for the blood of his friends.[1] Perhaps he remembered that earlier occasion when he had been deserted by Richard in that very building and had himself very nearly fallen a victim to lynch-law; it would have been strange indeed if that six-year-old memory had not been in both their minds.

The solidarity of the coalition survived with only minor exceptions throughout the course of the Merciless Parliament of 1388. The harsh vengeance visited upon the king's ministers and their abettors was demanded by all five Appellants in complete agreement. Only once did the two parts of the coalition take different sides on a matter of importance. All were agreed that Sir Simon Burley who was probably the chief architect of Richard's attempted *coup d'état* and therefore an object of particular loathing to the king's enemies, should be condemned. But when Richard and his queen begged that his life should be spared, Derby, Nottingham, and the king's other uncle, the Duke of York, who with his usual feebleness had taken no definite side hitherto, joined their prayers in favour of mercy—in vain. Burley had been the king's tutor before his accession in the days when Derby and Nottingham had been Richard's daily companions; he was advanced in years and had distinguished himself as a soldier when young and in spite of his responsibility for the king's evil courses they were prepared to give him his life. But all that they gained was beheading in place of the usual penalties of treason. Gloucester had the Commons on his side against them. Although this intervention gave them some claims on Richard's gratitude, it did not seriously injure their relations with their severer colleagues and cannot be interpreted as a split. Otherwise a united front was maintained and all five lords shared in the spoils of victory when £20,000 was voted for their expenses and the goods of their victims were divided between them. The fact that he had tried to save Burley's life did not prevent Derby from accepting for his own wardrobe some of the old knight's finery. Among his other

[1] *Knighton*, ii. 256. See also *Monk of Evesham, Vita Regis Ricardi II*, ed. T. Hearne (1729), p. 100.

spoils were some of the goods of Alexander Neville, the deposed Archbishop of York, and of the Duke of Ireland himself.[1] While it is fair to remember that 'the riding against the Duke of Ireland' (*equitacio contra ducem Hiberniae*) must have put the Appellants to considerable expense, there can be no doubt that they took care not to be out of pocket by it. A final piece of evidence that disagreements had not seriously divided them in 1388 is that when Derby's second son was born in London during that summer (it may have been as late as 29 September but I do not think so) he was christened Thomas after his uncle Gloucester.

This outward harmony was however deceptive. With the king's favourites eliminated, the younger Appellants were now prepared to give the king his chance. That does not necessarily mean that they despised him any less than their colleagues did, but they were not irreconcilable; they may have hoped to replace de Vere and de la Pole in his favour. In fact they underestimated the effect of the recent proceedings on the king, thinking it likely that he would acquiesce in what had happened—as a less sensitive and more sensible man would have done. They failed to recognize that Richard, outwardly calm and resigned, nevertheless lived for revenge. They did not assess correctly—though there were signs, had they been on the watch—the depths of Richard's powers of dissimulation, did not realize that for him the brutal murder of his friends was as much a blow at himself and his ideas of kingship as the proposal to depose him. They therefore became the cat's-paws of his revenge on Gloucester, Arundel, and Warwick; and only then were their suspicions aroused. Not until it was too late and their old associates were dead did they wake to a realization of their own isolation and its dangers. The history of the 1390s is a personal drama, not a constitutional conflict.

Richard did not wait for the return of Gaunt before making the first move. On 3 May 1389 he dismissed his protectors and declared himself of age to govern. Derby and Nottingham were

[1] M. V. Clarke, *Fourteenth Century Studies*, p. 119. DL 28/1/2, fo. 15^{v} records payments for bringing harness belonging to the archbishop and the duke from the Earl of Northumberland's house to Derby's residence at the Bishop of St. David's Inn.

restored to the Council immediately afterwards without their three associates and when Lancaster at last arrived in the autumn the king set himself to make much of him and his family. Lancaster's notions of kingship made him fair game for such a *rapprochement*. Moreover, like his father, he showed signs of premature senility; though only now approaching his fiftieth birthday and still outwardly imposing, he rapidly mellowed and lost his old energy and restlessness. For the rest of his life he was content to remain a steadfast supporter of the royal cause, even acquiescing in the banishment of his son and heir when Richard decided on it and making no protest at the murder of his youngest brother. As the elder statesman, he brought an air of respectability to the court which was essential if Richard was to succeed in his plans, and his death, long delayed though it was, greatly weakened Richard's position. The feeble, flighty Duke of York was no substitute for him.

Lancaster's influence undoubtedly helped to secure his son's allegiance and to isolate the three extremists among the Appellants. The immediate effect of his return was to reduce Derby's importance as the representative in politics of the Lancastrian interest. It seems to have been his policy to encourage his son to occupy his time in other things than politics; from 1389 to 1393 Derby devoted himself to his family and the typical employments of young and active noblemen, the tournament and the crusade. It was during this interlude from affairs of state that he steadily built up the reputation and the consequent popularity which was to serve him so well in 1399. We are so influenced by our impressions of Henry IV as a scheming usurper and care-worn ruler that we are apt to forget that in the 1390s he was worshipped as the conventional hero of chivalry. He is said to have conquered all hearts by his good looks, his liberality, his knightly skill and horsemanship, and by his reckless love of adventure. In his middle twenties the aptitude he had already shown as a jouster in 1386 reached maturity. In March and April 1390 there occurred one of those occasions for display that the age loved. The flower of French and English chivalry met for a prolonged tournament in the marches of Calais. This affair at St. Inglevert was one of the most notable international shows of the age, attended by every fighter of note in the west, and both French and English agreed that Derby was the outstanding performer of his nation. As in 1386 the experts agreed with the crowd. The fact that he practised the chivalric virtue of largesse and threw money away like water ensured that the writers who chronicled these proceedings would give him a good press.[1] In consequence he was invited to join the Duke of Bourbon's projected expedition to Barbary in North Africa. This ranked as a crusade and was a highly aristocratic party, though there were Genoese merchants in the background. Failing to be ready in time he decided instead to make his own expedition to aid the Teutonic knights in Lithuania, from July 1390 to April 1391. Many Englishmen like Chaucer's knight made this journey:

In Lettow hadde he reysed and in Ruce
No Christen man so ofte of his degre.

Accompanied by eleven knights, about twenty-seven esquires, and a number of servants, grooms and minstrels—the whole party probably numbered less than one hundred and fifty—he sailed from Boston on 19 July for Danzig.[2] It was largely as a result of his assistance that the Lithuanians were defeated at Kovno and Vilna besieged, but sickness and disputes between the English and their Teutonic hosts made it necessary to abandon the siege and return to Danzig in October.[3] Thereabouts Derby and his men remained throughout the winter before returning home in the spring. Next year the adventure was repeated.

In July 1392 Derby set off once more with about two hundred men for Prussia; but he was not wanted there and, abandoning

[1] Derby's presence at St. Ingelvert is noted in the *Chronique du Religieux de St. Denys*, ed. M. L. Bellaguet (Paris, 1839), i. 680, and in the part subsequently edited by J. Pichon as *Joutes de Saint Ingelbert* (Paris, 1863), p. 73. The *Chronique de Berne* speaks of his many gifts and abundant largesse and *Le Livre des Faits de Jehan Bouciquaut* describes how he jousted on behalf of his father as well as himself: Froissart, *Œuvres*, ed. Kervyn de Lettenhove (Brussels, 1872), xiv. 420, 450. Froissart, in his own long description of the jousts at St. Ingelvert, makes no mention of Derby, though elsewhere (*Œuvres*, xv. 82, 229) he leaves no doubt of Derby's high reputation.

[2] *Expeditions* . . ., pp. xxvii, xxxix–xlvi.

[3] Ibid., p. xxx and app. A, p. cvi.

his military crusade, he dismissed his army at Königsberg and set out with about fifty men by Prague and Vienna for Venice. His pilgrimage to the Holy Sepulchre—he was, I believe, the only medieval English king to accomplish this—was made in his own vessel between December 1392 and March 1393. It took him to Rhodes, Jerusalem, and Cyprus, returning by way of Venice, Milan, Pavia, and Paris. At each court he was magnificently entertained.[1] At Prague, for example, he stayed with the drunken Emperor Wenzel for what was probably an uproarious fortnight; at Vienna he met the Archduke Albert of Habsburg and the future Emperor, Sigismund of Hungary. As the guest of the Visconti court at Milan he met and charmed not only the archbishop, later Pope Alexander V, who still recalled his visit after seventeen years with affection and regard, but also the duke's niece, Lucia Visconti, who six years later refused to marry her family's choice because she had vowed herself to Henry of Derby.[2] The understanding of a less emotional kind which he established with Lucia's uncles was to prove more useful, only second indeed to that arrived at with the royal dukes of France whom he met at Paris in June on the next stage of his homeward journey. His first-hand knowledge of many of those who ruled Europe helped him during his reign to secure international recognition and eased the workings of his active diplomacy. The piety and unfailing industry with which he visited churches and the other sights of his long pilgrimage excited admiring comment from writers in many lands. The French, indeed, thought him excessively superstitious, but his piety was genuine; Henry was entirely innocent of his father's anticlericalism and indifference.[3] Not in a single respect did he fall short of the ideal of knightly accomplishment. Beside him Richard II cut a poor figure. The cost had been heavy —between £4,000 and £5,000 for each expedition. The larger part was provided by his father and transmitted to him through the duke's Florentine bankers.[4]

[1] Ibid., pp. xlvii–liv. For gifts to him in Venice see *Calendar of State Papers, Venetian, 1202–1500*, nos. 107, 108, 110.

[2] Wylie, *Henry IV*, iv. 128. *Calendar of State Papers, Milan* (1912), p. 1.

[3] Wylie, *Henry IV*, iv. 145–6.

[4] *Expeditions . . .*, pp. liv–lvi, lxxxvi.

His return to English politics in July 1393 was to a scene very different from that which he had left three years earlier. Richard had learnt his lesson—though how he read that lesson time was to show—and had set himself to lull the suspicions of his former opponents. He now did his best to win over to his side this young and popular kinsman. Lancaster acted as a go-between when needed and from now onwards Derby became a member of a new and differently constituted court-group. Richard was determined never again to allow himself to become isolated; a sufficient army of Cheshire men-at-arms at his back, a Council and Commons manned by trusty servants, and an imposing array of noble families among the lords on his side—all this had to be achieved and peace made with France before he could attempt to settle old scores with the Appellants. To win over Derby and Nottingham was the necessary first move.

So well did Richard play on the jealousies and cupidity of the baronage that from 1393 onwards he had the satisfaction of watching a series of more or less violent disputes break out among his former enemies; one between the Earl of Arundel and the house of Lancaster, another between the Earls of Warwick and Nottingham, completed the alienation of the two parties to the coalition of 1387.[1] To these can be added the dispute which arose even before the death of Mary Bohun between Gloucester and Derby over the division of their wives' inheritance, which was taken into the courts and even brought before the Winchester Parliament of 1393. How much expense and ill-feeling it produced can be gauged from the Lancastrian archives.[2] From the same source we find evidence of a similar quarrel between Derby and the Earl of Warwick in 1394 and 1395 over lands in Northamptonshire.[3] Nothing could have worked more fortunately for

[1] T. F. Tout, op. cit. iii. 483–5; see also, J. G. Bellamy, 'The Northern Rebellions in the Later Years of Richard II', *Bull. John Rylands Library*, 47 (1965).

[2] R. Somerville, *Duchy of Lancaster*, i. 68 n. 4, 132. DL 28/3/3 m. 5 records expenses of £27. 12*s*. 11*d*. in the lawsuit over the Bohun manors of Potton and Sutton, and DL 28/3/4, fo. 9v (Feb. 1392–Feb. 1393) records a further £23 paid 'diversis personis . . . super recuperacione maneriorum de Sutton et Potton'.

[3] Ibid. i. 68 n. 6. *Cal. Close Rolls, 1392–1396*, p. 325. DL 28/3/4, fo. 33v (Feb. 1394–Feb. 1395) records payments 'diversis personis ut pro rewardo et labore

Richard. The relations between Derby and his old associates were hopelessly compromised, while Nottingham had gone over even more whole-heartedly to the king—he was by nature a sycophant—and appeared to be high in his favour. When Richard was ready to strike, he was sure of the assistance or at least the neutrality of the two junior Appellants. The day for which he had waited so long and patiently came on 10 July 1397; Gloucester, Arundel, and Warwick were arrested.

Stubbs believed that their arrest was deserved. Right in 1387, they were wrong ten years later. They had overstepped the limit which separates legal opposition from treason and conspiracy; that was why Derby deserted them for the side of the king. Is there any basis for this suggestion? It is true that at the time of his arrest of the three lords, Richard attempted to pacify public opinion by issuing a proclamation which alleged conspiracy. There is no other evidence than the king's word that in 1397 Gloucester was engaged in any sort of political agitation.[1] So little did Richard himself put any trust in the charge of conspiracy that he did not repeat it or attempt to substantiate it when the three men were brought to Parliament for trial. Their fault, and the only fault with which they were charged in Parliament, was their conduct in 1386, 1387, and 1388. So greatly did Richard fear Gloucester's presence at the trial that he took care to have him murdered at Calais before the proceedings began. The confession which the duke dictated and signed when lying in prison proves that he too believed that it was for his misdeeds ten years before that he was being punished.[2] If therefore Gloucester was guilty in 1397, as Stubbs believed, his guilt was shared by Derby. Stubbs in fact did not grasp the retrospective character of the appeal of 1397.

suis et pro aliis diversis misis et custubus et solucionibus factis per ipsum computantem pro placito inter dominum et Comitem Warwici pro manerio de Bukby in comitatu Northamptonie'. Total £63. 13*s*. 4*d*.

[1] For discussion of this point see T. F. Tout, op. cit. iv. 21–2; A. Steel, *Richard II*, pp. 230–2; R. H. Jones, op. cit., pp. 76–7.

[2] The enrolled confession is in *Rot. Parl.* iii. 378–9; it is printed and discussed by J. Tait, 'Did Richard II murder the Duke of Gloucester?' in *Historical Essays by Members of Owen's College Manchester*, ed. T. F. Tout and James Tait (Manchester, 1907), pp. 193–216.

It is difficult to imagine what Derby thought of these proceedings. It does not seem very likely that he had genuinely repented of his part in the earlier attack on the court. He may have thought it safer to desert Gloucester now that he was lost. But when we find him acquiescing in the condemnation and execution of his old allies for actions in which he had himself taken a responsible part, it is impossible to regard him as consistent or to accept the strength of his constitutional beliefs. His most likely—indeed his only intelligible motive—was self-preservation.

CHAPTER III

The Usurpation, 1397–1399

PARLIAMENT met at Westminster on 17 September 1397. As Earl Marshal, Nottingham took a more prominent part than Derby in the proceedings which followed. Gaunt was High Steward in charge of the trial; perhaps for this reason his son was not one of the eight Appellants of 1397. Nottingham was, and glibly accused his old associates of the treasons in which he had shared. There is no reason for believing that Derby stood back because participation would have been unfitting or dishonourable. He brought a contingent of men-at-arms to Parliament for the king's protection and was at his father's side to taunt and give the lie to Arundel at his trial.[1] The only reference to the incongruity of two of the Appellants becoming involved in the charges against the remainder was a resolution of the Commons that in 1387–8 Derby and Nottingham had been 'innocent of malice' in their appeal of Richard's favourites.[2] The king, thereupon, vouched for their complete loyalty, as well he might, and made doubly sure by raising them both in September to the rank of dukes—of Hereford and Norfolk respectively. Nothing was stinted to guarantee their apostasy.

It was only after Gloucester and Arundel were dead and Warwick a dishonoured prisoner in the Isle of Man that one or both of the survivors began to awake to the perils of their situation.

[1] T. Rymer, *Foedera* viii. (1727), 14; *Monk of Evesham*, pp. 137–8; *Chronicon Adae de Usk*, ed. E. M. Thompson (1904), p. 14. DL 28/1/6 (Feb. 1397–Feb. 1398) and DL 28/1/9 (Oct. 1396–Oct. 1397) contain numerous references to Derby's expenses during the Parliament. Besides payments for banners, painted shields, and standards, 65*s*. were spent 'pro pictura xiii curlews xiii columbells et xiii popyngayes cum argento et aureo et aliis coloribus pro convivio facto domino Regi tempore parliamenti ibidem'. He also equipped himself with a new dagger at the cost of 11*s*.

[2] *Rot. Parl.* iii. 353.

This brings us to the last and most baffling problem of Derby's youth, one about which the evidence is for once really insufficient for a final solution. This is the Hereford–Norfolk quarrel.

The first difficulty lies in the fact that the only source is Hereford himself. To my mind his account is on the face of it so disingenuous as to raise the question of his veracity. Briefly it runs as follows. One day in December 1397 Hereford was riding from Brentford to London when he was overtaken by the Duke of Norfolk. The latter began the conversation by hinting darkly that 'we are about to be undone'. 'Why?' asked Hereford, all innocence. 'For what was done at Radcot Bridge' answered Norfolk. According to his account, Hereford expressed incredulity and reminded Norfolk that they had been fully pardoned by Richard II. But Norfolk persisted, affirming that Richard's oath was worthless even if he had 'sworn it on God's body' itself. For had not the other Appellants been similarly pardoned and what use had it been to them? Greatly shocked by all this, but not in the least disturbed about the king's good faith, Hereford reported news of this encounter to his father, from whom the story reached Richard's ears. The king at once took the matter up and ordered Hereford to set down what had happened in writing. The memorandum was then brought before the Committee of eighteen to whom Parliament had delegated its authority and considered by it on 31 January 1398.[1] When challenged, Norfolk hotly denied the whole affair, though he subsequently admitted to 'certain civil points' contained in the formal appeal which Hereford afterwards levelled against him. It is not known what these were, but on the main issue he entered a flat denial. Since neither party could produce any independent evidence a trial by battle was ordered, only to be countermanded by the king just as combat was about to be joined in the lists at Coventry on 16 September following. In order to avert further recrimination, the king said, he had decided to banish Norfolk for life and Hereford for ten years.[2]

What are we to make of this affair?

1. Is it possible to accept Hereford's story literally and to

[1] *Rot. Parl.* iii. 360. [2] Ibid. 382–3.

believe that he told not only the truth but the whole truth and nothing but the truth? To do so is to suppose that he was extraordinarily gullible. It is just possible to believe that before Norfolk spoke he had had no suspicions of the king's good faith, but only just possible and very difficult. That he should have remained convinced of the king's good faith after hearing Norfolk is inconceivable. Norfolk's insinuations against Richard were only too well founded and once uttered could not have been ignored; yet we are asked to believe that Hereford was not only simple enough to reject them but also blind to the effect that an exposure of Richard's undoubted duplicity towards the elder Appellants would have on the king. And as the sequel was to show, Hereford's accusation provided Richard with his opportunity and excuse. It is hard to believe that Henry was such a fool. His picture of himself as the incredulous confidant must be false.

2. Was Hereford's story substantially true, but told in order to create mischief? This is more reasonable on the face of it, but we know of no reason why he should have thought that to discredit Norfolk would be to his advantage. He had, as far as we know, no quarrel with Norfolk, though he may have been jealous of his favour with the king. Yet it was very risky to accuse one so high in Richard's favour of entertaining suspicions which it was only too probable he entertained himself. There is a more weighty objection. A man of Hereford's intelligence must have seen that if Richard still contemplated revenge he would scarcely buy his own safety by betraying Norfolk, his one potential ally. On only one score would such action be forced on him, namely if he thought that Norfolk had been put up by Richard to say what he did in order to trap him into an abortive conspiracy. If he believed that, then he may have thought that to accuse Norfolk was the only way out of a dilemma. I confess that this seems to me the most plausible theory we have so far considered, though it too has its weaknesses. *We* know that Norfolk had been involved in Gloucester's murder, but we do not know that Hereford did.[1] Would he be likely to suspect Norfolk of being irrevocably committed to the king's cause? And in any case would it be wise

[1] J. Tait, op. cit., p. 212 n. 37.

to denounce Norfolk unless he was absolutely sure? Would it not have been enough to reject his advances? This weakness is not fatal. It is possible that, intelligent man though he was, Hereford was hasty in deciding to act as he did. In the event it proved to be a false step.

3. What is there to be said for the view that the whole story was, as Norfolk claimed, a fabrication by Hereford? This has already been substantially answered. It would assume an amount of hostility towards Norfolk which the facts do not warrant. There is, however, one set of circumstances which may have forced such action on Hereford in self-defence, namely a situation in which the accusation was a *pis aller*. Admittedly this is sheer imagination, but since all other explanations have some unsatisfactory features it seems worth taking into account.

Suppose, therefore, that it was Hereford and not Norfolk who voiced his suspicions on the Brentford–London road and suppose that it was not Hereford but Norfolk who was incredulous.[1] This may at first sight seem to be open to the same objections as its opposite, but that depends on one's reading of the characters of the two men. While it is difficult, from what we know of his later life, to regard Hereford as a foolish or inexpert conspirator, there is not the same objection for so regarding Norfolk. He had been chosen by Richard to supervise Gloucester's murder at Calais and he may well have persuaded himself that he was the latest royal favourite. He was a scoundrel, but he seems to have been a pretty reckless and unthinking one. It was inevitable that Hereford should sound him, but if he proved unpersuadable the danger of his betraying Hereford to Richard would be great. Faced with this possibility Hereford may have decided that he had no choice but to get in first with an accusation of treason; after all he was the finer fighter and if it came to combat by battle he could rely on himself to win. If the fat were in the fire it was less dangerous to make the first move. To let it get to the king's ear through his father and then reluctantly to allow himself to be persuaded to speak would give the right impression of

[1] This, in fact, is how Froissart tells the story, although he systematically reverses the roles of the two magnates. *Œuvres*, xvi. 91–2.

honesty without too much forwardness. This explanation may be thought to be over-ingenious but it is certainly in character, and it is not easy to think of a better.

Hereford was fêted by the Londoners on his journey to the Continent where he had arrived by 13 October 1398. He was allowed an annuity of £2,000 a year for the period of his exile and was promised the succession to his father's duchy should the latter die before his return; his own children remained as hostages in the King's hands.[1] His exile was in no sense a disgrace—he had his popularity to thank for that—but Richard, as events were soon to show, hoped to turn the situation more to his advantage as soon as absence had reduced Hereford's hold on the people's affections. Hereford went straight to Paris where his reception was so warm that it provoked a diplomatic protest by Richard's agents. After that his close relations with the Dukes of Berri and Orleans were more discreetly arranged. It was in Paris that he heard of his father's death on 3 February 1399; Richard's avowal of his real intentions followed rapidly. In March Hereford was banished for ever, his estates confiscated, and his attorney condemned as a traitor. Having, as he no doubt thought, finally ruined his cousin, Richard blithely set sail for Ireland on 29 May leaving the kingdom in the incompetent hands of his uncle Edmund, Duke of York. It did not take Hereford long to see and seize his opportunity.

It would not be necessary to waste much time over the campaign of 1399 whereby Henry of Lancaster won the throne were it not for the fact that two very different versions of that campaign have survived, one official or Lancastrian and one unofficial and Riccardian.[2] It has been usual to accept the official one without question on the ground that it is enrolled on the Parliament Roll, whereas the Riccardian version is only preserved in a number of provincial and French chronicles. Yet an impartial review of the evidence proves that whereas the official version has only one source, the royal clerks who engrossed the roll, the Riccardian is based on a number of independent and unrelated narratives which

[1] *Cal. Pat. Rolls, 1396–1399*, p. 425; *Cal. Close Rolls, 1396–1399*, p. 339.

[2] See the discussion by M. V. Clarke and V. H. Galbraith, loc. cit.

cannot be disposed of so simply. To discuss all the evidence would be impossible in a short course of lectures. What I propose to do is to pass briefly over the period which is not in question, i.e. before Richard's arrival in Wales, merely emphasizing the salient points, and then to continue with what I believe to be the true narrative of the deposition and usurpation, without producing the evidence for and against at every stage. Finally I shall discuss Henry's motives—they are pretty obvious ones—for putting a false story into circulation. That it is a false story is, I would maintain, clear from internal evidence alone: from impossible chronology as well as from the less certain guide of false psychology. It is in fact a skilful but obvious fake.

Henry's reception of the news from England was intended to lull Richard's misgivings and it certainly did. As a Frenchman put it, with characteristic English duplicity he pretended a gay indifference.[1] But he was joined by the exiled Archbishop Arundel and his nephew the young earl, son of the executed Appellant. From this source and from English merchants he was kept informed of the violence of the popular outcry against Richard's tyranny. His own popularity at home seems to have been undiminished. Then, when his preparations were complete, he travelled secretly to Boulogne accompanied by the Arundels and a few others—in all a party of some twenty men. Driven off from Dover by a force under the command of the Earl of Wiltshire, he landed at the mouth of the Humber early in July 1399. This was close to his ancestral land and he soon occupied his own castle of Pickering without opposition. The rest of his campaign was a triumphal progress. Everywhere the tenants of Lancaster crowded to join him while the common people welcomed him, poor fools that they were, as a deliverer. The accession to his banner of the northern barons was a more notable gain, but the final success was the decision of the wretched Regent York to join him when the royal army showed that it would not resist his march. The overwhelming character of his conquest was due to three causes.

First there were the follies of Richard's government in the years

[1] 'Anglicana usus astucia': *Chronique du Religieux de St. Denys*, ii. 676.

1397–9. The imposition of arbitrary taxes had alarmed all who had property, and Henry saw fit at Knaresborough to announce that all taxation would be abolished.[1] No one had known what Richard intended next; his arbitrariness and vindictiveness had become intolerable. Much was expected of Henry and he would find it hard not to cause disillusionment everywhere once the 'revolution' was accomplished. Few can resist a triumphal progress which, in the words of one contemporary, resembled the coming of Our Lord,[2] but to think what he had to live up to might well have alarmed the usurper. Second, the common people, like the propertied classes and with even less reason, saw in Henry a saviour. Nothing substantial had been done since 1381 to relieve the causes of urban and agrarian distress. Even the peace with France had brought no benefit to trade, since the piracy which had ravaged English shipping continued unabated in the Narrow Seas. The dislocation of industry and commerce had produced widespread unemployment and a good deal of economic distress. For this, too, Henry was expected to find solutions, and here again disillusionment would be the result.

Finally Henry won the support of the baronage by the moderation and conservatism of his programme. He had come to claim his ancestral lands and to purge Richard's court of its new crop of obnoxious favourites. Or so he said. Before they joined him, his first aristocratic allies, the Earls of Northumberland and Westmorland, made him swear on the host at Doncaster that he would not take the crown. Even in those perjured days, it was not believed that so perfect a knight as Henry of Lancaster would disregard so sacred an oath. The barons trusted him and gave him their support. It will never be known for certain whether Henry had already decided to seize the crown, but he was soon to be forsworn.[3] So cunningly, however, did he play his cards that his

[1] T. Gascoigne, *Loci e Libro Veritatum*, ed. J. E. T. Rogers (Oxford, 1881), p. 230. For a recent discussion of the financial exactions of Richard II, see C. M. Barron, 'The Tyranny of Richard II', *B.I.H.R.* 41 (1968), 1–18.

[2] *Anglia Sacra*, ed. H. Wharton (1691), ii. 363; Thomas Bekynton, *Official Correspondence*, ed. G. Williams (R.S., 1872), i. 152.

[3] Since this was written, evidence has come to light that the Earl of Northumberland had tacitly underwritten Henry's design on the crown by accepting from

duplicity was not revealed until it was too late to counter it. That is to say he led a large proportion of the English aristocracy up the garden path. It is not surprising that his first years as king were darkened by their wild but impotent rebellions.

Richard was slow in getting back from Ireland and the kingdom was as good as lost before he could raise a finger. His few trusted supporters were cut off, captured, and executed at Bristol on 29 July. Otherwise there was not even a show of resistance. All that remained was to obtain possession of the king's person. Without this the rebellion might have proved abortive: a free Richard was a menace, especially as Henry's allies and followers were determined to regard him as still their rightful sovereign. If Henry coveted the throne it was essential to have Richard under lock and key. This, then, was the chief purpose of the campaign of August 1399.

Richard had left his most reliable servants behind him in England. About him in Ireland were mostly traitors and fools. One of the former, his cousin Aumale, son of the Duke of York, persuaded him to divide his army and to send half under the Earl of Salisbury to North Wales to raise the Welsh and the men of Chester for his cause, while the other half with the king made for South Wales to get into touch with those who were resisting Henry around Bristol. Richard set sail about 24 July and landed in Milford Haven a day or two later. He arrived too late. Henry had been too quick for him. Soon after his landing, Aumale and Thomas Percy, Earl of Worcester (brother of Northumberland, one of Henry's chief supporters) and his other baronial captains deserted him and joined the enemy. Failing to raise the men of Glamorgan as he had hoped, and finding his army melting away and unreliable, Richard decided to disband it and to make his way to Salisbury's camp in North Wales where he expected to find the means of resistance in his palatine county of Chester.

Again Henry's decision forestalled him. Moving on interior lines he was able to reach Chester, the very heart of Richard's

him, on 2 Aug., the grant of the wardenship of the West March under the seal of the duchy of Lancaster. See J. M. W. Bean, 'Henry IV and the Percies', *History*, 44 (1959), 219–20.

country, on 9 August while the king was hurrying up the west coast to Salisbury at Conway. The wretched Salisbury, after failing to raise the North Welsh and having no good news of the king, had likewise disbanded his army the day before Richard's arrival. Thus, thanks to the treachery and incompetence of his lieutenants for which he must take much of the blame, Richard found himself practically deserted at Conway; about the same time Henry, with a growing army, had occupied Chester in force. The only thing to do was to negotiate. He was still a free man; Conway could not be easily taken from the east; there was shipping in the estuary by which he could escape to France via Ireland should negotiations fail. All was not lost for ever as long as he could preserve his liberty. So he sent the Dukes of Exeter and Surrey as envoys to Chester. Meanwhile the Earl of Northumberland and Archbishop Arundel, armed with full powers, had set out for Conway on a similar mission from Henry; they reached the king's presence on 11 August. Speaking on Henry's behalf and as representatives of the rebellious lords, they offered Richard easy terms. Henry had returned, they said, only to enjoy his life, lands, and inheritance; he was the king's loyal subject. If Richard would consent to refer to Parliament Henry's claim to be hereditary Steward of England and to permit the trial of five of his unpopular councillors, he should be *couronnez haultement, Roy et seigneur*. Those whom he had dispossessed, it was understood, were to be restored. 'Duke Henry . . . wisheth for nothing but his land and that which appertaineth to him; neither would [he] have anything that is yours, for you are his immediate rightful king.' It is not surprising that these terms should appear to Richard good enough to justify surrender. Not that he had any intention of abiding by them any longer than was necessary. As he said in the hearing of one chronicler: 'There are some of them whom I will flay alive.'[1] But he decided to feign agreement until he could safely take his revenge. This does not excuse Henry's treachery but it makes it difficult to feel much sympathy for his victim. Like Charles I, Richard thought that his divine authority justified

[1] *Jehan Creton, Histoire du Roy d'Angleterre Richard*, ed. J. Webb for the Royal Society of Antiquaries (London, 1819), pp. 135–40, 355–8.

any duplicity. However, it was three days before he decided to trust Northumberland's and Arundel's professions. Henry's envoys were very persuasive, probably because they too were their leader's dupes. At any rate they voluntarily swore on the host, consecrated for the purpose—no mere formality for an archbishop—that there was no deceit in their offer. On the host they swore that Richard *staret in suo regali potestate et dominio.*[1] Then Richard decided to accompany them back to meet Henry at Flint, thereby placing himself in his enemy's hands. He soon knew his fate. At Flint he was treated as a captive.

By taking possession of Richard's person at Flint, Henry had successfully completed the second stage of the 'revolution'. He had conquered England and he had the king under lock and key. To secure the throne he had still another obstacle to surmount, the reluctance of some of his own strongest supporters to accept a Lancastrian king. First among these was the Earl of Northumberland, head of the powerful Percy clan and allied by marriage with Richard's acknowledged heir, the young Earl of March. It is not certain how widely this reluctance stretched among the baronage, but in view of the oaths at Doncaster and Conway it cannot be regarded as an unimportant factor. The attitude of the Arundels is obscure, but if it is true that Richard was told at Flint by Henry and the archbishop that 'he should no longer reign',[2] the latter was soon won over to condone Henry's perjury and to consent to his own. It is probably of greater significance that at Flint Northumberland had a longish conversation with Henry alone;[3] from subsequent events we may deduce that this was the scene of their disagreement and it is by no means certain that Arundel sided with the proposal to depose the king. Here at least Henry showed his hand. It remained to be seen whether he would succeed in carrying the day. It is possible that the Percies were prepared to consider a deposition which placed March on the throne but not one that passed him over in favour of Lancaster.

[1] *Dieulacres Chronicle* (in *Bulletin of the John Rylands Library*, 14, 1930), 173; cf. *Creton*, p. 141; *Traison et Mort de Richard II*, ed. B. Williams (London, 1846), pp. 48–50. The archbishop's presence is mentioned by *Usk*, p. 28 and in *Rot. Parl.* iii. 416.

[2] *Continuatio Eulogii*, ed. F. S. Haydon (R.S., 1863), p. 382.

[3] *Creton*, p. 372.

Evidently it was decided to postpone the issue to a Parliament and one was summoned in Richard's name for 30 September at Westminster. The barons opposed to Henry may have thought that the assembled lords would be able to resist his claim. It remained for him to do his best to outwit them. Meanwhile an outward show of agreement was preserved. From Chester on 20 August letters were sent under Richard's great seal to all the sheriffs announcing that his dearest kinsman Henry, Duke of Lancaster, had come to redress the defects of his government and that he, Richard, unwilling to endure any longer the evils from which the realm was suffering had with the advice of Lancaster, Archbishop Arundel, the Earls of Northumberland and Westmorland, and the other magnates, ordered them to proclaim the king's peace and put down all disturbances.[1] Richard had transferred his royal authority to his captors. He was now led forth to London by Henry 'in strong and mighty ward'. After that he practically disappears from view. According to the Lancastrian propaganda he received all this cheerfully, *hillari vultu*, with a joyful mien, but one of his friends who saw him reports more convincingly that he was 'pale with anger'. His chances of flaying his opponents alive were diminishing. At Lichfield he tried to escape through a window by night, but was caught and brought back, and at least one attempt was made by his supporters to rescue him on the road to Coventry.[2] In London he was lodged under Henry's guard in the Tower.

Once they had arrived in the capital, the lords began to debate their differences. Parliament was to meet on 30 September and the issue remained in doubt. Henry's greatest asset was his immense popularity, the tide of which continued to rise during these days, and the magnitude of which must have seriously upset his opponents' calculations. This was backed by the overwhelming force of the Lancastrian and other retainers whom it brought to his standard. If he could only seize the initiative, the northern earls and their sympathizers would be outmanœuvred. Committees

[1] *Cal. Close Rolls, 1396–1399*, p. 522.

[2] *Traison et Mort*, p. 211; *Annales Ricardi Secundi*, ed. H. T. Riley (R.S., 1866), p. 251; *Creton*, p. 177.

of experts preparing the case for Parliament rejected his claim to be the heir of Henry III to the exclusion of Richard II himself—a revival of the old Lancastrian myth about Edmund Crouchback—and Chief Justice Thirnyng set his face against a claim to the throne by conquest.[1] Cutting through all this obstruction—a warning to him of what would follow if he hesitated when Parliament met—Henry decided to present his opponents with a *fait accompli*. When the estates met in Westminster Hall on 30 September it was to learn that Richard had *already* resigned the throne which stood vacant in their midst. They had ceased to constitute a legal Parliament since the king was no longer king. The confusion was still further magnified by the presence of a great mob of Londoners and Lancastrian supporters who cried out for Lancaster to be king.[2] As soon as Richard's abdication had been accepted, Henry stepped forward to claim the vacant throne; the words he used are important:

> In the name of Father, Son and Holy Ghost, I, Henry of Lancaster, challenge this realm of England and the crown with all the members and the appurtenances, as I that am descended by right line of the blood coming from the good Lord Henry third, and through that right that God of his grace hath sent me with help of my kin and of my friends to recover it, the which realm was in point to be undone for default of governance and undoing of the good laws.[3]

I will come back to the significance of that claim presently. Meanwhile let us follow the narrative to its end. Acclaimed by this disorderly assembly, Henry took his seat on the throne. His opponents, confronted by the fact of Richard's abdication and by the overwhelming character of the popular clamour, and realizing the effect of this abdication on the legal existence of a Parliament called in the late king's name, found it necessary to acquiesce in what had been done. The ground was cut from under their feet. Those who were opposed to deposition were answered by an abdication; those who had looked for the removal of Richard in favour of the Earl of March were answered

[1] *Usk*, pp. 29–31; *Annales*, p. 282.
[2] *Monk of Evesham*, p. 159; *Creton*, pp. 200–1.
[3] *Rot. Parl.* iii. 422–3.

by a tumultuous acclamation of Henry IV. Both were hopelessly outwitted, and the usurper's reign had begun.

How had Richard's abdication been obtained? The answer is scarcely in doubt: by third degree. It was extorted under pressure and finally given in exchange for a promise that his life would be spared, after the king had fruitlessly asked to be heard by Parliament in his own defence.[1] Only one man, Thomas Merks, Bishop of Carlisle, attempted to get him a hearing, and that availed only to lose him his bishopric. Richard, after prolonged pressure, signed away his throne under threat of death. In those circumstances he could not be allowed to appear to answer his accuser.

The death of Richard by foul play at Pontefract in March 1400 was the last inevitable stage in this shameless usurpation, Henry's final exercise in the art of perjury. While it is difficult to feel much sympathy with Richard, who had set an example of faithlessness scarcely less thorough, it is impossible to overlook the load of guilt with which the usurper had weighed down his conscience, a conscience which may not have been constitutionally tender but which disaster, disease, and the approach of death were to harass increasingly as his reign wore on.

Such are, I believe, the stages by which Henry achieved his ambition. When the throne was his, it was advisable to set about the task of giving them a more respectable look. Hitherto there had been no time to consider appearances, but afterwards the stability of the 'revolution' demanded that it should be made to look less barefaced and more constitutional; as constitutional as was possible in the circumstances. It could not be made to look regular—revolutions defy such attempts—but by a certain amount of judicious manipulation it could be made to look less irregular, less illegal. Henry had perhaps wanted to regard the assembly of 30 September 1399 as a Parliament; although he did not want to owe his throne to Parliament—in that sense Stubbs's talk of a parliamentary title is anachronistic—he may have desired to obtain the acceptance by Parliament of his *right* to the throne. However, too many doubted whether that assembly was a Parliament for him to be satisfied. The next best thing was to

[1] *Usk*, pp. 30–2; *Traison et Mort*, pp. 67–70.

summon a Parliament at once to recognize the *fait accompli* and to settle the succession on his eldest son, and this was done. In the interval a document was prepared, known as the 'Record and Process', a version of the 'revolution' of September 1399 which did its best to make it appear in a favourable light. The duping of the lords at Doncaster and thereafter, the duping of Richard at Conway, the fact that Richard had resigned under duress and after being refused a hearing in Parliament, were all things which could not be mentioned. Instead a story had to be put about which made Richard's abdication legal, that is to say free and voluntary, which placed it at Conway when he was at liberty and not after he became a captive, and which made Henry's succession as far as possible unimpeachable. This the 'Record and Process' did with as much skill as the haste with which it was composed and the difficulties of the task allowed. It was then enrolled on the Parliament Roll and widely circulated in the country; so the story gained currency. How well it succeeded is shown not only by the fact that it formed the basis for the accounts of the 'revolution' in the majority of the chronicles, but by Stubbs's unshaken faith in Henry's 'parliamentary title' and in the constitutional character of the 'revolution' of 1399.[1]

Yet even in the 'Record and Process' there is no basis for supposing that Henry desired a parliamentary title in Stubbs's sense. Henry neither owed his position to Parliament nor wished it to be thought that he did. He claimed the throne by *right*; acceptance of that claim was the most that he desired. This is proved beyond a doubt by the words which he used on 30 September and which were enshrined in the 'Record and Process'. Well known though these words are, they seem never to have been critically examined, least of all by Stubbs. For him the significance of the proceedings was contained in the assent of the estates to Henry's claim. Coming thus to the throne, he 'made the validity of a parliamentary title indispensable to royalty'. If Stubbs turned a blind eye to what he felt to be a mere 'fabrication', others, notably Wylie, have empha-

[1] For the dissemination of the official version in the chronicles see C. L. Kingsford, *English Historical Literature in the Fifteenth Century* (Oxford, 1913), p. 20.

sized the element of election. But there was no election, whatever some contemporaries liked to believe. Henry claimed the throne in the first place by blood, *de jure* and not *de facto*, by right of his descent from Henry III through Edmund Crouchback, in spite of the fact that this descent was denied by the committee of lawyers who examined it. Their objection was overruled by the acclamation of clergy and people. But while claiming the throne *de jure*, he claimed *secondly* (and the order is important) by conquest: 'Through that right that God of his grace hath sent me with help of my kin and of my friends to recover it.' Even so it is only a recovery: it was his by right but he had had to secure it by force. Those are the only two grounds which he stated but a third is hinted at in order to soften the effect that his words might produce: 'the which realm', he adds in a subordinate clause, 'was in point to be undone by default of governance and undoing of the good laws'. But he does not *claim* it for that reason; it is a mere observation on the effect of Richard's last tyranny. To have claimed by conquest alone, as Henry had first thought of doing, would have put a premium upon rebellion; as it was a dangerous example had been set and many were quick to learn the lesson in the coming reign. But a convincing *de jure* title was not to hand; that was possessed by Richard II and the Mortimer heir, both safely under lock and key. It was difficult to claim that the crown was entailed on the male line and could not be transmitted by a female. So the descent from Henry III, though already condemned, was reintroduced in a vague form—'I that am descended by right line of the blood coming from the good lord King Henry Third'—to join his claim by conquest. That was the best that he could do. How wrong are those who emphasize election is suggested by the word 'challenge': 'I Henry of Lancaster challenge this realm of England.' Henry was offering to fight any rival claimant, not submitting his claim to the impartial examination of the assembly; of course no one answered the challenge.[1]

[1] *Rot. Parl.* iii. 423. S. B. Chrimes and A. L. Brown, *Select Documents of English Constitutional History, 1307–1485* (London, 1961) (hereinafter cited as 'Chrimes and Brown'), p. 191.

The effect of introducing conquest into the claim was to put the realm in the conqueror's mercy, in that all lands were at the conqueror's disposal. For Henry to claim so dangerous a power would have been unwise; indeed had he tried to exercise it he would have seemed worse than Richard. He therefore began his reign by a second pronouncement in English from the throne to the assembled estates:

> Sirs I thank God and you spiritual and temporal and all the estates of the land; and do you to wite it is not my will that no man think that by way of conquest I would disinherit any man of his heritage, franchise or other rights that him ought to have, nor put him out of that that he has and has had by the good laws and customs of the realm; except those persons that has been against the good purpose and the common profit of the realm.[1]

The rights of property were secured by this wise moderation. Only Richard's friends need fear the effect of conquest, but the fact that it was a conquest was necessarily emphasized

Had Henry's descent justified his claim, it would be possible to believe that he was inspired by constitutional principles; but it was not and he knew it. He knew too what deceit had been practised to render the usurpation successful. It was based on a series of unconstitutional actions and upon at least three major acts of perjury of which many of the new king's ostensible supporters were as much the victims as Richard himself. It provided a most inauspicious start to the new reign and it is difficult to understand why Stubbs was so easily pleased with it. Far from being 'strong in constitutional beliefs' down to 1399, Henry had shown himself to possess none at all. It remained to be seen whether he would develop any as king.

[1] Chrimes and Brown, p. 192.

CHAPTER IV

Henry IV's Government: The Magnates

THE English state to which Henry succeeded in 1399 was for its size probably more centralized than any other, but the king's government was not only in theory but still more in practice severely limited. The 'revolution' of 1399 had shown what happened when a king acted without a due regard for the realities of his position. Although Richard in many of the details played his hand skilfully, his powerlessness in the face of Lancaster's attack proved only too clearly how dependent the Crown in fact was upon the willing co-operation of at least its more important subjects. The king governed and was expected to govern but unless he could carry a tolerable number of his magnates with him he was asking for trouble. Richard in 1387 had hoped to beat down resistance by drawing on his estates in the north-west, only to find that he could not overcome the combined army of the five lords. For the next decade he pursued a wiser policy, but his easy victory in 1397–8 made him overestimate the extent of his advantage. By seizing the vast duchy of Lancaster he no doubt hoped to increase his preponderance, but he had not time to divert the loyalty of the Lancastrians from their ancestral lord to himself; in 1399 they rallied to Henry. Richard seems to have seen his danger. His visit to Ireland was believed with justice to be part of a plan for using Irishmen to overawe England; and he was also credited with the hope of buying support from France. A more patient and less clumsily executed scheme *might* have been successful. Richard threw away his chances by his wild precipitancy, but the chances themselves were slight. The natural supports of monarchy, namely the baronage, could not be replaced so easily. A royal army drawn from other sources large enough to impose his wishes upon his subjects was almost certainly beyond his reach.

What, however, could not be done by force could be achieved by management. It was only by flouting the traditions of his office that Richard got himself into the position where force was his only hope. He was too impatient and too autocratic to be a good political manager for long. Yet it was only by such management that the late medieval polity could be made to work. And it could be made to work even by so average an intelligence as Edward III's. The fact was that power was not concentrated in the hands of the king but distributed very unevenly among a large class of persons of whom the king was only one, if the greatest. Henry's first problem, therefore, was his relations with his lay magnates. Of these during his reign the number was always under fifty.

What fluctuations there were between 1399 and 1413 were, apart from forfeitures for treason, without significance. Henry IV made only three new peers and these were all members of the family of Lancaster: his eldest son, Henry, was naturally made Prince of Wales, Duke of Cornwall, and Earl of Chester in 1399; on 9 July 1412 his second son Thomas was made Duke of Clarence and Earl of Aumale; and on 5 July 1412 Henry conferred the Earldom of Dorset upon his youngest half-brother, Sir Thomas Beaufort. That apart from these Henry made no peers at all has not I think been noticed by historians.[1] Edward III had been lavish in new creations; so had Richard II whose numerous dukes were contemptuously referred to as *duketti* by the chroniclers. He had also created a new grade of nobility with his marquesses. Henry V, like his father, was to confine his creations to the royal family. It was under Henry VI that a host of new barons would appear and older families be advanced to higher rank. The new Lancastrian nobility was to be the work of Henry VI's Council. Henry IV, however, set an example of abstinence, and even practised reduction. Richard II's wholesale

[1] For a recent discussion of the limitation of the peerage under Henry IV see J. E. Powell and K. Wallis, *The House of Lords in the Middle Ages* (London, 1968), pp. 427–50.

creations of 1397 were reversed and those honoured degraded to their former rank; the rank of marquess disappeared and that of duke was restricted to the royal family. When rebels were condemned as traitors, even though their families were treated reasonably and not deprived of all their lands, they forfeited their dignities. As a result the total number of magnates in Parliament was reduced between 1399 and 1413. In only one direction did Henry do less than he might have done to bring about a reduction. He recognized the practice of summoning the husbands of baronial heiresses in the right of their wives. When for example the old Lord Cobham died in 1408 leaving a granddaughter as heir, her husband, Sir John Oldcastle, received a summons in his place. The same happened to the heirs of Audley and Bourchier. A barony by writ was coming to be thought of as descending in default of male issue through the female issue along with the lands which enabled the holder to support his dignity. The time was in fact passing when the Crown could reasonably refuse a writ in such cases, but the custom was still unsettled in 1399 and if Henry had had a deliberate plan to reduce the number of peers he could almost certainly have disregarded it. That he chose not to may have been because he himself had assumed without royal grant the style of Earl of Hereford and Northampton after his marriage with Mary Bohun. However he certainly refrained from increasing them; his reason I am inclined to think was as much sympathy with baronial exclusiveness and disgust at Richard's want of discrimination as fear of strengthening baronial opposition. He was, however, so generous in rewarding service by grants of land that he laid the foundations of several of the new baronial houses of the next generation, notably the Tiptofts and Hungerfords.[1]

The immediate practical effect of his policy was however to reduce the number of parliamentary magnates, for apart from forfeitures several baronial families became extinct by failure of heirs during his reign. Excluding the house of Lancaster itself,

[1] Summaries of the careers of Sir John Tiptoft and Sir Walter Hungerford will be found in J. S. Roskell, *The Commons and their Speakers in English Parliaments, 1376–1523* (Manchester, 1965), pp. 367, 357.

only forty-one lay peers were summoned to his last Parliament in 1413 as against forty-nine to his first. At that rate the peerage would have dwindled slowly to vanishing point or become wholly royal. This process was taking place without any dangerous concentration of territorial power in the hands of a single magnate; in 1413 there was no one whose position was remotely comparable with that of John of Gaunt in Richard II's reign. The only possible candidate for such a position was Edmund Mortimer. This young man, who came of age in 1412, was the heir not only of the great marcher family but of his grandmother, Philippa, heiress of Clarence and Ulster. Since Henry kept him in captivity and retained his estates he was no more than a candidate. The king was afraid of him not because he was territorially powerful but because after Richard's death he was the heir of Edward III and the inevitable centre of any plot against the Lancastrian dynasty.

The forty-nine temporal lords summoned in 1399 consisted of four dukes, a marquess, ten earls, and thirty-four barons. Unknown to the government one baron had in fact died leaving an infant heir.[1] As far as can be ascertained the remaining forty-eight were present in Parliament. In addition there was an equal number of spiritual lords, consisting of two archbishops, eighteen bishops (Bangor was vacant), twenty-five abbots and two priors. Since their numbers remained constant (except for temporary vacancies) the spiritual peers were therefore in a majority before the end of the reign, but apart from a handful of bishops they were completely overshadowed in influence by the temporal lords.

So much for the baronage as a body. Turning from the general to the particular, it is necessary to classify and select. Some barons of lesser rank were obviously influential as individuals apart from their class but they cannot be given detailed treatment here. What I propose to do is to confine myself to the great baronage, those of the rank of earl and over, and to a few of the more important bishops, merely mentioning their principal associates in order to give some idea of the size of their following.

It was part of the legacy of Richard II's political manœuvres

[1] William, Lord Dacre, died 20 July 1399. His son was a minor until 1412.

and of the violence with which he had turned on his enemies in 1397 that the magnates were split into groups. Among the lords in 1399 were his surviving victims and the heirs of those who had not survived; there were also those who had helped him in his work of revenge. The methods by which the usurper had gained the throne had done nothing to improve the position; those of his initial supporters whom he had outwitted added their bitterness to the common stock. The result was a body divided by personal feuds which were apt to break out in Parliament in challenges and counter-challenges and accusations of treason, and filled with men by turns apprehensive and vindictive and above all lacking in any sense of loyalty to the new dynasty. The baronage was Henry IV's most serious problem and it was six years before he emerged from its shadow. By 1405, however, that danger had passed, though it had taken a heavy toll of the magnates of 1399. In those six years nature removed four and seven more had disappeared by violence.[1] Only a minority had remained consistently loyal to the Lancastrian king.

The simplest classification would distinguish three obvious groupings:

(*a*) Those who had been involved in the recent troubles as victims of Richard's tyranny.
(*b*) Those who had been the willing or unwilling instruments of Richard's tyranny.
(*c*) Those who had succeeded in remaining aloof.

(*a*) It was natural that Henry, who himself belonged to the first group, should find some of his most faithful supporters in it. Thomas Mowbray, Duke of Norfolk, with whom his relations were compromised by the dispute of 1398 was removed by death before he could return from exile. His son and heir, another

[1] *Natural death*: Thomas Mowbray, Duke of Norfolk, d. 1399; Aubrey de Vere, Earl of Oxford, d. 1400; Thomas Beauchamp, Earl of Warwick, d. 1401; Edmund, Duke of York, d. 1402. *Violent death*: Thomas Holland, Duke of Surrey, d. 1400; John Holland, Duke of Exeter, d. 1400; John Montagu, Earl of Salisbury, d. 1400; Thomas Despenser, Earl of Gloucester, d. 1400; Edmund, Earl of Stafford, d. 1403; Thomas Percy, Earl of Worcester, d. 1403; Thomas Mowbray, Earl of Nottingham, d. 1405.

Thomas, was a minor of fourteen in the new king's ward. He was already betrothed to Constance Holland, the daughter of Henry's sister Elizabeth, whom he married in 1402. There was therefore some hope of attaching him to the house of Lancaster. Of the remaining Appellants of 1387 only Warwick survived. He was, however, discredited by his craven behaviour in 1397 when Richard II contemptuously spared his life. He was liberated from prison by Henry's triumph but was coldly received by the usurper. Although he was the head of the ancient house of Beauchamp he was hardly worth conciliating; he was ailing and died in 1401. His son and heir Richard, the future paragon of chivalry, succeeded on coming of age in 1403. One of his first exploits was to fight bravely for Lancaster at the battle of Shrewsbury. Thenceforward he was closely associated with the future Henry V and one of his most outstanding lieutenants in France.

Of more immediate importance were the Arundels. Archbishop Thomas, now in his forty-seventh year, was immediately restored to the primacy, his supplanter Walden being driven out. A bishop since his twentieth year, Chancellor 1386–9 and 1391–6, and the partner of Henry's exile and return, he was obviously one of the outstanding figures in Parliament. As a spokesman of the opposition in 1386 he had not been afraid to threaten Richard. As Chancellor for the best part of a decade he had moved into a more central position aloof from faction until Richard turned on him unexpectedly in 1397. There was every reason why he should have wished for Richard's punishment but the part he had played at Conway makes it difficult to believe that he was in favour of deposition. He was, however, prepared to accept the *coup d'état* and to crown Henry king. If we may judge from the speech with which he opened the first Parliament of the new reign he stood for what may be called the traditional baronial theory of government. The government he said, would not be 'by the voluntary purpose or singular opinion' of the king alone but by 'the advice, counsel and consent' of 'the honourable wise and discreet persons of his realm'.[1] This was as much a warning to Henry as a manifesto on his behalf. Arundel was evidently not altogether happy at the

[1] *Rot. Parl.* iii. 415. Chrimes and Brown, p. 194.

way the new king was already behaving. It was only gradually that Henry and the Primate came together. When Arundel became Chancellor in 1407—taking an office which clerical purists regarded as incompatible with his dignity—both he and his master were isolated. The younger generation of the nobility, including the archbishop's own nephew, was rallying to the leadership of the heir to the throne. For the rest of the reign the former spokesman of the baronial opposition became the defender of the liberties of the Crown. We shall see later how this came about. But at first Arundel maintained his old role, being even suspected on one occasion—in February 1405—of having knowledge of a plot to put the young Edmund Mortimer on the throne. He was probably innocent (at least Henry believed him so) but it was indicative of the middle position he then still occupied. It only remains to add that as Primate, Arundel was a conscientious and efficient ruler, a worthy successor of Courtenay. He was a man of munificence and taste and his one appearance in the book of Margery Kempe reveals his charity and common sense.[1]

The new Earl of Arundel, Thomas Fitzalan, was a better man than his father. When he fled the country in 1399, he was under eighteen years old. While in captivity in the hands of Richard's half-brother John, Duke of Exeter, he had been treated with great indignity and harshness, being, as he alleged, obliged to black his captor's boots. Exeter had been granted the castle and honour of Arundel by Richard, and there was no doubt of the young heir's willingness to assist in the deposition. As a reward he was allowed to recover his inheritance in October 1400, two years before the end of his technical minority. Most of the rest of his life was passed fighting against the domestic and foreign enemies of the house of Lancaster. From 1405 onwards he gravitated towards the circle of Henry, Prince of Wales, and when he died in 1415 it was of disease contracted in that master's service at the siege of Harfleur.

The chief victim of 1397, Thomas of Woodstock, left an only

[1] Archbishop Arundel's career up till 1397 has been studied by M. Aston, *Thomas Arundel* (Oxford, 1967).

son Humphrey, born about 1382 and therefore a minor in the king's ward. Richard took him with him to Ireland for security in 1399. Released from captivity in Trim Castle in August 1399 he died on his way home to England soon afterwards. Of his three sisters one was a nun and another died unmarried in 1400. The third, Anne, who thus became sole heir to her father took his lands to her husband, Edmund, Earl of Stafford. He was twenty-four years old, and the Parliament of 1399 was his first. The grandson of a great soldier and of a like spirit, he was one of Henry IV's most trusted supporters. In 1403 he was killed fighting by the king's side against the Percies at Shrewsbury, leaving an heir only a year old, Humphrey, later first Duke of Buckingham.

So much for Richard's victims. Their record is uniform: to a man they or their heirs rallied to the support of Richard's supplanter. They at least gave no comfort to the enemies of Lancaster.

(*b*) There were in the first place Richard's eight Appellants. Two had already disappeared from the scene, Norfolk by plague in exile, William Scrope, Earl of Wiltshire by execution in Bristol. The remaining six had to run the gauntlet of a Parliament determined to undo the acts of Richard's tyranny.

Chief among them was John Holland, Earl of Huntingdon and created Duke of Exeter in 1397, Richard's surviving half-brother. He was born about 1350 and owed everything to Richard's generosity. A violent brawler, a skilful jouster, and the young Arundel's unchivalrous warder, he was bound to be troublesome. In 1386 he had first seduced and then married Henry's sister Elizabeth; he had also served with credit under John of Gaunt in Spain. His ties with the house of Lancaster were therefore close and Henry seems to have been anxious to secure his allegiance.

Under his influence was his nephew Thomas, Earl of Kent and created Duke of Surrey (1397), son of Richard's elder half-brother. Born in 1372 he had only succeeded his father in 1397. He was a dashing and thoughtless young lord of whose prowess Froissart greatly approved. He was only too easily led into trouble.

The third was John Montagu, Earl of Salisbury, fifty years old in 1399 and one of the few genuine friends Richard had. He was something of an intellectual and was rightly suspected of possessing Lollard sympathies. It was he whom Richard had sent in December 1398 to protest to the French court at its friendly reception of the Earl of Hereford. Henry bore him a grudge for this and was only persuaded by his sister Elizabeth to include Salisbury in the general amnesty.

The fourth, Edward, Earl of Rutland, created Duke of Aumale in 1397, was the elder son and heir of Edmund, Duke of York and therefore first cousin of both Richard II and Henry IV. Less ineffectual than his father, he was unstable and treacherous; it is impossible to see any consistency in his actions. He had helped to betray Richard and he was to betray both sides after 1399. But though untrustworthy he was no coward and his contemporaries seem to have found something to admire in him. He was held to have made atonement for his disloyalty by dying of suffocation on the ground at Agincourt.

Rutland's sister Constance was married to the fifth Appellant, Thomas Despenser, Lord of Glamorgan and after 1397 Earl of Gloucester. She was a thoroughly bad lot and seems to have acted in close association with her brother before and after her husband's death. The latter was born in 1373 and enjoyed Richard's sudden favour in 1397. We shall probably be right in regarding him as little more than a hanger-on of Aumale's.

Lastly Henry IV's own half-brother, John Beaufort, Earl of Somerset and Marquess of Dorset. He was born about 1371 and makes his first appearance on the scene as the bastard of Lancaster in the jousts of St. Inglevert in 1390. Slightly younger than Henry he had been with him as a boy and frequently appears in Henry's accounts. His parents' marriage had been followed by his legitimation by Richard in Parliament in February 1397 when he was created Earl of Somerset. In the autumn when the *duketti* were created he was rewarded with the title of Marquess of Dorset. A favourite of his father, his part in the appeal of that year was the result of Richard's careful humouring of the old duke; it did not mean that he was committed to Richard's cause. In fact he deserted York for Lancaster early in the 'revolution' and probably was responsible for the collapse of York's pretence of resistance to Lancaster's advance.

The first business of the Parliament of October 1399 was to reverse its predecessor's acts. All the judgements, statutes, and ordinances of the Parliament of 1397–8 were utterly annulled and repealed with general approval. But when the Commons petitioned for an inquiry into the responsibility of those who had advised Richard's misdeeds, it was the turn of his Appellants to face a hostile assembly.[1] Amid stormy scenes of accusation and angry denial—on one occasion twenty hoods were thrown down in challenge—it became increasingly clear that the stability of the new king's throne depended upon a policy of amnesty. After all though not himself an Appellant, Henry IV had played a part in the proceedings against his old associates. The uproar against Richard's advisers may well have been intended to produce the embarrassment it obviously did. Henry had the sense too to see that the elimination of the Appellants of 1397 would have the result of leaving him more than ever exposed to the demands of those who had helped to make him king and who expected rewards greater than he was prepared to give. He was already sure of his half-brother and he could reasonably expect to attract the support of his brother-in-law John Holland and his cousin Aumale. The rest were probably not irreconcilable; none of them, except perhaps Salisbury, had served Richard from love rather than self-interest. They were needed as a counterbalance to the Percies and Arundels. Henry, as I hope to show, shared Richard's determination to maintain the liberties of the Crown in the face of baronial pressure; he felt no reluctance in employing Richard's human instruments for that purpose, though the methods he adopted were more cautious and therefore better calculated to achieve the desired results. No courtier of his predecessor would be debarred from his service. He therefore attempted pacification. The six were deprived of the titles conferred on them by Richard in September 1397 and reverted to their former rank; they were also stripped of all more material rewards received since the day

[1] *Annales Henrici Quarti*, ed. H. T. Riley (R.S., 1866), pp. 303 ff.

of the Duke of Gloucester's arrest.[1] Beyond being threatened with the penalties of treason if they should ever again raise a finger on Richard's behalf—he was still alive at Pontefract—they were otherwise let off and reinstated. It was not a popular decision but it was a wise one; not condemned by the fact that it largely failed. If John Beaufort alone adhered to Henry, Aumale, now again Rutland, was at least temporarily detached from his old colleagues.

The latter, with the help of a few of Richard's other friends who had escaped retribution, now entered into a wild plot to effect his restoration. The only result of their ill-considered and premature action was to bring about his elimination and their own. Hoping to seize Henry and his family while they were celebrating Twelfth Night (6 January) at Windsor, they were betrayed by Rutland before they could strike. In the plot with them were Roger Walden the deposed archbishop, Thomas Merks the ex-Bishop of Carlisle, William Colchester, the abbot of Richard's favourite monastery of Westminster, and Ralph, Lord Lumley. The inclusion of the last is interesting since he was a retainer of the Percies; he never seems to have enjoyed Richard's favour and unless his participation was merely irresponsible his close connections with the Earl of Northumberland suggest that his master was cognizant of the plot and waiting, as was his wont, to see how it went before declaring himself. The ecclesiastics also remained inactive. Some of the rebels had managed to call out a few of their more devoted followers but the majority of their retainers evaded service. These affinities which had been swollen in the days of their lords' greatness were now in dissolution. Within a few days the leaders had been captured and lynched by the populace who still believed in the usurper and did not wait for Henry to collect an army. A small number of knights and servants were executed by Rutland himself, acting on the king's orders. The clerks were merely imprisoned. But Richard's murder followed as a matter of course. This removal of Huntingdon, Kent, Salisbury, and Despenser materially altered the balance of forces within a few months of the beginning of the reign.

[1] *Rot. Parl.* iii. 451–2.

(*c*) Those magnates who were neither Richard's victims nor his Appellants naturally formed a more miscellaneous group since it comprised those who had been less conspicuously associated with Richard's revenge, others who had held aloof from policy or from indifference, and yet others prepared to co-operate with those in power at any time. The least important figures were York, Oxford, Suffolk, and Devon. It is unnecessary to waste any time over Edmund, Duke of York; he ended his undistinguished career in August 1402 when Rutland succeeded to his title and estates. The Earl of Oxford in 1399 was Richard's old friend Aubrey de Vere, who had been restored to the earldom in 1393 after Robert de Vere's death without issue. He was tactfully dropped by Richard thereafter and took no part in the proceedings of 1397, probably because of his senility; he died in the spring of 1400. Michael de la Pole, the Earl of Suffolk, was also the heir of a victim of the Merciless Parliament. Though he had been restored to his family honours in 1397 he was an insignificant person and was wisely allowed to retain them two years later. He never gave Henry the least trouble but on the other hand his services were inconspicuous. If Suffolk was by nature a nonentity, Edward Courtenay, Earl of Devon was one by accident. Over forty in 1399, he had had a distinguished military career in his youth but his sight failed in the 1390s and he was totally blind for many years before his death in 1419.

Of principal significance were the Nevills and Percies, the two great northern families whose adherence early in the 'revolution' had ensured its success. Ralph Nevill was the head of the family which had held the lordship of Raby in County Durham since the reign of Henry I. By a series of fortunate marriages the Nevills had become great landowners in Yorkshire and the neighbouring shires. In the fourteenth century they had been conspicuous in the French and Scottish wars and had added considerably to the wealth and prestige of their house. Ralph Nevill had succeeded his father in 1388 and was aged thirty-eight in 1399. His father had been one of John of Gaunt's principal retainers and supporters and his son maintained the connection. This was cemented when on the death of his first wife he married

Joan Beaufort, the Duke of Lancaster's youngest daughter. He was by his father-in-law's side at the trial of Arundel in 1397 and received his reward, the earldom of Westmorland, that September. He was, however, a Lancastrian not a Riccardian, and as John of Gaunt's principal executor it was natural that he should have welcomed Henry's return. On 30 September 1399 he was made Marshal of England for life. Henry always described him as the 'king's brother' and throughout the reign he remained a member of the Lancastrian family group along with his Beaufort kinsmen. In October 1399 he was granted the great honour of Richmond for life. He became a member of the new king's Council and from 1403, when the Percies had proved their unreliability, was in charge of the marches towards Scotland, and the king's principal lieutenant in the north. As such he foiled the baronial rebellion of 1405 and prevented any further danger from the Percies. Henry IV owed his security on the throne more to Westmorland than to anyone else. The earl had two brothers who were also barons. One, Thomas Nevill, had married the heiress of the Furnivalls of Sheffield. He was only slightly younger than Ralph and had been summoned to Parliament from 1383. As a member of a trusted family he was early taken into Henry IV's service. Until 1404 he was chiefly employed in the northern marches but in the spring of that year he was named a member of the Council. In November 1404 the king placed him in charge of the proceeds of the special income tax voted by Parliament for the defence of the realm, and in December he became Treasurer of England; his death in office in March 1407 deprived Henry of a valued servant. John Nevill was the only son of the old Lord Nevill by his second wife Elizabeth, heiress of the Latimers of Corby, a baronial family whose land lay chiefly in Northamptonshire and Cleveland in Yorkshire. Born in 1382 he was still a minor in 1399 but on attaining his majority in 1403 he joined his older half-brothers in Parliament. The Nevill interest was a strong one therefore and well situated to keep the Lancastrian influence predominant in the north. The Earl of Westmorland had twenty-three children, many of whom became important later; but in Henry IV's reign, only John, the eldest, associated with his father in the government of the marches, was old enough to gain any prominence. Both as Warden of the Marches and, while the wardenship was held by the king's son, John, as principal member of his Council, Westmorland was kept fully occupied to the end of the reign. As lord of the castles of Raby, Richmond, Middleham, and Sheriff Hutton, he was supreme everywhere north of the Humber once the Percies had been vanquished.

The Percies were a family of even greater antiquity than the Nevills and, until the rebellion of 1403, probably of greater wealth and influence. Henry Percy was fifty-eight in 1399 and had succeeded his father over thirty years before in 1368. From 1359 onwards he had been an active soldier and his association with the marches dated from his majority. Like the Nevilles the Percies were protégés of the house of Lancaster, but trouble had begun early as a result of John of Gaunt's ambition to monopolize the marches during Edward III's dotage. In 1376 Percy had been bought over with the office of Marshal and in the following year with the earldom of Northumberland. For a time he had seemed satisfied, but the hollowness of his friendship was revealed in 1381 when the Peasants' Revolt seemed to leave Gaunt defenceless. When the duke on his return from Scotland had sought entry to Alnwick castle he had been refused admission by Northumberland's orders and obliged to take refuge again at the Scottish court. For this miscalculation he had been summoned at the duke's complaint to answer to Richard II's Council. After the usual violent quarrel Northumberland had been constrained at length to humbly beg the king's and duke's pardon, in return for which he had been left unchallenged in the marches. From 1383 to 1403 the wardenships were pretty continuously in the Percies' hands, and though Richard seems to have attempted in 1389–91 to insert Nottingham into their preserve, he soon desisted.[1] The earl's son, Henry Hotspur, born in 1364, was usually associated with his

[1] For the wardenship of the marches in this period, see R. L. Storey, 'The Wardens of the Marches of England towards Scotland, 1377–1489', *E.H.R.* 72 (1957), 594–603; J. A. Tuck, 'Richard II and the Border Magnates', *Northern History*, 3 (1968); J. M. W. Bean, 'Henry IV and the Percies', *History*, 44 (1959).

father. In 1386–8 and again in 1397 the Percies had avoided taking sides in Richard's troubles busying themselves in the north, but by 1399 they were not afraid to come out as critics of the king's violence. News of their words reached Richard just as he was departing to Ireland; his threats of what he would do to them on his return are enough to account for their decision to join Henry. When the latter made himself king their acquiescence in this undesired result of the rebellion had to be heavily paid for. Henry probably hoped to buy them over permanently. Northumberland received the office of Constable for life, the lordship of the Isle of Man in tail and the wardenship of the West March for ten years. He was also allowed to farm two thirds of the Mortimer inheritance until the heir should come of age. Hotspur became Warden of the East March, Constable of Chester, Flint, Conway, and Caernarvon and Justiciar of Chester for life; he was granted the lordships of Anglesey and Denbigh and in 1402 was appointed the King's Lieutenant for all North Wales.

There was a third Percy, Thomas, Northumberland's younger brother. Born about 1344 he had pursued one of the many careers open to a younger son, an official one, as a royal curialist. In 1378 he had been retained to stay with the king for life, having previously served in France under Sir John Chandos as Seneschal of Poitou. After various military and diplomatic appointments including that of admiral in John of Gaunt's Spanish voyage, in 1390 he had secured the post of under-chamberlain previously held by Sir Simon Burley, and in 1393 had been promoted to the stewardship of the household, a position he held until Richard's fall. In 1397 he had been created Earl of Worcester with an annuity of £400. He never quarrelled as his brother did with John of Gaunt and was one of the duke's executors. Of the Percies he was the one that Henry was most prepared to trust. Appointed admiral in 1399, he was almost immediately restored to the stewardship of the household. In 1402 he was made the King's Lieutenant in South Wales and chief councillor to the Prince of Wales.

Henry was faced with a difficult choice. If he trusted the Percies, he would have to place key posts and the power to do him great harm in their hands; if he mistrusted them he would almost certainly drive them into opposition and revolt on the ground that their just claims were being denied. He decided to take the risk of liberality. As Northumberland admitted in 1403, they received more than £40,000 from him in less than four years; they claimed that it ought to have been £60,000.[1] Generous as he had been they were not content. Dissatisfied at not being allowed to pocket the ransoms of the Scottish prisoners they took at Homildon Hill in 1402 and alleging that Henry had refused to ransom Hotspur's brother-in-law, Sir Edmund Mortimer, March's uncle, who had been captured by Owen Glendower, they decided to risk an armed throw in 1403. There is little doubt that they had never really accepted the usurpation. They tried to get as much as possible in return for their acquiescence and when Henry failed to pay the high price they expected they determined to destroy him. Contemporaries excused the treachery of Northumberland and Hotspur, but Worcester's was regarded as unpardonable. Not only had he been treated generously but he was the king's household servant. Northumberland's hesitancy in taking up arms enabled the king to strike first at his son and brother at Shrewsbury. Hotspur died fighting and Worcester was executed after the battle. The result was that Northumberland was able to escape punishment. In spite of the king's desire to bring him to justice the lords preferred to believe that he was innocent and he got off, but he lost his offices and received no further rewards or employment. This merely caused Northumberland to prepare another plot in 1405. This time he was joined by the young Earl of Nottingham, Lord Bardolf, and the Archbishop of York, but with the help of Westmorland the rebels were again surprised before they could concentrate; Nottingham and Scrope of York were captured and executed while their accomplices fled to refuge in Scotland. That ended the danger from the Percies, for although in February 1408 the earl and Bardolf attempted an invasion, they were met by a local force under the sheriff and defeated at Bramham Moor near Tadcaster in Yorkshire. Both lost their lives in the battle. The Percies were beaten because, although they

[1] See J. M. W. Bean, op. cit., pp. 223–4.

were brave fighters, they mismanaged their rebellions. Henry was the more skilful soldier, quick to take advantage of any division in their forces, while the loyalty of the Percies' great local rival, Westmorland, put them at a disadvantage at the very centre of their power. The majority of the baronage and gentry remained unmoved by their appeals.

One of the most important results of these rebellions was to put the lands of the defeated at the king's disposal. Already the addition of the duchy of Lancaster to the possessions of the Crown had greatly increased the king's direct influence in local affairs, and this was further enlarged by the forfeitures of 1400, 1403, and 1405. There could for example be no threat from the marcher lordships of the west when nearly all of them were in the king's hands—the Despenser lands in Glamorgan, the Bohun lordship of Brecon, the Hastings land in Pembroke, the Mowbray lordship of Gower, the Lancastrian castles and lordships in South Wales and Monmouthshire, and the great Mortimer lordships in the central March, while there was already a royal preponderance in the north. In fact the only independent marchers left were the Beauchamps of Bergavenny, the Earl of Arundel in Clun and Oswestry, and the Greys of Ruthin, all loyal servants of the Lancastrian king. The same result followed in the north from the fall of the Percies. Although the revenues of the forfeited lands were considerable in the aggregate they were only sufficient to meet a small part of the king's normal expenditure, for the lands were mainly used to endow the king's younger sons and to reward loyal service.[1] The grant of Richmond to the Nevills was typical, however, in that it was only for life; Henry made no permanent alienations except to his own family. Most of the lands were farmed on a temporary basis by men he could trust; it gave them local influence, benefited the Treasury, and kept the property under direct royal control. The result was that most of it was still in the king's hand when Henry V decided to reinstate most of the rebels' heirs. But during his father's reign reinstatement was generally undesirable and owing to the youth of most of the heirs unnecessary; only the heirs of Kent and Salisbury achieved it.

[1] e.g. *Cal. Pat. Rolls, 1405–1408*, pp. 42–8.

Kent's brother and heir Edmund Holland had taken no part in the treason of 1400; he was a minor in the king's ward and was allowed to work his passage home, fighting with Henry at Shrewsbury and with the king's son Thomas at sea. When he came of age in 1403 he was restored to his family honours only to die without male heirs in 1407. Salisbury had left a son of twelve and he too obtained reinstatement in 1409 on attaining his majority. It was no part of Henry IV's policy to penalize the families of the rebels if they proved their loyalty, but it was a great advantage for the time being to have their estates in his keeping. It is for that reason that 1405 can be taken as the turning point of the reign. Treason had not succeeded and the dynasty was thenceforward secure.

A second result was the break-up of many affinities. Comparatively few of the gentry were involved in the three rebellions; and of those that were, most were pardoned. But they emerged into a world that had changed. They had lost their protectors and employers, whose lands were now in the hands of the Crown. Henry wisely confirmed the pensions and annuities which their late lords had granted them for life, but he could not take them all into his service. In any case he had his own followers to reward and there were many of Richard's whose experience and abilities made them too useful to discard. In time most of the abler ones found their niche in his employment but for a time there was clearly a loosening of old ties. A good example of this is provided by the career of quite an obscure Oxfordshire esquire, John Willicotes of Great Tew.[1] He belonged to a family attached to the service of Richard and his first queen. In the last years of the fourteenth century John Willicotes was retained for life by Thomas Despenser, Earl of Gloucester. The latter's fall and death in 1400 did not involve his esquire, who soon got Henry IV to confirm his retaining fee. Willicotes then attached himself to Edmund, Earl of Stafford and was employed by him both on his estates and in the king's service in Wales. But Stafford was killed at Shrewsbury and his heir was a minor in the king's ward. So

[1] For Willicotes's career, see K. B. McFarlane, 'Bastard Feudalism', *B.I.H.R.* 20 (1945), 172.

Willicotes looked for a new patron and found one in the young Earl Marshal. Again the choice was unfortunate and the earl was executed at York in 1405; his pension to Willicotes was soon afterwards confirmed by the king. This time Willicotes succeeded in being taken up by the Prince of Wales and his fortune was at last made. He ended his life as a confidential servant of Henry V and receiver-general of his duchy of Cornwall. The unsettlement caused to many affinities by the events of 1399–1405 had its repercussions in Parliament. Not only were the lords weakened and divided, but the gentry were forced into relying more on themselves. The prominence of the Commons and their initiative in the criticism of the government in the Parliaments of 1401, October 1404, and 1406 were products of that enforced self-reliance. The removal of so many baronial families left the gentry to speak for the governed. That they spoke with so little uncertainty is the best proof of their political maturity; their voice was their own, not the lords'.

CHAPTER V

Henry IV's Government: Council, Parliament, Finance

HENRY had raised great expectations in 1399 and had disappointed them. Yet by contemporary standards he proved a capable king. He not only seized the throne which Richard by his folly had thrown away, but he showed himself able to hold it without any diminution of the royal authority. His dynasty was far from secure at his death, but he had defeated piecemeal the various attempts to dislodge it. He handed on what he had captured to his successor. This was no inconsiderable achievement and the qualities responsible for it deserve to be recognized. He had overcome the counter-revolution in favour of Richard; he had dealt successfully with the unwilling king-makers of 1399 when they attempted to imitate his example on their own behalf; he had forced England's neighbours to accept the fact of the change of dynasty. He or his lieutenants had gained a number of notable victories in the field against the Scots, Welsh, French, and rebels of English blood. As far as military success could make his throne secure Henry had won through by 1408. It was not until the very end of his reign that he could feel the same confidence of success in a less bloody struggle—that in defence of his royal prerogative against the pressure of his critics in Parliament.

The keynote of Henry's government was that he had retained, and therefore should enjoy, all the royal 'liberty' that his ancestors, kings of England, had claimed and enjoyed. The 'revolution' of 1399 did not curtail the royal power; the king did not abandon any of his rights. The fact that Richard had been guilty of a want of governance, a misuse of royal authority, did not affect the nature of that authority; this remained intact. Henry promised to respect the rights of others—as Richard, it was claimed, had not always done—but his own rights were to be respected too. In that sense and that sense only was he a constitutional king, since 'constitutional' properly means: in accordance with the law and custom of the constitution as it was at any given moment. Henry recognized no innovations unless he was forced to; as he told Parliament in 1411 he would have 'no manner of novelty' there.[1] His prerogatives, or as he preferred generally to call them his liberties, were as great and as inviolable as those of his predecessors and must stand untouched. In promising to respect the liberties of others he had promised no more than was implicit in the coronation oaths of every king since the conquest. By adopting this position, Henry made it clear that he did not regard 1399 as a revolution at all and it is perhaps a mistake that we should continue to use the phrase. We do not talk of the 'revolutions' of 1327 or of 1461 or of 1485. 1399 is not like 1689: the constitution underwent no alteration in that year. It is not a *constitutional* landmark.

Even those who criticized Henry's government in Parliament would have agreed with this view. They neither denied nor refused Henry's claims; on the contrary they confirmed them when specifically asked to do so. They, like Henry, were out to safeguard their rights. If they overstepped the bounds occasionally in their zeal, they were easily abashed. They were less concerned on the whole with asserting principles than with obtaining tangible advantages. The methods they chose were sometimes new, but they were more often old and pushed rather further than before. Without, however, being clearly aware of the constitutional implications of their actions, they were in their practice feeling their way towards a new conception of the respective roles of king and Parliament in government. To state what that conception of government was is dangerous. They themselves never formulated it distinctly, and it can only be done in words which have acquired a wealth of associations by their later use. But it is less perilous than not to formulate it at all.

Perhaps we can best start with a negative. The king's critics had no desire to undertake the burden of government themselves. They might devise limits to the king's freedom of action, but it

[1] *Rot. Parl.* iii. 648. Chrimes and Brown, p. 234.

was not in order that they might assume a share of responsibility. Though many of their number may have been ambitious of place in the royal service, they did not claim for Parliament, still less for the House of Commons, a part in the executive. They were not partners in government, but petitioners and critics. They paid the piper and would, if they could, call the tune; but they had no great wish to play the tune themselves. If they were the king's opposition, they were never an alternative government. They had their grievances, they were anxious that these should be remedied and they were forced by circumstances to devise machinery to make their wishes the more effective. They even went so far as to threaten dire consequences should their grievances be ignored or shelved too long. However they accepted no responsibility; the king's government was the king's affair. They did not ask for representation on his Council; his ministers and councillors were of his own choosing. But he must choose well and those whom he chose might in certain circumstances be held answerable to Parliament for what they had done. They claimed the right to examine, to criticize, to indict and to condemn. In so doing they were taking the first hesitating steps towards such claims as the redress of grievances before supply, the responsibility of ministers, at least in matters of finance, not to the king alone but to the king in Parliament, the appropriation of taxation to particular uses and the parliamentary audit of the king's accounts. Concern with all these things can be detected in varying degrees in the parliaments of Henry IV's reign. But it must be remembered how fragmentary is our knowledge of their proceedings. We have the Rolls of Parliament, but no Journals—Rolls recording the decision, not Journals recording the debates. This means that an unproductive deadlock may leave no trace and that a protracted struggle may be concealed behind a plainly recorded decision. What is more, the decisions were selected and edited by the royal officials, while independent evidence from the chronicles is extremely rare.

Henry's government came into existence before Richard had theoretically ceased to reign. It was the hasty product of an emergency and it naturally bore traces of its haphazard origins.

The king had brought a bare handful of personal servants back with him from exile; he had been joined by many old officials of his duchy, and the majority of Richard's civil service left behind in charge of the kingdom when he went to Ireland were quickly reconciled with the conqueror. The first holders of the three great offices of state may serve as illustrations of the mixed origins of the new administration. Henry's first Chancellor was John Scarle, appointed by Richard on 5 September 1399. Scarle was a Chancery clerk of some standing; he had been already in the office in 1378. From 1384 to 1397 he had been the Clerk of Parliament, from 1394 to 1397 Keeper of the Rolls and, in the absence of the Chancellor, head of the Chancery. The thing that commended him to Henry apart from his experience was no doubt that he had been John of Gaunt's chancellor of the County Palatine as early as 1382 and had held that office until 1394.[1] He retired in 1401 to the archdeaconry of Lincoln and died in 1403. The new Treasurer was John Norbury, again appointed by Richard on 3 September 1399. Norbury was by origin a Hertfordshire esquire whose career can be traced back to 1380. He was then fighting in Aquitaine and in 1385 he was one of a number of English adventurers who took service with the King of Portugal and helped to win the battle of Aljubarotta. I find him next in the service of Henry Bolingbroke in 1390; he seems to have been his personal esquire. He was with him in Prussia and accompanied him into exile in 1398. He was also on John of Gaunt's establishment as an esquire and his daughter Joan was married to Gaunt's treasurer of the household, Nicholas Usk. In fact he was a devoted Lancastrian and the new king was godfather to his son Henry. He was generously rewarded—but characteristically his grants were mostly for life. The chief of them was the castle and lordship of Leeds, Kent; hence he appears as a considerable landowner in the home counties in 1412. He held the office of Treasurer until the spring of 1401.[2] The Keeper of the Privy Seal was a clerk, Richard

[1] Somerville, *Duchy of Lancaster*, i. 475. For references to his career, see T. F. Tout, *Chapters*, vi. 388.

[2] Norbury's career has been studied by M. Barber, 'John Norbury, *c.* 1350–1414, An Esquire of Henry IV', *E.H.R.* 68 (1953), 66–76.

Clifford, a connection of the border family of the Lords Clifford, and a close intimate of Richard II and by repute his chosen boon-companion at table. His service with Richard went back before 1388 when as a clerk of the royal chapel he had been removed as obnoxious to the Appellants. He had soon come back and from 1390 to 1398 had been Keeper of the Great Wardrobe. In November 1397 Richard made him Keeper of the Privy Seal and Henry continued him in that office. He was a great pluralist and supple enough to survive his master and to prosper under a new. He became Bishop of Worcester in 1401 and soon after resigned his seal. Translated to London in 1407, he died in 1421.[1] These three were typical of Henry's first servants; there were to be changes later.

Council and Parliament

The term 'king's Council' when used for the early fifteenth century is unfortunately incapable of precise definition, for the very good reason that its character was nebulous and indistinct. The king's Council was a number of different bodies which faded into one another and were not distinguished formally by contemporaries. Their membership was rarely constant and their functions were not specialized. The king could take counsel in many ways. Parliament itself was only a particularly ceremonious way of taking counsel. By 1400 its form was set but it was the only kind of Council that was not to some degree amorphous and elastic. A Council might be attended by all the barons and by more knights than attended Parliament, but a meeting of the three great officers of state was equally a Council. Yet a distinction was beginning to be drawn between the Great Council on the one hand and the Continual Council on the other; it was not a hard and fast distinction, but it was a contemporary distinction and it is useful to adopt it. A Great Council, attended by a varying number of people, was a reinforcement of the Continual Council for more solemn deliberation. In Henry IV's reign it was roughly an annual affair, though there were two in 1401 and two in 1402.[2]

[1] See references to him in T. F. Tout, op. cit. vi. 205.

[2] Sir N. H. Nicolas, *Proceedings and Ordinances of the Privy Council of England* (1834), i. 155, 179 (hereinafter cited as *Proc. and Ord.*). A. L. Brown, 'The Commons and the Council in the Reign of Henry IV', *E.H.R.* 79 (1964), 29 (for the

Its usual business was to prepare the agenda for Parliament, but there were normally other matters to discuss as well. It might, as in March 1401, consist of only five persons but it normally included some thirty or forty and on three occasions when several knights from every shire were summoned (not elected) it consisted of more like two hundred.[1] These were, however, special occasions: the ordinary business of government was in the hands of the Continual Council, which had a total membership usually of twenty to twenty-five but which often consisted of a mere handful of its nominal membership; from time to time it was afforced for particular business by experts.

The great obstacle to the solution of most of the problems of conciliar history is the fact that the Council rarely, if ever, kept a full record of its acts. The materials for its history are scattered among the archives of the great departments of state and the vast majority have perished or been mislaid. It is practically impossible to follow its daily workings before 1390 and there are serious gaps in our knowledge even after that year. The Clerk of the Council, seconded from the office of the Privy Seal, kept a journal—though only a select one—for 1392 which has survived and there is another, also selections, for the period 1421–35. For the first half of Henry IV's reign, down to 1407, a great mass of memoranda, minutes, and warrants still exist, mostly unprinted, which enable us to watch the Council at work more continuously than ever before and to understand its importance as an organ of government for the first time in its history. Against this must be set the almost total disappearance of records from 1407 onwards. The reason for this gap is not clear, but it is not confined to the Council's papers; even most of the returns of members to the House of Commons for the same period are missing. There is an unexplained loss of records for this period which makes it the darkest in fifteenth-century history. Lamentable though this is, the main lines of conciliar development had been laid down in the

Great Council of Mar. 1401). For a discussion of Great Councils, see ibid., p. 4, and 'King's Councillors in Fifteenth-Century England', *T.R.H.S.*, 5th ser. 19 (1969), 97.

[1] *Proc. and Ord.* i. 155–6; ii. 85–9, 98–9.

preceding years and it is unlikely that the loss is fatal to our understanding of the main story.[1]

Henry IV's Council came into existence in the same rough and ready fashion as his government. It was not publicly appointed; it merely grew. With the officers as a nucleus it was gradually augmented by the king until by November 1399 it was a fairly considerable body, meeting regularly at Westminster but rarely with anything like a full attendance. During parliamentary sessions a good many lords made their appearance at its meetings and at most times the presence of a few of them is recorded, generally those whose services or official position made their advice of practical value to the government. Thus the Earls of Westmorland, Stafford, Somerset, Worcester, and Northumberland attended whenever their duties elsewhere allowed them to come to London. But perhaps Henry's most significant action was to appoint a number of the members of his first Parliament as feed councillors: seven knights of the shire including both Speakers, Sir John Cheyne and John Doreward, and three citizens of London.[2] The fact that they were paid ensured their fairly regular attendance. It is often suggested that the king procured the return of a certain number of his councillors to the Commons in order that they might take charge of his business there; but on this occasion at any rate the roles were reversed; prominence in the Commons earned these men places in the king's Council. None of them is known to have had any previous connection with the house of Lancaster; one at least, Sir William Sturmy, was an old servant of Richard II. The Lancastrian interest was represented by Sir Hugh Waterton, who had been Henry's Chamberlain as Earl of Derby and Sir Thomas Erpingham, who was Henry's Chamberlain as king. Apart from these there were the bishops and royal clerks. Of the bishops the most important after Arundel were

[1] For a discussion of the early clerks of the Council and the records kept by them, see A. L. Brown, *The Early History of the Clerkship of the Council* (Glasgow, 1969).

[2] The London citizens were William Brampton, Richard Whittington, and John Shadworth. Other M.P.s were Thomas Coggeshale and John Fernyngham. John Curson M.P. was appointed but not paid. See J. L. Kirby, 'Councils and Councillors of Henry IV 1399–1413', *T.R.H.S.*, 5th ser. 14 (1964), 35–66.

Henry Beaufort of Lincoln, another of the king's half-brothers, Edmund Stafford of Exeter, Richard Yonge of Bangor, Walter Skirlaw of Durham, John Trefnant of Hereford, and William Wykeham of Winchester. Of these Stafford, Skirlaw, and Wykeham were old political hands with long experience of royal administration. There were also a number of king's clerks who were soon promoted to vacancies on the episcopal bench.

In its mode of operation Henry IV's earliest Council differs in no respect from that which was functioning in the last decade of Richard II's reign. As before, while bishops and lords were often present in small numbers, the main brunt of the work fell on the officers and the feed clerks, knights and esquires. Since all kings were generally absent from Westminster for a good many months of the year, either on campaign or more usually moving about the country from palace to castle, manor-house, or hunting-lodge, the routine work of government was largely in the Council's hands. It rarely left the capital unless a Parliament or Great Council was meeting elsewhere and not always then *in toto*. On the other hand all questions of policy and all major decisions had naturally to be referred to the king. There was therefore a constant passing to and fro of councillors and messengers between the court and Westminster. The three officers had their departments at the capital and their presence was usual at the council-table. The household officers and many of those councillors attached to the household, like Waterton and Erpingham, were usually with the king but were frequently sent to convey the king's views to the Council and to bring back the advice of the Council to the king. Moreover the secretary in charge of the Signet was at court to write at the king's dictation to Westminster. It is important not to over-emphasize the existence of this division between the Council at Westminster and the Council in attendance on the king; but the division existed and foreshadows a distinction which was to become obvious under the Tudors.[1]

[1] For a discussion of the functions of the Signet and Privy Seal in this context, see A. L. Brown, 'The Authorization of Letters under the Great Seal', *B.I.H.R.* 37 (1964), 125–56.

It had particular importance at times of crisis when the king was in disagreement with the policy demanded by Council and Parliament. It is only another example of the fissiparous nature of the medieval Council.

It is not sufficiently realized that the Continual Council was beginning to develop its own *esprit de corps* and a distinct constitutional position *vis-à-vis* the king which caused it to seek the confidence of Parliament and to become an independent source of criticism of the royal policy. It was the king's Council and its members were chosen and appointed by the king, but it was there to exercise a measure of control over his actions and when backed up by Parliament could be a formidable obstacle to his freedom. He was not to rely upon his 'voluntary will and singular opinion' but upon the advice of those worthy to give it. In other words it would be highly rash to assume that a king's councillor was a king's pawn. Yet that is one of the assumptions, commonly made, which has done most to obscure the limitations of Henry IV's constitutional position. The outspoken speaker of the Parliaments of 1401 and January 1404, Sir Arnold Savage, was a councillor; we have no right to assume that his outspokenness was eyewash or that it was any less evident at the council-table than at the bar of the House.

The best starting-point for our purpose is 'an ordinance for the government of the king's Council', passed on 8 March 1390 which defined the procedure to be followed now that Richard II was of age.[1] This ordinance assumed a daily meeting of the Council for the transaction of the business of the realm. It assumed that in important matters the king's wishes would be discovered before a decision was taken, but declared that no gift or grant that decreased the revenue should be made without its advice and without the assent of two of the four chief councillors named. Those councillors below the rank of baron were to be paid a wage; the barons were to be rewarded for their trouble on the advice of the Council. As far as it is possible to judge these were no innovations. The rules may not always have been kept, but it is difficult to find any evidence that Richard did not comply

[1] *Proc. and Ord.* i. 18a.

with them down to 1397. The Parliament of that year was induced to confer special emergency powers on a Committee of eighteen which seems largely to have replaced the Council (the membership was practically identical) until Richard's departure to Ireland.[1] This Committee seems to have done his will without question, which is scarcely surprising since it had been carefully selected. Henry IV's Council merely stepped into its shoes. From the first, however, Henry made many grants, great and small, without consulting it, sending orders direct to the Chancery. It is clear from a mass of evidence that in this respect the ordinance of 1390 was a dead letter from the beginning of his reign. When in 1399 the Commons asked him to make no grant save by the advice of his Council, his answer was a temporizing one 'saving his liberty'.[2] Although he left much of the routine-work of government in the Council's hands, and took its advice on most questions of policy, domestic, commercial, and foreign, that was unlikely to satisfy anybody. Medieval politics were largely concerned with the spoils of office, the granting of places of profit and influence, and not with the broad questions of policy as we understand them. Governance was for most men a question of the distribution of patronage, upon which the whole structure of political power was based; when men talked about the king's singular opinion as undesirable they were thinking mostly of his exercise of the enormous patronage at his disposal. A clash was bound to come if Henry reserved all grants and appointments to himself.

The first signs of trouble came in March 1401. It is a good example of the reticence of the Parliament Rolls that they contain no reference to what was done by the Commons on that occasion. Had not Henry left London unexpectedly before Parliament was dissolved, so that the Council was obliged to put its views on paper in a letter to him, we should be unaware that the question was even discussed. That letter has never been printed. A summary of it is given by Professor Baldwin but he misdated

[1] On this Committee and its work, see J. G. Edwards, 'The Parliamentary Committee of 1398', *E.H.R.* 40 (1925), 321–33, and Chrimes and Brown, pp. 175–8.

[2] *Rot. Parl.* iii. 433.

it 1404 and did not fully understand its purport.[1] It is indeed difficult to interpret, difficult even to read, and part of it has entirely perished. It survived in two completely different forms; one is a draft letter, endorsed with a long note of what was recommended, extensively corrected; the other a fair copy of the letter without any endorsement. The letter explains that the Council had met on Friday 18 March 1401[2] to discuss the estate of the king and realm and had postponed its decision to the following morning only to learn that the king had departed early for the country (he is next found at Leeds in Kent). It therefore sent John Doreward, one of the councillors and Speaker in 1399, to declare its advice to the king; the latter was asked to hear him in the presence of the Earls of Somerset and Worcester (respectively Chamberlain and Steward of the Household) and to express his approval. Now the endorsement, which was presumably a note of what Doreward was to say, makes it clear that the Commons had asked that the members of the Council, the three officers of state and the three officers of the household, should be appointed and charged or sworn in full Parliament to hold office until the next Parliament 'so that the Commons before their departure could have knowledge of these persons and of their charge to the great comfort of the same Commons'. The king had agreed to the household officers being charged outside Parliament with two or three of the Commons present to witness the ceremony. But the rest seems to have appeared to him against 'the estate and prerogative of the king'. The Council, however, recommends

[1] The correct date of this document and its importance was first referred to by McFarlane in *The Cambridge Medieval History*, viii (Cambridge, 1936), 369. The Advice is printed in Chrimes and Brown, pp. 205–6, the letter in *E.H.R.* 79 (1964), 29.

[2] The letter merely says 'hier le Venderdy', giving no date. In assigning it to 18 Mar., Mr. McFarlane seems to have been influenced by the document he cites below, recording Doreward's report to the Council of the king's decisions on certain matters under discussion (E 28/11, no. 15, 16 Oct. 3 Henry IV). It is clear from this, however, that the matters under discussion were the provision to be made for the heirs of the Earls of Oxford and Salisbury and that Doreward's report did not refer to the matters raised in Parliament. The Parliament ended on 10 Mar. and the reasons for assigning this letter to Friday 4 Mar. have been set forth by A. L. Brown in *E.H.R.* 79 (1964), 3. The earliest reference to the king being at Leeds seems to be on 30 Mar. (*Cal. Pat. Rolls, 1399–1401*, pp. 470, 472).

that the same procedure should be followed with the ministers and Council. If, however, the king will not agree to this, then perhaps he will consent if the councillors when taking the oath make protestation that 'they do not take this charge by force of any request of the Commons, but at the pleasure . . . of the king'. The Council finally suggests that to avoid hardship the councillors should take their place by turns at the table, provided that a sufficient number of each estate (prelates, lords, and those of lesser estate) are always present. This should make it possible for every grant or appointment to be made by the common advice and assent of the Council. Doreward did his mission and reported the king's answer on 21 March. A note in the council minutes records that he brought the king's consent to certain matters, but it is unfortunately not clear that his agreement covered everything that was suggested to him. It *is* clear, however, from this highly important document that the object of having the Council (and officers) nominated in Parliament was to ensure that they should hold office until the next meeting and to make them responsible for giving advice and assent to all grants and appointments. Further, it is clear that Henry pleaded his prerogative as a reason for refusing and that the Council itself was urging a compromise on the king which would save his face and yet give the Commons what they wanted. It was in this same Parliament that a request for the redress of the Commons' grievances before the grant of taxation was rejected by the king as unprecedented.[1] The Parliament of 1401 in fact prepares the way for those of January 1404 and 1406. It was significantly followed by a change of ministers.[2]

The Parliament of Michaelmas 1402 was, as far as we know, uneventful. That of January 1404 saw the election of the same Speaker, Sir Arnold Savage, as that of 1401; it again made the same demands, this time with more public success. As a result, on 1 March Henry announced that 'at the strong instances and

[1] *Rot. Parl.* iii. 458. Chrimes and Brown, p. 202.

[2] The political significance of these changes has been investigated by A. Rogers, 'The Political Crisis of 1401', *Nottingham Medieval Studies*, 12 (1968), 85–96.

special requests made at divers times in this parliament by the Commons, for the ease and comfort of his whole realm, he has ordained certain lords and others to be of his great and continual Council'.[1] The composition of this body was approximately the same as hitherto, for the king's right to choose his own councillors as he pleased was not yet questioned. It was given absolute responsibility for overseeing the expenditure of all money collected from the land-tax granted at the same time, for which it was to be answerable to the next Parliament. If anything was said about the Council's control of appointments and royal grants it is not recorded, but there is sufficient evidence to suggest that this was implicit in the public announcement of the Council's appointment. The only result was to determine Henry to summon a more subservient Parliament to release him from his bonds. In the summer of 1404 he left London for the Lancastrian estates in the midlands from which he gave orders to the Chancery direct, without consulting the Council at Westminster. On 25 August he held a Great Council at Lichfield at which it was decided to have a Parliament at Coventry, in Lancastrian country, on 6 October.[2] This Parliament is famous as the Unlearned Parliament since the king forbade the sheriffs to return any lawyers; there is also evidence that an attempt was made to influence the choice of the electors positively in the government's favour.[3] The result was a victory for the king; the Council was not reappointed publicly and the arrangements for the expenditure of the land-tax were altered so as to transfer control to two royal nominees.[4] But the victory was only temporary and had the effect of intensifying the determination of the king's critics in the next assembly which met on 1 March 1406. This Parliament had been originally summoned to meet at Coventry where Henry probably expected to repeat his earlier success. Pressure was, however,

[1] *Rot. Parl.* iii. 530. Chrimes and Brown, p. 212.

[2] *Report on the Dignity of a Peer* (London, 1820–9), iv. 790; *Cal. Close Rolls, 1402–1405*, pp. 519–21.

[3] *Eulogium Historiarum*, ed. F. S. Haydon (R.S., London, 1863), iii. 402.

[4] These were the Treasurer of England, Thomas, Lord Furnival, and Sir John Pelham, a knight of the King's Chamber. Both were members of the Council nominated in Apr. 1404. *Rot. Parl.* iii. 530.

brought to bear on the king by the councillors who were now encouraged by the support of the Prince of Wales, and the venue was changed to Westminster. Ever since the summer of 1404 Henry had been more and more openly at loggerheads with the Council and had attempted to short-circuit its influence by an increasing recourse to the use of the signet and of sign-manual warrants to the Chancellor,[1] who since February 1405 had been the Lancastrian clerk Thomas Langley, Dean of York. The group of councillors round Prince Henry ably led by Bishop Beaufort, who had succeeded William Wykeham at Winchester in November 1404, and backed up by the 'Long Parliament' of 1406, was instrumental in bringing the king to the greatest surrender of the reign.

The Commons began the proceedings by a demand for 'good and abundant governance'. It was not until 22 May that Henry was constrained to give way and to announce the appointment of a Council of a far more aristocratic composition than any of his previous ones. It consisted of five bishops, nine barons, and three knights, and before Parliament broke up the three knights had asked to be excused. In order to ensure regularity of attendance it was agreed at the Commons' request that all members of the Council should be paid. A series of ordinances were drawn up—again by the Commons—which had the effect of transferring all power to the hands of the councillors: 'In all matters the king should govern by the advice of his councillors and trust them.'[2] All warrants, whether signet, sign manual, or other, were to be submitted to the Council for its approval, and without an endorsement by the Council should be invalid. 'A reasonable number' of the councillors should remain continually about the king's person and consult their colleagues regularly. Not satisfied with all this, before taxation was granted in December the Commons insisted that the councillors should publicly swear in the presence of Parliament to abide by a long list of articles drawn up

[1] A more cautious assessment of the number of warrants to the Chancellor under the signet is made by A. L. Brown, *B.I.H.R.* 37 (1964), 141.

[2] *Rot. Parl.* iii. 572–3. Chrimes and Brown, pp. 218–20. Discussed by Brown in *E.H.R.* 79 (1964), 14–19.

to regulate their conduct; and that a record of these transactions should be enrolled on the Parliament Roll in the presence of six of their number.[1] There is evidence that this policy was temporarily effective. Until another Parliament met at Gloucester in October 1407 the Council ruled the king almost as if he were a minor. But at Gloucester he again succeeded in turning the tables on his critics. As he indiscreetly boasted to a Hanseatic envoy, he had found a Parliament to do his bidding. As a result he was graciously pleased to discharge the Council and to resume his freedom.[2] Such was the position when the disappearance of the records plunges us into comparative darkness.

For two years the king managed to carry on without a Parliament, but his financial needs made one necessary in the autumn of 1409. He tried again to repeat the tactics of October 1404 and October 1407 and summoned a Parliament to Bristol for January 1410. An obscure crisis followed, terminated by what may have been a Great Council in December 1409. The Chancellor and Treasurer resigned and were not replaced for more than a month, and Westminster replaced Bristol as Parliament's meeting-place. When it met it procured a fresh royal surrender, but only after a struggle which lasted until May. On 23 April the Commons presented a series of demands, among them the inevitable request that the king 'should ordain and assign in the present Parliament the most valiant, wise and discreet lords to be of his Council' and that these should be publicly sworn.[3] It was some time before the king was able to announce his team; those whom he first considered excused themselves and it was only on 2 May that he selected seven lords to serve with the three officers. Two of them, the Earl of Westmorland and Bishop Langley, were his staunch supporters, and these were replaced by others before Parliament was dissolved. The Council as finally constituted was entirely composed of the Prince of Wales's supporters and clearly enjoyed the confidence of the Commons.[4] Until November 1411

[1] *Rot. Parl.* iii. 585–9. Chrimes and Brown, pp. 220–5. See A. L. Brown, *E.H.R.* 79 (1964), 20–6.

[2] *Rot. Parl.* iii. 609. Chrimes and Brown, pp. 227–8. Wylie, *Henry IV*, iii. 120.

[3] *Rot. Parl.* iii. 623. Chrimes and Brown, pp. 229–30.

[4] *Rot. Parl.* iii. 623, 634. Chrimes and Brown, pp. 232–3.

it was in complete control. An attempt, however, to bring about the king's abdication on grounds of health then enabled Henry to dismiss them. At the Parliament of 3 November 1411 he was in the ascendant and made short work of the prince and his supporters. Announcing that he intended 'to stand as free in his prerogative as any of his predecessors' he thanked the Council for its services and discharged it.[1] No new councillors were appointed and for the rest of the reign, with an occasional crisis which he was able to surmount, Henry governed with as much freedom as he had at the beginning.

Viewing these fourteen years as a whole we see that it was a ding-dong struggle between king and parliaments to enforce different conceptions of the place of the Council in government; that the object of the Commons was to limit effectively the king's liberty to act independently of his publicly appointed councillors and to render the latter answerable to Parliament for their charge; and that the king, bowing to pressure, was frequently constrained to admit in practice what he was never prepared to allow in theory. That he died free was after all an accident. On each previous occasion the opposition had staged a come-back and each time for a longer period. The defeat of 1411 had been due to the Prince of Wales's unwisdom, but the pressure would not have been relaxed and the Parliament sitting when Henry died in March 1413 was already preparing his defeat.

It is obvious that the source of Parliament's power was its ability to withold necessary taxes. So far I have said little of the financial struggle which was running parallel to the struggle over the Council. They interacted on one another but it is best to deal with them separately.

Parliament and Finance

Henry's rash promise in 1399 'to live of his own' was to cause him endless trouble.[2] If he had attempted to keep it he would have

[1] *Rot. Parl.* iii. 658. Chrimes and Brown, p. 235.

[2] For a discussion of the demand that the king should live of his own, not treated in the following pages, see B. P. Wolffe, 'Acts of Resumption in Lancastrian Parliaments', *E.H.R.* 73 (1958), 584–93.

found himself with a net income (after deducting the cost of collection and the many annuities and grants paid before the revenue reached the Exchequer) of less than £12,000 a year.[1] This was derived in part from the royal demesne, the profits of the shires, escheats, and wardships and in part from the hereditary customs on wool. The possessions of the Dukes of Lancaster about doubled this revenue, but Henry kept these separate and treated the income from them as personal. In fact the hereditary revenues of the Crown were insufficient to meet the expenses of the king's household. Henry was therefore in the bad tactical position of having to go to Parliament for money within a few months of having offered to do without taxation, an offer which had materially assisted his usurpation. In 1399 he only succeeded in obtaining a grant of a subsidy on wool for three years though at slightly higher than the normal rate. This may have yielded him about £33,600 a year, but he received neither a grant of direct taxation nor the usual tonnage and poundage. In 1401 he was more successful, though the tonnage and poundage he received was at a lower rate than usual; he also obtained a tenth and a fifteenth, the usual form of direct tax. It would be tedious to enumerate the grants of each subsequent Parliament, but here is a summary of Henry's revenue from these sources.

He collected a whole tenth and fifteenth in every year from 1403 to 1408 with the exception of 1406; he collected a half tenth and fifteenth in every year from 1409 to 1412; and in 1404 and 1412 he received the proceeds of the special income-taxes on land. Thus, except in 1406 he received direct taxation of some sort in every year from 1403 to 1412 inclusive. As for indirect taxation granted by Parliament, he received a subsidy on wool at a high rate from 1399 to 1404 (50*s.* the sack for native exporters, 60*s.* for aliens, worth about £33,600) and at the normal rate for the rest of the reign (43*s.* 4*d.* the sack for native exporters, 53*s.* 4*d.* for aliens, worth about £30,000 p.a.); tonnage and poundage

[1] This figure is probably taken from the estimates presented by the Treasurer in 1411 (*Proc. and Ord.* ii. 10), although these sources are there said to yield just over £6,200 and the addition of tonnage and poundage, estimated at £5,333 6*s.* 8*d.*, would be needed to raise it to the figure given by McFarlane.

at a low rate from 1401 to 1403 (2*s.* the ton and 8*d.* in the pound) and at the normal rate for the rest of the reign (3*s.* the ton and 1*s.* in the pound, said in 1411 to bring in 8,000 marks, i.e. £5,333. 6*s.* 8*d.*). Convocation followed Parliament in usually granting a tenth. There were ten clerical tenths from Canterbury during the reign, each worth about £13,000.

As a result of this taxation Henry's revenue in a good year, that is in any of the seven years when a full one-tenth and one-fifteenth was paid, rose to something over £90,000. And after 1402 it probably never fell below £75,000. Income in the middle ages, however, was always anticipated. As soon as a tax was granted and long before its collection was due, the government was giving its creditors drafts on it in lieu of cash. This policy of assignment—future taxation was assigned for present needs—meant that expenditure was always ahead of revenue. So the grant of two-tenths and two-fifteenths in October 1404, the collection to be spread over two years, put much more money at Henry's disposal in 1404 itself than in 1405 when most of it was due.[1] Henry was always in debt and always assigning his revenue several years ahead. Ready money he obtained by borrowing. Henry borrowed about £150,000 in the course of the reign. This was not, of course, revenue, since it had to be repaid. Since he had to pay discount (concealed usury) on his loans it is probable that he lost about £30,000 of good revenue by borrowing. It tided him over bad periods but at some cost. He put his hand on £120,000 but had to repay £150,000.[2]

It is must more difficult to speak of his expenditure. There are two fragmentary budgets for the reign, one of June or July 1401, the other of March 1411, which afford us glimpses of the extent of his commitments. On the former occasion the Treasurer

[1] In June 1405 the Council rehearsed in a long letter to the king the assignments made on the subsidy which had had the effect of diminishing severely its current yield (*Proc. and Ord.* i. 268–70).

[2] For the extent of Henry's borrowing, see A. Steel, *The Receipt of the Exchequer, 1377–1485* (Cambridge, 1954), pp. 112–13, 125–48. On the question of interest, discussed by K. B. McFarlane in 'Loans to the Lancastrian Kings: the Problem of Inducement', *Camb. Hist. J.* 9 (1947), 51–68, cf. G. L. Harriss, 'Aids, Loans and Benevolences', *Hist. J.* 6 (1963), 1–19.

calculated that, apart from the household and some minor items, the king's needs for one year amounted to £131,000.[1] Since the normal cost of the household was reckoned at £16,000[2] and often exceeded that figure, we have an estimated expenditure of about £150,000 in 1401. In 1411 the details given by the Treasurer add up to about £65,000.[3] At that point he abandoned the enumeration of items, but noted that nothing had been included for the keeping of the sea, the rewards paid to councillors, annuities payable at the Exchequer, or for embassies. He then adds the significant remark that the debts of Household, Wardrobe, and Exchequer amount *ad grossam summam*. There is no reason, in short, for supposing that the position had improved since 1401. Henry IV, in spite of taxation at a rate not noticeably below that of Richard II, and with no major war to finance, was chronically indebted and therefore very dependent upon the willingness of the taxpayers to treat him generously.

I do not propose to treat Henry's relations with Parliament over finance in strictly chronological order, but to take in turn the principles for which the Commons were fighting one by one and to cite examples from the Parliaments of the reign of each.[4]

Redress of grievances before supply. This had indeed been long enunciated as a principle and is not merely a deduction from practice. It appears in the *Modus Tenendi Parliamentum*, composed as is now generally agreed in or about 1322. In 1401, as we have seen, Henry IV was actually requested by the Commons to agree to it as a constitutional rule. He declined, but although the principle was thus repudiated by the king, it was obviously part of the Commons' programme and it was virtually impossible not to allow it in practice. The king needed money and he was

[1] *Proc. and Ord.* i. 154.

[2] The total for all departments of the household in the first eighteen months of the reign averaged £58,000 p.a. (A. Rogers, op. cit., p. 89) though this was exceptional. From 1408 the household was provided with an allocation of £16,000 p.a. and in 1408–9 and 1409–10 it in fact received over £18,000 from the Exchequer (E 101/405/23; E 101/406/3).

[3] *Proc. and Ord.* ii. 7–13.

[4] For a recent discussion of this aspect, see A. Rogers, 'Henry IV, the Commons and Taxation', *Medieval Studies*, 31 (1969), 44–70.

obliged to bargain for it. In every Parliament where the grant of taxation is dated it will be found that it was voted on the last day after the concessions had been made. The Parliament of 1406 lasted from 1 March to 22 December because the Commons refused taxation until their demands had been met. The history of every Parliament of the reign shows that this was the Commons' strongest weapon and that it was regularly used, but it must be admitted that it was not wholly effective; I will mention later the reasons for this.

The responsibility of ministers to Parliament at least in matters of finance. This was, as I have already suggested, the object of the Commons in asking for the publication of the names of the king's councillors and that they should be charged and sworn in Parliament to hold office until the next Parliament. Conceded in the Parliament of January 1404, it was carried another stage in the Long Parliament of 1406. Not only did the king undertake to submit all warrants involving expenditure to the Council for its endorsement; not only did the councillors swear to obey the articles drawn up by the Commons for their guidance; but the Commons also made a further request. Here again the Parliament Roll is silent but the St. Albans Chronicle tells us that the Commons were so suspicious of the Council's good faith that they asked that its members should be held individually responsible out of their own pockets for any expenditure improperly incurred between that Parliament and the next. It was a proposal that the councillors found intolerable and on their advice it was rejected.[1] So obstinate were the Commons, however, that they held out until 22 December before they would agree to a grant on other terms.

Appropriation of supply to particular uses under the supervision of specially appointed treasurers. The germ of this lay in the doctrine that all parliamentary grants were extraordinary, the king living of his own for all ordinary purposes. Henry could not complain if the purpose for which the tax was granted was defined, but he was reluctant to approve the creation of special machinery to

[1] *The St. Albans Chronicle, 1406–1420*, ed. V. H. Galbraith (Oxford, 1937), pp. 2–3.

make such appropriation more effective. The best example of this dates from the first Parliament of 1404. As Walsingham puts it: 'In this Parliament there was granted to the king a novel tax, galling to the people and highly oppressive. I would have given a description of it here, except that those who suggested it and those who granted it [presumably the Council and the Commons respectively] would prefer that it should remain for ever secret.'[1] As a result no mention of it will be found in the Parliament Roll, nor in the Exchequer records, for all documents connected with its assessment and collection were subsequently destroyed in order that it might not serve as a precedent. Hence it is difficult to say anything about its yield. Fortunately they forgot to destroy the writs ordering its collection which were enrolled in the Chancery. The details of the tax are not relevant to the present discussion, interesting though they are. It was partly an income-tax of 1*s.* in the pound on all land-incomes of £1 p.a. and over, partly a tax of £1 on every knight's fee and partly a tax on chattels. It is the first of two income-taxes collected in Henry IV's reign, in that respect as novel as the tax on knight's fees might be thought to be reactionary. But it is with the fate of the proceeds that we are concerned. £12,000 of it was to be paid to the king 'to dispose thereof at his pleasure', while the rest, the bulk that is, was to be expended on 'the defence of the realm'. 'If reasonable ordinance and provision' for this purpose had not been made by 15 May 1404, namely for a reasonable force to put to sea to safeguard the same and similarly for an army to defend the shores against French invasion 'then the grant . . . shall be void and of none effect'.[2] That is to say, Henry had first to prove that the purpose for which he had asked for money was a genuine one by committing himself to the expenditure before the tax was collected. If he did not, he could not get it. Parliament then appointed four special 'treasurers of the wars' to receive the proceeds of the tax from its collectors, to 'keep it safely' and to use it only for the purpose assigned 'and to no other use', 'as they will answer therefore to the next Parliament'. Three

[1] *Historia Anglicana*, ii. 260.

[2] *Cal. Fine Rolls*, xii. 251–64. Chrimes and Brown, pp. 212–14.

London merchants and a clerk were chosen as treasurers.[1] What was done in March 1404 for a special tax with special treasurers was repeated in October 1404 with an ordinary parliamentary grant and with the Treasurer of England himself. Appropriation of supply was no longer an aspiration. Twice in 1404 and again in 1406 it was an achievement.

The demand for a parliamentary audit of accounts. This was implicit in the phrase just quoted about the four treasurers of the wars of March 1404 being answerable to the next Parliament. Although this foreshadowed a demand for audit it did not clearly arrange for one to occur. Yet when Parliament met in 1406, an audit was one of the first things requested. Henry took—or rather attempted to take—his usual high line: 'kings were not wont to render account', and we are told somewhat vaguely by the chronicler that every sort of obstruction was resorted to by his ministers to prevent an inquiry into their expenditure. But the Commons prevailed. On 19 June 1406 they voted tonnage and poundage for one year on condition that they might audit the accounts for the 1404 taxes.[2]

The destruction of the records prevents us from knowing how thoroughly the audit was carried out, and it is possible, though hardly likely, that the Commons may have been satisfied by a formal victory; nevertheless the principle of a parliamentary audit had at least been conceded. Wrongly as he may have meant it, Stubbs was right in saying that this Parliament was 'an exponent of the most advanced principles of constitutional life in England'. In fact Lancastrian constitutionalism was not the fruit of a happy partnership between king and Commons but of the concessions made by a would-be autocrat hampered by financial weakness.

Henry dealt with this persistent and galling pressure partly by a flat refusal, taking his stand firmly on his prerogatives, partly by skilful opportunism: he yielded when forced, only to recover

[1] The treasurers were John Oudeby, clerk, John Hadley, Thomas Knolles, and Richard Merlawe, citizens.

[2] *Eulogium Historiarum*, p. 409; *Rot. Parl.* iii. 577. Chrimes and Brown, p. 220.

when more favourably placed; and rigged every turn of events in his own favour.

In his obstructive tactics Henry was helped by a good many factors, the first of which was the want of continuity between successive Parliaments. They only sat as a rule for a few weeks, the intervals between them were often more than a year, and once they had been dissolved, their wishes could often be ignored with reasonable hope of impunity. Many statutes were still-born because the king did not raise a finger to enforce them. He exercised his royal prerogative to dispense people from obeying them; it was not necessary to suspend or annul them; they could merely be neglected. That is why so many statutes of the fourteenth and fifteenth centuries represent no more than pious hopes. If their enforcement depended upon royal action Parliament had no means of ensuring that they would be carried out; it could only re-enact them from time to time.

Secondly, membership of Parliament was not a whole-time profession. Although those returned always wanted to be in Parliament, members were generally anxious to cut the proceedings short and to get back to their home counties. Their professional work or their harvests were being neglected. Lawyers with much business in the courts at Westminster may have been glad to remain there during term, but the majority had their local interests to consider. The Commons resisted taxation; they were driven by the desperation of their grievances to draw up plans of reform; but they had only a limited staying power. If the king could hold out long enough, weariness would cause them to give way. Only up to a point could this be relied upon; it was unsafe to try them too hard, and in many cases the king himself could not afford to wait.

Thirdly, the Commons were a little unsure of their ground and probably unsure of the staunchness of their own members. Some at least were timid about venturing too far along new tracks. They feared the vindictiveness of the king. Before the dissolution in 1401, for example, the Commons petitioned for pardon 'if they or any of them had through ignorance or negligence done anything in word or deed against the royal estate which might in any wise turn to the displeasure of his royal person'.[1] They felt exposed to the perils of retribution once they had dispersed. The Parliament of November 1411 provides an even better example of this. The king's critics had been compromised by the proposal of the Beauforts that Henry should be deposed in favour of his son. Henry's sharp action in refusing to hear any manner of novelty was followed by a statement that he would 'stand as free in his prerogative as any of his predecessors'. The Commons were cowed, and hearing, as they said, that the king's heart was heavy against them, humbly begged and procured from him a declaration of his faith in their loyalty before they went anxiously home.[2] When Parliament was summoned to places where the king enjoyed territorial power or indeed to anywhere away from the capital, resistance was never so pronounced as at Westminster.

Lastly, as we have seen, the king had some influence—as in the Unlearned Parliament—to exclude his most determined critics. It is obvious that he often had friends in the House and it is not without significance that electoral reform was one of the main concerns and achievements of the Long Parliament of 1406.[3] Considering what a number of trump cards the king held, his occasional successes are not surprising. What is really surprising is the dogged persistence and intermittent achievements of his critics. With everything loaded against them, they scored a number of points. He was able to nullify many of their efforts by a persistence even greater than theirs, but he did not emerge unscarred.

[1] *Rot. Parl.* iii. 466. [2] Ibid. 658.

[3] *Statutes of the Realm*, ii. 156. Chrimes and Brown, p. 226. The statute stated that the election of knights of the shire was to be made 'by all those who are there present' in the shire court. See J. G. Edwards, 'The Emergence of Majority Rule in English Parliamentary Elections', *Trans. Roy. Hist. Soc.*, 14 (1964), p. 177.

CHAPTER VI

Father and Son

HENRY IV's treatment of his Parliaments is typical of his method of dealing with the problems facing his government. It exhibits fully the qualities which retained him his throne—his vigilance, patience, tenacity, opportunism. Beaten again and again, he awaited a suitable moment for recovery and used it with wary moderation yet with sufficient firmness to gain his ends. He did not defeat his object by turning each victory into a triumph of self-glorification and personal revenge, as Richard would have done. Occasionally his temper got the better of his prudence—as for instance in his summary execution of Archbishop Scrope—but this happened rarely. Usually his acts of violence, such as the murder of Richard II, were the result of calculation and he forgave more often than he punished. As a result he achieved what Richard had desired and, for all his perseverance, failed to achieve for long—the obedience of his subjects. Even if he soon lost their love and failed to bring them the blessings for which they had foolishly hoped, he managed them too firmly to be gainsaid in the end. He was still master of England in 1413 and he left a peaceful kingdom to his heir.

It must be doubted whether this was what he had looked forward to when he coveted and seized the crown. Kingship brought him singularly little joy, though it called forth the use of all his powers, and it is not surprising that he regretted his usurpation and died an embittered man. For this his health was no doubt partly to blame. There is little reason to believe that he suffered abnormally from illness before 1405, though this has sometimes been assumed from the references to doctors and medicines in his early household accounts. As a matter of fact these references are of extremely rare occurrence and do not justify any inferences. That he was a normally healthy man at least is suggested by his record of activity, his success in tourney and war, and the praise of his physique by admiring contemporaries.

On 8 June 1405 while riding in Yorkshire he was stricken quite suddenly, 'so that it seemed to him he had felt an actual blow'. That night 'he was vexed with a nightmare so that he raised his chamberlains by a great noise, shouting "Traitors! Traitors! ye have thrown fire over me". And he was stricken by a manifest leprosy.' The fact that earlier that day he had executed Archbishop Scrope of York for his share in the Percy rebellion made it obvious to his subjects and himself that this was a judgement of God. It was not, however, leprosy since he was soon fully recovered.[1] In June 1408 he had a second seizure and became unconscious. He was thought to be dead 'but after some hours the vital spirit returned to him'.[2] He was never the same man again. In the winter of 1408–9 he was seriously ill for several weeks, his children were summoned and his will was made. These attacks were intermittent but each left him weaker and less capable of conducting the business of government. Finally, in the autumn of 1412 he became a more or less complete invalid until a last seizure proved fatal in March 1413. What this illness was remains something of a mystery. It was not leprosy. It may have been syphilis; a disease which, it seems, was not then unknown, as is sometimes alleged. It may have been a series of clots of blood in the brain—what is technically called cerebral embolism or thrombosis. It seems to have been accompanied by other disorders, an unpleasant skin disease on the face and a prolapse of the rectum which prevented him from sitting a horse. In short we have a steady and crippling breakdown in health after 1408. An exceptionally active man, he was condemned to physical inactivity, a thing always hard for an ex-athlete to bear. Coupled with this he was haunted by the thought, which contemporary belief encouraged, that it was a punishment for his sins and a foretaste of the eternity which awaited him. There are traces of this in the unusually abject will—the first royal will in English since the

[1] Wylie, *Henry IV*, ii. 246–7; *Anglia Sacra*, ii. 371; Gascoigne, *Loci e Libro Veritatum*, p. 228.

[2] *Thomae Otterbourne Chronica Regum Angliae*, ed. T. Hearne (1732), p. 263.

conquest—which he dictated at Greenwich on 21 January 1409, beginning 'I, Henry, sinful wretch' and going on to refer to the 'life I have mispended'.[1] Curiously enough these phrases are echoed in the will of Archbishop Arundel whose perjury in 1399 had betrayed Richard into his enemies' hands; it looks as if Arundel shared his master's sense of guilt. There is nothing like their two wills outside those of some repentant heretics.

Henry had always been a devout man, a conventionally devout man perhaps, but by contemporary standards (and they were high) above the average in punctilious devotion, a pilgrim as well as a soldier, and one who had earned widespread commendation abroad for his regularity at mass, and alms-giving. There can be little doubt that his last years were made miserable by remorse. He knew that he ought to offer amends by abandoning his usurped throne, but he knew also that his sons would wish him to retain it for his dynasty and that there was therefore no release for him that way. His eldest son's obvious impatience to succeed him roused all his old tenacity and so, racked by sickness and remorse, he clung to his royal power until his death on 20 March 1413. The chief problem of his last years was his son.

Henry of Monmouth was born on 16 September 1387. Like most royal princes, he was soon given his own household and it is not probable that he saw much of his father during his early years. The Derby accounts suggest that his education was on fairly normal lines, though perhaps more than usually bookish.[2] The story that he resided for a time at Queen's College, if true—and the evidence is late and bad—must refer to 1398 when his father's half-brother Henry Beaufort, described as his tutor, was Chancellor of the University. It may have been then that Beaufort won his confidence. Richard II took him into his own charge when his father was exiled and with him he went to Ireland. Richard, who seems—it is an interesting trait—to have exercised an easy fascination on children and peasants, completely won his

[1] *Collection of all the Wills . . . of the Kings and Queens of England*, ed. J. Nichols (1780), pp. 203–5; Wylie, op. cit. ii. 234–8. See also below, pp. 218–19.

[2] See below: Chap. VII, p. 115.

heart. One chronicler tells how the usurper Bolingbroke had to order him with threats to leave the king at Chester in August 1399 and that he only obeyed when Richard reminded him of his filial duty. He never forgot Richard and when he became king one of his early acts was to bring his body to Westminster for honoured burial among the royal tombs. This is the background of the opposition between father and son which was further to darken Henry IV's last years. At first all went well and from 1403 to 1407 Prince Henry was occupied in winning his spurs as viceroy in the Welsh Marches. As Henry IV put it, he had sent 'his first-born son into Wales for the chastisement of the rebels'. This Prince Henry did with energy and resource, but by 1407 the Welsh danger was over and he was looking for new worlds to conquer. He was a man of terrific vitality and driving force and, as time was to show, justified in regarding himself as a potential military genius.

Experience of baronial treachery, parliamentary obstruction, and a host of other difficulties and disappointments had rendered his father cautious and pacific. Ever since his abortive Scottish campaign in 1400, Henry had abandoned the offensive against his numerous foreign enemies. The Percy victory at Homildon Hill had, indeed, put an end to danger from the Scots and Henry had been lucky in capturing James I at sea in 1405. But in that year the French had landed in Wales; Looe, Plymouth, Poole, and the Isle of Wight were burnt and plundered by French and Castilian pirates, and though English reprisals undoubtedly were equally damaging, the command of the sea was not recovered. By a series of treaties with Flanders and Brittany in 1407, and with the Hanseatic League in 1408, peace was gradually being restored—but as usual the peace policy seemed to the patriotic opposition pusillanimous and cowardly. What is more, the beginnings of civil war in France suggested the advantages of interference, to revenge recent humiliations and to recover the empire of Edward III.

The formation of a group among the nobility and members of the Council who were dissatisfied with the king's want of initiative and who desired a more active and bellicose policy at home and abroad had begun in 1405. It was already in active existence in the following year when Bishop Beaufort went on embassy to France and confidentially told the French court that Henry IV would soon abdicate in favour of his son.[1] Henry, however, had no such intention. As his grip on the details of government slackened after 1407 he came to delegate as much as possible to his old political associate and fellow exile Archbishop Arundel. Arundel was a calculating and ambitious man and between 1405 and 1407 he was won over to the king's side. His appointment as Chancellor on 30 January 1407 bitterly disappointed those who had regarded him as the spokesman of the baronial theory of government; as Walsingham said, he accepted office 'against the will of those who loved his honour'.[2] The Beauforts already disliked him; he had also a private quarrel with the earl, his nephew, while the baronage regarded him with all the hostility which is the lot of the lost leader. During 1407–9 he was the king's deputy during his illnesses which were frequent and severe. These repeated illnesses encouraged the Prince of Wales to think that his own day was dawning; the king's recoveries were more than his patience could bear. It was thus inevitable that the discontented should have gravitated to the prince's side and have egged him on with their own careers in view. By 1407 Prince Henry had become the centre and nominal head of a strong and largely baronial opposition to the king and archbishop, composed mostly of men of the younger generation. Such were the young Earl of Arundel, Richard Beauchamp, the talented young Earl of Warwick, Henry, Lord Scrope of Masham, and Hugh, Lord Burnell; most of them had seen service with the Prince in Wales. More important was the allegiance of the slightly older Beaufort family. Bishop Henry Beaufort of Winchester, the prince's half-uncle, had been his tutor at Oxford. He had become a bishop in his early twenties and was only thirty in 1406. He was already a cautious and experienced politician and he was a valuable adviser for this group of young men. His elder brother, John, Earl of Somerset, was scarcely less judicious, while the youngest, Sir Thomas Beaufort, became and remained the most trusted personal

[1] E. de Monstrelet, *Chronique*, ed. L. Douet D'Arcq (Paris, 1857), i. 126.

[2] *The St. Albans Chronicle*, p. 10.

friend and minister of Henry V. Lastly must be mentioned a number of bishops afterwards high in Henry V's favour: Henry Chichele, Bishop of St. David's—a civil servant attached to the prince's household; Thomas Langley, Bishop of Durham, and Nicholas Bubwith, Bishop of Bath and Wells.

With the fall of Harlech in February 1409 Prince Henry was finally released from active service in Wales. Almost immediately his presence at the Council table galvanized the constitutional opposition among the baronage into action. In the autumn of 1409 he and his friends determined to rid the king of his minister and to take the government into their own hands. On 26 October 1409 the Chancellor, Arundel, issued writs for a Parliament to meet at Bristol on 27 January 1410. That was still the assumption at the beginning of December,[1] but early in that month the king met with opposition in the Council over finance, and on 11 December Sir John Tiptoft was relieved of his office as Treasurer. The king countermanded the Council's decisions by signet letters to the Customs' collectors. He was, however, overborne.[2] On 18 December new writs transferred the meeting place of Parliament to Westminster and three days later Archbishop Arundel resigned the Great Seal. From then until 19 January 1410 the king retained the seal in his own hands, probably refusing to accept the prince's nominee for the office. During this period, while the king was at Eltham, the seal was attached to letters at his oral command by a clerk. On 19 January it was entrusted to John Wakering, Keeper of the Rolls of Chancery, and it was not until 31 January that Sir Thomas Beaufort took office as the first lay Chancellor of the reign.[3] But already on 6 January Henry, Lord Scrope had become Treasurer and on 19 January the king was obliged to repudiate his previous signet letters and confirm the earlier decisions of the Council. These dates are important for they provide our only clues to what was happening. The transfer of power and office to the prince's party had thus been accomplished by the time Parliament met at Westminster on 27 January.

[1] *Cal. Pat. Rolls, 1408–1413*, p. 173.

[2] *Cal. Close Rolls, 1409–1413*, pp. 25–6.

[3] Wylie, *Henry IV*, iii. 284 n. 1, 301. H. Maxwell-Lyte, *The Great Seal*, p. 228.

The formal announcement of a Council composed of the prince's friends was made in response to a petition of the Commons on 2 May. Already on 18 March the prince had been appointed Captain of Calais on the death of the Earl of Somerset—a significant indication of where his interests lay. Henry IV meanwhile had withdrawn from Westminster to take up residence with the archbishop at Lambeth; now, before the end of May, he withdrew to Windsor and did not reappear in the capital until the following year.

For nearly two years, from January 1410 to November 1411 a Council consisting of the prince and his friends administered the country in the king's name. A resolute attempt to restore order in financial policy was pursued concurrently with active intervention in France. In September 1411 a small force under the Earl of Arundel was sent to assist the Burgundians, as the advance guard of a larger expeditionary force under the prince himself. They distinguished themselves at the battle of St. Cloud and a Burgundian embassy to secure further aid reached England early in the new year. By then, however, English policy towards the parties in France had changed with the king's reassertion of power. The circumstances attending the prince's fall are quite as puzzling as those of his seizure of power. The first indications that his position was being undermined came in the late summer of 1411 when Archbishop Arundel successfully conducted a visitation of Oxford University to extirpate Lollardy in spite of the prince's protection of the university.[1] At about the same time, writs were issued for a Parliament at Westminster on 3 November. When it met the prince was absent on a progress through the shires in search of support.[2] A few weeks earlier six knights of his household, including his steward Sir Roger Leche, had been arrested.[3] The trial of strength came in the Parliament itself. The Beauforts put up a proposal that the king should be deposed in favour of his heir. This was too much for Parliament; the chroniclers tell us that it was formally debated and then dropped. The king's

[1] Wylie, op. cit. iii. 447.

[2] *Incerti Scriptoris Chronicon Angliae*, ed. J. A. Giles (London, 1848), p. 63.

[3] *Cal. Close Rolls, 1409–1413*, p. 244.

warning to the Speaker that he would suffer no novelties in this Parliament, showed that he meant business. The prince and his friends were removed from the Council and from the offices of state and the king resumed his personal rule and recovered his health and spirits.

In the summer of 1412 Henry IV planned an expedition to France to assist the Armagnacs. This was in direct opposition to the Burgundian alliance favoured by the Prince of Wales, and the king seems to have suspected his son of proposing violent opposition to this policy. The first evidence we have of this obscure crisis is an open letter from the prince dated at Coventry on 17 June 1412.[1] In this the prince recalled that it was well known that the king intended to lead an army overseas for the recovery of Aquitaine. The king, he said, had agreed that he should accompany the expedition with a limited number of followers, but he had considered the number too few either for his honour or for his security and, in the king's presence, had insisted that 'in so far as his serenity would think it worthy to license us' he should be allowed to confer with his friends to find ways and means of increasing the numbers and services for his security and honour and for good of the realm; to which request, as he thought, the king gave his permission. But as he was going towards 'our own city of Coventry', with the king's permission, neither armed nor with a mass of people, but as simply as honour would allow, certain sons of iniquity, sowers of discord, etc., suggested to the king that the prince contemplated rebellion with a view to seizing the Crown of England in his father's lifetime. Rumours were also spread that the prince was trying to prevent the conquest of Aquitaine. Both rumours were false, spread by those who sought to stir up civil war in place of peace. As God knew, he felt nothing but love, obedience, and filial humility towards his father and would strive with all his power for the recovery of Aquitaine and the other rights of the Crown. His purpose in drawing up this letter was to declare his true intentions on this matter.

Having dispatched messengers to various parts of the country

[1] *The St. Albans Chronicle*, pp. 65–7.

with this proclamation, Prince Henry came to London on 30 June 1412 'with much people of lords and gentles'.[1] He took up his residence outside the city in the Bishop of Durham's Inn in the Strand. The king was at St. John's Hospital, Clerkenwell until 3 July; then he went to the Bishop of London's palace by St. Paul's until 8 July when he moved to Rotherhithe for a Council, which sat for three days; the Prince of Wales was not present.[2] The king and all lords had their retainers with them and there was serious danger of civil war. Although the prince's court 'was at all times more abundant than the king his father's', moderation prevailed, and during the period 9–11 July peace was patched up. In reply to the prince's demand for the dismissal and punishment of his slanderers—virtually a request for the trial of Archbishop Arundel and the king's second son Thomas, of whom the prince was jealous—'the king seemed indeed to assent to his request but asserted that they ought to await the time of Parliament that these might be punished by the judgement of their peers'.[3] The prince had to be content with this. For the rest Henry IV decided that both he and his heir should remain in England, but that their followers should proceed to France under the leadership of Thomas of Lancaster, now made Duke of Clarence, the Duke of York, and Sir Thomas Beaufort, now made Earl of Dorset. This compromise veiled a merely nominal reconciliation. In fact the prince was outmanœuvred, he was stripped of his swollen contingent and no Parliament was summoned to try his slanderers; it is not surprising that he remained dissatisfied and shortly afterwards withdrew once more into the provinces, where he was soon again at his old tricks.

His enemies about the king lost no opportunity to discredit him with his father. He was accused by rumour of having misappropriated the wages of the Calais garrison.[4] This provoked him to another throw. Having collected a fresh army and having

[1] *A Chronicle of London from 1089 to 1483*, ed. Sir N. H. Nicolas and E. Tyrell (London, 1827), p. 94.

[2] Ibid.; *Proc. and Ord.* ii. 30–1. See *The First English Life of King Henry V*, ed. C. L. Kingsford (Oxford, 1911), p. xxiv.

[3] *The St. Albans Chronicle*, p. 67.

[4] *Proc. and Ord.* ii. 34.

issued new proclamations (now lost), he again arrived in London on 23 September 'with a huge people'.[1] The king was ill at Westminster, surrounded by the prince's enemies. The prince now adopted a curious procedure.[2] First he solemnly confessed himself and took the sacrament; then he dressed himself in a remarkable costume: 'he disguised himself in a gown of blue satin or damask made full of eyelets or holes and at every eyelet the needle wherewith it was made hanging there by the thread of silk; and about his arm he wore a dog's collar set full of S's of gold and the terets [rings for them] of the same also of fine gold.' Thus apparelled, he appeared at Westminster with a great company of lords. In order to prove that he had no evil intent he forbade these to advance beyond the fireplace in Westminster Hall. Advancing alone, he made salutation to the king and requested a private audience. Henry IV was then carried in his chair to his secret chamber and in the presence of three or four of his confidential servants he commanded the prince 'to shew the effect of his mind'. The prince made a longish speech, then falling on his knees drew his dagger and presented it to the king saying 'Father I desire you in your honour of God, for the easing of your heart, here tofore your knees to slay me with this dagger. My lord and father my life is not so desirous to me that I would live one day that I should be to your displeasure nor I covet not so much my life as I do your pleasure and welfare. And in your thus doing here in the presence of these lords, and before God and the day of judgement, I clearly forgive you my death.' The king was harrowed at these words, cast the dagger from him, burst into tears and forgave his son. The reconciliation seems this time to have been complete and lasting. They 'fully were accord of all matters of which they were discord' as John Hardyng put it in his rhyming chronicle.

[1] *A Chronicle of London*, p. 95.

[2] The story of the prince's disguise first appeared in *The First English Life of King Henry V*, derived from information supplied by the Earl of Ormonde. It appears in Stow, *Annales* (1631), p. 339 and was used in *The Famous Victories of Henry the Fifth* (1598). C. L. Kingsford (*The First Life*, p. xxv) refers it to the July crisis on the ground that in August Ormonde sailed with the Duke of Clarence to France. On the other hand, in July the king was not at Westminster, where Ormonde locates the interview, and where the Council met in September.

The prince delivered his two rolls of his account as Captain of Calais to the King; and on 21 October 1412 the king declared in Council that after an inquiry his son stood blameless and exonerated.[1] Archbishop Arundel remained Chancellor. For the rest of the reign there was peace.

Henry IV was now seriously ill; the French parties had sunk their differences—temporarily only—and had bought off the English invaders. The prince and his friends were at length prepared to await with patience the inevitable event. In December the king was for periods unconscious. He rallied at Christmas but after another seizure died in the Jerusalem Chamber at Westminster on 20 March 1413. The survival in many forms of stories of a death-bed interview with his heir suggest that some discussion about the future did actually take place. It would be rash to accept the reported conversations in detail. For example the anonymous author of the so-called *First English Life of Henry V* puts into the mouth of the dying king a touching but improbable sermon on justice and mercy.[2] However there is sufficient evidence that two or three subjects weighed on Henry IV's mind. Undoubtedly he had feelings of guilt at his usurpation. His confessor John Tille, it is said, urged him to repent and to find a remedy; whereupon the king answered that he could alas do nothing 'for my children will not suffer the regalia to go out of our lineage'.[3] He also feared that the next king would revenge himself on his younger brother Thomas. Prince Henry is reported to have replied 'I shall honour and love my brothers above all men, as long as they be to me true, faithful and obedient as to their Sovereign Lord. But if any of them fortune to conspire or rebel against me, I assure you I shall as soon execute justice upon any one of them as I shall upon the worst and most simplest person within this your realm.' Clarence worked faithfully for Henry V until his death at Beaugé in 1421. Finally, the dying king was uneasy about his debts. His creditors were never paid.

[1] *Proc. and Ord.* ii. 37–9.

[2] *The First Life*, pp. 13–16; cf. pp. xxvii–xxix.

[3] J. Capgrave, *The Chronicle of England*, ed. F. C. Hingeston (R.S., 1858), p. 302.

Henry V, if he made his father any promise, broke it when he seized his father's goods and prevented his executors from acting. On his death-bed in 1422 he repented and ordered his father's as well as his own debts to be settled, but his command was ignored under Henry VI.[1]

When Henry IV died a Parliament which had been summoned for 3 February was still in session. It was dissolved by his death and there are no recorded proceedings. On 21 March the new king dismissed Archbishop Arundel and made Bishop Beaufort his first Chancellor. At the same time he put away all his disreputable friends and prepared to dedicate his life to military conquest.

Thus ended 'the unquiet times of King Henry the Fourth'.

[1] *Rot. Parl.* iv. 5; *Cal. Pat. Rolls, 1413–1416*, p. 54. For a discussion of the administration of the wills of Henry IV and Henry V, see J. S. Roskell, *The Commons in the Parliament of 1422* (Manchester, 1954), pp. 113 ff.

CHAPTER VII

Henry V: A Personal Portrait

WHEN I was invited to talk to you about Henry V, I was told that you wanted a personal portrait—with not too much background. That was, I take it, a warning; I am to say as little as possible about the political situation and the military problems that confronted Henry the ruler and conqueror, but to devote the best part of my time to the man. Family background on the other hand cannot be wholly omitted.

Henry was born at Monmouth on 16 September 1387 and died of dysentery at Bois de Vincennes on 31 August 1422. That is to say that he did not live to see his thirty-fifth birthday. This short life falls into three roughly equal parts. For his first twelve years Henry of Monmouth was a member of the high nobility, grandson and heir of John of Gaunt, Duke of Lancaster, first cousin once removed of King Richard II. For the next twelve and a half years, thanks to his father's usurpation of the throne, Henry was Prince of Wales. Finally for nine and a half years—the shortest period of the three—he was king.

His parents, Henry of Bolingbroke and Mary Bohun, married in 1380, when the bridegroom was fourteen and the bride at most twelve; they had a son who died soon after birth in 1382 and then, between September 1387 and July 1394, four sons followed by two daughters; the mother died in childbirth at the age of twenty-four. Her widower did not remarry until 1403—and then only, it seems probable, for political reasons; he needed a queen more than a wife. His eldest son was not yet seven when he lost his mother. That she meant something to Henry V is suggested by one of the actions he took when he became king. She had been buried in the great Lancastrian chantry of St. Mary in the New Work at Leicester, but her husband had spent little on her grave and chose to be buried himself elsewhere—at Canterbury. Soon after his accession Henry V paid a London coppersmith £43 for making a figure of his mother to be placed on her tomb.[1] That he neglected to carry out his father's will may indicate the balance of his filial sentiment. His attachment to his mother's memory was perhaps kept alive by the survival of his maternal grandmother until 1419. Joan, Countess of Hereford, whose strength of character and addiction to good works remind me of her grandson, was certainly held in affectionate veneration by Henry of Monmouth. His 'dearest grandmother' is twice mentioned in the will he made in July 1415 on the eve of his first French expedition, and she received many benefits at his hands in her last years.[2]

The household accounts of Henry's father and grandfather preserve some evidence of his upbringing and early education. Though born at Monmouth his childhood seems to have been passed, during his father's absence on crusade, with his mother at Peterborough. We know the name of his nurse and the clothes that he wore, that he shared a *valet de chambre* and a bedchamber with his brothers, and also at first a governess. He seems to have consumed surprising amounts of soap and shoes; he had a broad black straw hat.[3] In 1395 among these trivial details appears something more significant. At the age of eight he was learning Latin, for seven books of Latin grammar bound in one volume were bought for him in London.[4] By this time his mother was dead and although his father was home the children had their own tiny household and did not often see him. This household made more than one move before, at the beginning of 1397, it seems to have been broken up. Henry at least visited his grandmother, the old countess, though the greater part of his time seems to have been spent with his father's father, John of Gaunt. His brother Thomas

[1] J. H. Wylie and W. T. Waugh, *The Reign of Henry V* (Cambridge, 1914), i. 232.

[2] T. Rymer, *Foedera* (1729), ix. 291. She is bequeathed a cup and ewer of gold, value 100 marks. For grants to her, see *Cal. Pat. Rolls, 1413–1416*, pp. 152, 168, 171, 258; ibid. *1416–1422*, pp. 2, 172, 177.

[3] A number of these details will be found in Wylie, *The Reign of Henry IV* (1884), iii. 326–8, and iv, app. A. They are from DL 28/1/3, 28/11/4, 28/3/3, 28/3/4, 41/10/43.

[4] DL 28/1/5, fo. 32. The book cost 4*s*.

was with him for a time and then for a time disappears. The third brother, John, lived at Framlingham castle with another dowager, Margaret, Countess Marshal. The two girls were sent to live at Eaton Tregoes in Herefordshire in the household of Sir Hugh Waterton, a trusted Lancastrian retainer. There their youngest brother Humphrey visited them for six weeks in the late summer of 1397.[1] The girls' household seems to have consisted of an esquire, two waiting women, and two pages; Humphrey came accompanied by his own esquire and his own tutor; but by the following winter his sisters, aged nearly six, and three and a half respectively, were receiving instruction when two books of alphabet were ordered for them in London.[2] The education of these children of the house of Lancaster was not scamped. It is not without interest that the most bookish group of royal princes in medieval England was one *not* educated for the position, but for a humbler station; it contradicts a prevailing notion that when it came to literacy the royal family left the baronage far behind. Of the brothers Thomas alone seems to have been indifferent to learning; at least no books are mentioned in his will. Of Humphrey's book-collecting and patronage of native and foreign scholars, his library in Oxford is still evidence enough. But his brothers Henry and John ran him close. John, afterwards Duke of Bedford and Regent of France, not only commissioned such a splendid show-piece as the Bedford Book of Hours, but for the not inconsiderable price of £2,300 odd he bought the library of more than 1,200 volumes collected over the years at far greater cost by two royal bibliophiles, Charles V and Charles VI of France; besides, instigated by his councillor, Sir John Fastolf, he founded the school of law that became the Norman University of Caen. Henry's life was cut short before he could equal the attainments of his younger brothers; but his own library was for his time,

[1] The young lords were at Tutbury for Circumcision and Epiphany 1397; by 18 Mar. Henry had moved to Pleshy. In August John was at Framlingham, while Humphrey was at Eaton, where his sisters had moved in April. John was still at Framlingham in the winter of 1397. DL 28/1/9, fos. 2, 14^{v}–15^{v}; 28/1/6, fo. 26^{v}.

[2] D 28/1/6, fo. 39: 'Et pro ii libris de ABC pro juvenibus dominabus erudiendis emptis ibidem (London) xiii^{o} die Februarii 20 d. per manus Ade Garston.'

rank, and other tasks, remarkably well stored and, it was believed, much read. A list of 110 volumes in his possession at his death has been preserved; this includes much law, a good many of the fathers, Seneca's letters, Cicero's *Rhetoric*, some history, and some logic.[1] But it does not exhaust the known contents of his shelves. In 1421 a London scrivener received £12. 8*s*. 0*d*. for making copies of twelve books on hunting.[2] A year later, at his death, the king had failed to return two chronicles of the Crusades which he had borrowed from his able aunt the Countess of Westmorland, and a complete set of the works of Gregory the Great which had belonged to Archbishop Arundel.[3] When the poet Lydgate describes him as given to the study of ancient histories, it was not pure flattery. His copy of Chaucer's *Troilus* still survives.

Well-read, if not a scholar, Henry is the first king of England whose state papers, written with his own hand, have been preserved for us. Richard II's minutes, a brief record of approval, survive in some numbers in the archives of his government. A few letters, a telling marginal note here and there in one of three languages, Latin, French, and English, bear witness to Henry IV's literacy and addiction to business. But with Henry V, the king who kept personal control of every branch of government, we enter on a period in which it is not unusual to find the royal wishes set out in the king's own hand, especially matters too secret for another's knowledge. To read a man's own words is to know his mind more intimately than at second-hand. Henry V's writing, unlike that of many of his wordy and florid contemporaries, is what might have been expected from a man of decision; it is unadorned, brief, and very much to the point. The instructions that he penned for the eye of his ambassador to the Emperor, Sir John Tiptoft, in January 1417, have the ring of authority.[4] The document is a long one for it deals with a complicated international situation; I can only quote the opening words to illustrate Henry's tone of command:

'Tiptoft, I charge you by the faith that you owe to me that ye

[1] See Appendix C.

[2] F. Devon, *Issues of the Exchequer, Henry III to Henry VI* (London, 1837), p. 368.

[3] T. Rymer, *Foedera*, x. 317.

[4] Ibid. ix 427.

keep this matter, hereafter written, from all men secret save from my brother the Emperor's own person, that never creature have witting thereof without mine especial commandment of mine own mouth or else written with mine own hand and sealed with my signet. Keepeth this charge as ye will keep all that ye may forfeit to me . . .' That bald beginning 'Tiptoft' is characteristic. Even in those letters which the king dictated one gets to recognize the informality and the tone of voice. During the years when he was absent from England on campaign, a stream of letters to the councillors and ministers at home left them in no doubt about his wishes. He has received a complaint of misgovernance in the provinces and writes 'Call the justices unto you and by their advice ordain that both parties have no cause to complain for default of justice.'[1] On another occasion comes a message: 'We have granted the Archbishop of Cologne, our vassal, an annual fee of 500 marks. Pay it without delay and in haste!'[2] He hears that a Breton ship has been captured by Cornish pirates and orders immediate restitution in accordance with the treaty 'betwix us and our . . . brother of Brittany. And knoweth well that our will and desire is that the said truces be kept as justly for our party as we would that they were kept towards us for his party, and in such wise that neither he nor his said subjects have no cause reasonable to complain unto us hereafter for this cause, nor for none other semblable, for default of right.'[3] In his concern for justice and in the abruptness with which he expressed his will, Henry V reveals his character in his letters. A letter written in 1419 from Normandy, ordered a careful watch to be kept upon one of his prisoners taken four years before at Agincourt. The Duke of Orleans was then in Pontefract castle, but was so little confined that he was allowed to visit the country place of Robert Waterton at nearby Methley to hunt and disport himself. Hearing of a Scottish plan to rescue him, Henry writes: 'I will that the Duke of Orleans be kept still within the Castle of Pomfret

[1] E 28/33, no. 4, 12 July 1419.

[2] E 28/33, no. 6, 20 Sept. 1419.

[3] P.R.O. Chancery Warrants, C 81/1384, no. 61. Signet letter of 8 June 1418 written 'in our host afore Loviers'.

without going to Robert's place or to any other desport; for it is better he lack his desport than we were deceived.'[1] Once more the incisive phrase.

The language, you may have noticed, is always English. Though he could read, write, and speak Latin and French—and that for pleasure—Henry was the first King of England who preferred to conduct business in the vernacular and to encourage its use by others. It is recorded among the memoranda of the London Brewers' Company that in 1422 it was resolved to keep their records in English: 'Whereas our mother-tongue, to wit the English tongue, hath in modern days begun to be honourably enlarged and adorned, for that our most excellent lord King Henry V hath in his letters missive and divers affairs touching his own person, more willingly chosen to declare the secrets of his will, and for the better understanding of his people, hath with a diligent mind procured the common idiom (setting aside others) to be commended by the exercise of writing.'[2] Three and a half centuries had passed since the Norman conquest before a king harked back to Alfred's example and encouraged the use of English rather than scholarly Latin or polite French to record the decisions and actions of government. This is all the more remarkable when his conquest of France and his assumption of the succession to the French crown involved his captains in the use of a different language across the Channel. If it was Henry's aim to unite in his person the kingdoms of England and France, one would have thought that such a union would have been eased and enforced by encouraging the use of French (still the traditional language of polite society in England) in the government of both countries. There is something incongruous in the king's preference for the vernacular; for he can hardly have hoped to make it the spoken language of the governing class in his second kingdom. And yet he may have done! It is perhaps this encouragement of the English tongue that has persuaded some French historians that he was (in the words of one) 'the first King of England who had some English blood in

[1] H. Ellis, *Original Letters Illustrative of English History* (1824), i. 2.

[2] *A Book of London English, 1384–1425*, ed. R. W. Chambers and Marjorie Daunt (Oxford, 1931), p. 139.

his veins'. In fact he had no more than his two predecessors. Like every previous member of the royal family since Henry II he had Norman, Gascon, French, and Spanish blood in his veins. The tiny fraction of Anglo-Saxon ancestry (getting smaller in each generation) derived from one source only: Henry I's marriage with Edith of Scotland, and even though Henry V was descended by three or four lines from her, he was further away than any king before him. Most of his blood was Norman or French.

It would be odd to leave the treatment of Henry's education without a reference to the tradition that he resided for a time at Queen's College, Oxford, under the charge of his uncle Henry Beaufort, afterwards Bishop, first of Lincoln, and then of Winchester. Beaufort, who was only a dozen years older than his nephew and who was certainly his political mentor at the beginning of his public career, had been educated at Peterhouse, Cambridge, before he migrated to Oxford; he had rooms in Peterhouse in 1388, but was paying for a set at Queen's in 1393–4. In 1397–8 he was Chancellor of the University and it is argued that it was then that his nephew came into brief residence. In its favour this theory of an Oxford education can cite the learned works he was afterwards to read and possess; the titles in his library are thoroughly academic and, compared with his brother Humphrey's humanist leanings, old-fashioned as well. But he was ten years old in 1397 and there is no time after 1398 (when he was still only eleven) that he can have been here. He was too young to have been able to benefit much from the curriculum of the university. What is more there is no hint anywhere in his father's accounts for 1397–8 that he was residing at Oxford; the references there are to London, Hertford, Pontefract, and Kenilworth; and although there is recorded the purchase of a Latin grammar (Donet) for his brother John, the iron chain that was bought for Henry's greyhounds suggests that he was differently occupied.[1] The Queen's tradition must be regarded as suspect.

At the beginning of October 1398 his father's exile brought about a change in Henry's life. King Richard, treating the boy as a surety for the Duke of Hereford's good behaviour, kept him

[1] DL 28/1/6, fo. 39.

in his own household under his own eye. When, in May 1399, Richard set out for Ireland, Henry went with him; he was well treated by the king and is said to have been knighted by him in Ireland, though only in his twelfth year. Meanwhile Hereford had landed in Yorkshire and made himself master of Richard's kingdom. Leaving young Henry at Trim, Richard crossed to Wales and was tricked into putting himself in his enemy's hands. While this was happening Hereford sent from Chester to Ireland for his son. It was at Chester in August 1399 that the king, his captor, and the latter's young heir met in a curious scene which was to set Henry of Monmouth's course as Prince of Wales. On arriving by sea from Ireland, he seems to have gone at once to Richard who had won his affectionate loyalty during his father's exile, and took up his place in attendance on his king. Here he was found by his father when Hereford came to speak to Richard:

and after departed; and in the departing, Henry, the son and heir of the said duke, came to his father and knelt down before him and welcomed him, as him ought to do; and there forthwith his father charged [him] the next day to come from the king and wait upon him. Then this young knight Henry [aged twelve, remember] brought the king to his chamber with a sorrowful heart, for cause he should depart from his godfather and his sovereign king, for he loved him entirely. And when he came into the king's chamber he told the king how he must the next day after, wait upon his father by straight and hard commandment. And then the king said to him these words: 'Good son Henry, I give thee leave to do thy father's commandment, but I know well there is one Henry shall do me much harm and I suppose it is not thou. Wherefore I pray thee be my friend, for I wot now how it will go.' And so on the next day after Henry took his leave of the king his godfather with a heavy heart and went to his father. And after that was the king arrested in the same castle by the said duke, and all his meyny that were about him put away and such men were put about him as the duke would.[1]

This was written by a partisan of Richard II and the sentiment has doubtless been exaggerated. But at the back of the new Prince of Wales's growing estrangement from his father was a

[1] *The Brut*, ed. F. Brie (E.E.T.S., 1908), ii. 545.

boy's ardent loyalty for the king his father deposed and murdered. How far Henry V was from forgetting his first lord is emphasized by one of his earliest actions as king. After his murder Richard was buried in the church of the Black Friars at Langley in Hertfordshire. The beautiful tomb he had caused to be built beside his first wife's grave at Westminster Abbey remained empty throughout the reign of Henry IV. Henry V had his body brought there for reburial and set to work to complete Richard's unfinished nave. His devotion to the abbey was as great as Richard's, and it was there too that he chose to lie when his time came.

The second period of Henry of Monmouth's life—the reign of his father, 1399–1413—can be briefly dismissed. Its most striking episodes, his capture of the Council in 1410 and 1411, his exclusion from power, the king's fear that he was contemplating armed rebellion, and their final reconciliation, were dealt with in my account of Henry IV. Between his twelfth and twenty-fifth birthdays the Prince of Wales grew up and learnt his trade. From September 1400 until the surrender of Aberystwyth in the autumn of 1408, with the advice of a council of tried soldiers, he was engaged in the recovery of his Welsh principality overrun by Owen Glendower. As Henry IV put it, he had left his 'first-born son in Wales for the chastisement of the rebels'. Wounded in the face at Shrewsbury when not yet sixteen, he had also experienced a war of sieges and the importance of artillery; he had found himself as a general in the company of such noble captains as Hotspur, Richard Beauchamp, Earl of Warwick, the Lord of Powys and Sir John Oldcastle. But after 1406 his attention was turned more and more to English affairs where his father's illness invited his interference. Henry seems to have been impatient of the king's weakness and impatient to succeed to his inheritance. From 1408 onwards he was deeply involved in the work of the Council until at Christmas 1411 his services were abruptly dispensed with. During that period a determined attempt had been made to set the royal finances in order, to restore good diplomatic relations with the other maritime powers, in particular Flanders, and to intervene on the Burgundian side in the French civil war. There is here a foretaste of Henry's achievements as king. But although much of his time had been taken up in the camp and the council chamber, his growing energies had not been fully expended in the tasks of government. For they were insatiable; and his vision of what he could do was limitless. If he died in his prime of dysentery, it was because he had asked more of his body than it could give. Until he became king—especially for so long as his suspicious father deprived him of responsibility—his ambition was thwarted, or rather perverted into less worthy channels. Thus were provided the materials for the legend of Prince Hal.

For Henry was one of those men about whom legend gathers. As the art of biography revived in the generation after his early death, memories of his wild youth came to replace the full story of his devotion to duty and hard work. It was on these memories that Shakespeare built. They were up to a point accurate memories. Disbelieved by Victorian scholars, they have been proved to have contemporary support. In contrast to his self-discipline and single-mindedness as king, his youth had had its disorders as well as its achievements. That with some wild friends he had lain in wait and robbed his own receivers, that he attracted to himself low and riotous company, that if not dissolute himself he was at least far from chaste, and that William Gascoigne, the Chief Justice, had then so far offended him as to be dismissed at the beginning of his reign, can now hardly be doubted.[1] The interest lies in the suddenness and completeness of the reformation at his father's death. So long as Henry IV lived, wrote Tito Livio in 1438, the prince 'exercised equally the feats of Venus and Mars'; thereafter 'he reformed and amended his life and manners so that there was never no youth nor wildness that might have any place in him, but all his acts were suddenly changed into gravity and discretion'.[2] 'As soon as he was made King,' wrote his much older contemporary Walsingham, 'he was changed suddenly into another man, zealous for honesty, modesty and gravity.'[3] Now he had work to do. All the chroniclers in fact say the same thing: 'suddenly he

[1] See C. L. Kingsford, *Henry V* (London, 1901), pp. 86 ff.

[2] *The First English Life of King Henry the Fifth*, p. 17.

[3] *The St. Albans Chronicle*, p. 69.

became a new man'. It was an instantaneous and lasting conversion, which happened literally overnight. His father died in the Jerusalem Chamber at the west end of Westminster Abbey on 20 March, 1413. That night the new king came to confess himself to an anchorite who occupied a cell near St. Benet's chapel in the south transept of the abbey; just as Richard II had come as a boy thirty years before, after Wat Tyler had been killed in his presence. Henry remained there all night in secret converse with his ghostly adviser, dedicating himself to his new purpose.[1] There was an end of hesitation and there was no room for the weaknesses—or for the boon companions—of his youth. One small result of this was wonderingly noticed by the chroniclers. From the day of his father's death until his marriage with Katherine of France in June 1420, Henry is said to have kept himself entirely chaste.[2] This presumably contributed to his reputation as a lover of priests, of being that rarely popular figure 'a priests' king'. But if some of his closest friends were clerks, Henry was nothing of the mollycoddle that phrase usually implied.

As to his personal appearance, the chroniclers are agreed and their descriptions tally with the traditional portraits. Unlike his father who was short, Henry of Monmouth was above the average in height, slim, and small-boned; his thick brown hair was, in obedience to the fashion of his day, cut fairly short and confined to the crown of his head; he was clean shaven all round to a line well above his ears. He had a long, oval face, a deeply indented chin, and clear, expressive hazel eyes. He spoke little and that—like his writing—strictly to the point. Considering what he did to it, even though his exertions killed him young, his lightly made body was tough; to his contemporaries he seemed tireless, driving himself and others to the limit of endurance.

In nine years he accomplished much. In 1422 he was the arbiter of Christian Europe, dwarfing Emperor and Pope; and he had transformed the spirit of his own people. Unfortunately he had counted upon more than nine years and he died with nothing finished; worst of all for the historian, leaving his ultimate inten-

[1] *Thomae de Elmham Vita et Gesta Henrici Quinti*, ed. T. Hearne (1727) (Pseudo Elmham), p. 15.

[2] *The First English Life of King Henry the Fifth*, p. 5.

tions uncertain. When he died he was recognized, but by scarcely half the population, as Regent of France and heir to that kingdom. Had he lived for as little as two months more he would have been crowned its king. Instead he was succeeded by a child, less than nine months old. So, not only was his first great task incomplete, but his death has deprived historians of any certainty about his goal and even less about his chances of achieving it. On his death-bed he asserted that had he lived, he would have united Christendom against the Turk and 'built again the walls of Jerusalem'; some doubt about the seriousness of such aims is understandable. The age of the Crusades was over and that of world empires not begun. But it is possible to believe that Henry V might have bridged the gap that divides Napoleon from Godfrey de Bouillon, and have succeeded where Richard I and St. Louis had failed. It did not happen. Within thirty years what Henry *had* done had been completely destroyed. He did not change the course of history; to some historians that amounts to saying that he never could; that is, of course, nonsense. But though it would be foolish to be certain that his vast designs were attainable, I for one must doubt the contrary. His particular brand of far-sightedness, combined with a most unvisionary attention to detail, his military genius and diplomatic resource, made a forceful combination which it would have been difficult for his opponents to withstand. And they were in no case to resist. He had profited from 'a France full of faction'; why should 'a Europe ruled by puppets' have presented greater difficulties? He was faced by no one he needed to fear. Had he been living in 1450, there is no reason why he should not have rolled up the map of Europe as in nine years he had rolled up that of France. Indeed it is hard to believe anything else. That is enough of might have beens; it is time to consider what was done and how.

In 1411 the small English army under the Earl of Arundel which was sent to intervene in the French civil war accomplished nothing. It was too small. That which followed in 1412 under Henry's brother Thomas, now Duke of Clarence, only drove the opposing French princes into a temporary peace among themselves as a result of which the invader was persuaded to take himself off.

Henry seems to have learnt the lesson of these experiences though in neither expedition was he present. The parties to the French civil war must somehow be prevented from forgetting their quarrels in the face of a foreign invasion: that was the aim of diplomacy, though it involved tortuous negotiations with both sides. 'Open agreements openly arrived at' formed no part of Henry V's method; he aimed not at peace but at success in war; it was the diplomat's business to prevent a junction of his enemies, to create the conditions favourable to victory. Hence modern French historians are really paying him a deserved compliment when they recoil in anger from 'his duplicity . . . his pretence of defending right' and consign him to the age of the Italian tyrants to which in any case, like his enemies whose double-dealing failed, he belonged.[1] Henry's diplomacy was thoroughly tortuous and those who were deceived cannot escape the jibe of being fools. But he was not the one Machiavelli in an innocent world; he merely played the usual game with uncommon skill. In war one hopes to deceive.

Diplomacy does not win victories unsupported by force of arms. As a soldier Henry had two immediate tasks: to persuade the French to fight a pitched battle and to beat them. The danger was that, remembering the strategy of the 1370s, the French would refuse battle. Indeed at the critical moment the old Duke of Berri was in favour of letting Henry return home unmolested. A successor to Crécy and Poitiers was needed to make the English enthusiastic for war and willing to pay for the cost of its early stages and to demoralize the already divided French. Then conquest might be attempted. But the purpose of the carefully prepared expedition of 1415 was not conquest but a victorious battle. It was achieved by taking enormous risks. Harfleur at the mouth of the Seine was assaulted in the middle of August; it held out for a month, not surrendering until 14 September. At this late season Henry imitated the strategy employed by Edward III in 1346; it was rewarded by a second Crécy. By cutting his numbers and equipment to a minimum and by giving the French the impression that he was afraid to fight, he lured an enormously larger

[1] E. Perroy, *The Hundred Years War* (trans. D. C. Douglas, 1965), p. 235.

army into attacking his skilfully chosen, though hastily prepared, position. It was cut to pieces with scarcely any loss on the English side. Henry's army reached Calais laden with royal and noble prisoners on 16 November.

Round one had gone entirely according to plan. Henry prepared for round two without hurry, making all ready for a war of sieges, of artillery, and siege engines. Meanwhile in 1416 a Franco-Genoese fleet which attempted to retake Harfleur was destroyed by Henry's brother, John (Duke of Bedford) in the mouth of the Seine. And the diplomatic offensive was kept up. Then between August 1417 and May 1420 Normandy was conquered; the fall of Rouen after six months of heroic resistance on 13 January 1419 may be regarded as the decisive stage in this uniformly successful operation. The Treaty of 1420 merely recognized what had been achieved. The intervening period had seen a remarkable transformation of the conquered duchy. The fiefs of its lords—most of whom had retreated before Henry's advance—were shared out among the English captains; between July 1418 and June 1419 six Norman counties were conferred upon their leaders. Henry V's plan here was like William I's Norman conquest in reverse; the English revenge for 1066. Those of the native population who were willing to accept an alien master were left in possession, but they had also to receive and obey an alien governing-class. The lordships and castles passed into the hands of Henry's English earls, barons, and mercenary adventurers. The campaign of 1417–19 brought great rewards for the conquerors.

A pause followed for the king's marriage and the coronation of his queen. For six months in 1421 England and the need for reinforcements claimed Henry's attention; and then he returned with fresh troops and arms for the final effort. Until May 1422 his piece-meal conquest of northern France gathered momentum, when at the taking of Meaux on the Marne he contracted the disease from which he died. For more than three months he fought against it until he was too weak to ride a horse. His last hours were embittered by a sense of work unfinished, of the dangers for his infant heir, of the infidel in the Holy Places.

It is recorded that his end was peaceful—'like one who fell asleep'; but just before he had started up crying: 'Thou liest, thou liest, my portion is with the Lord Jesus Christ' as if he were boldly addressing the evil spirit. He had reason to be disturbed. The French had practically abandoned hope when his death saved them; it is unlikely that their resistance would have stood another pounding. As it was it took them twenty-seven years to win back what he had gained in less than seven.

It is surprising to find that the French writers of the fifteenth century treat Henry more generously than do their modern successors. The defeat of their countrymen did not blind them to the qualities of their enemy. It is different when we turn to the French historians of the nineteenth and twentieth centuries. I have already cited some of their unchivalrous judgements and more are available. Among the 'unpleasant features' discovered in Henry by the best of them are 'the affectation of piety', a 'hypocritical devoutness', cruelty, senseless ambition, and utter lack of scruple.[1] Part at least of this immoderate indictment is baseless and most of the rest comes from a determination to judge Henry by standards inapplicable to his time. This is seen by comparing it with the views of his contemporaries, both friends and foes.

The suggestion that Henry's piety was a pretence, that his religion was a hypocrite's, is based neither on the testimony of those who knew him nor on anything that he himself said or did. Though he was the friend of Oldcastle, his own orthodoxy was never suspect. It was as conspicuous before his accession as it was later. His interest in the reform of the Church seems to have been equally genuine. During his visit to England in 1421 he found time to address a meeting of some sixty abbots and more than three hundred doctors and monks of the English province of the Benedictine order 'on the early religious observance of the monks, on the devotion of his ancestors and of others in founding and endowing the monasteries and upon the negligence and carelessness of the moderns'. Nor was he content with mere exhortation; he presented the assembly with a list of thirteen respects in which the brethren fell short of what he regarded as right. Had he

[1] Perroy, op. cit.

returned once more from France, it was not in his character to have been content to find nothing done.[1] He himself founded two monasteries, of Carthusians at Sheen and of Bridgettines at Syon, orders notable for their asceticism and spiritual fervour. Not all the churchmen he employed or had about him were as good as they were able; but those whom he chose as his friends and confessors included most of the best Catholic minds of the kingdom, distinguished scholars and reformers like Stephen Patrington and Thomas Netter, Robert Hallum, Robert Gilbert, and Richard Courtenay. It was not entirely flattery that made the learned Richard Ullerston—another advocate of reform—refer to Henry's 'desire for spiritual study' and commend him for his familiarity with the scriptures.[2] And it is difficult to believe in the hypocrisy of the man who in the early morning before Agincourt recalled that 'Now is all England praying for us.'[3] The worst that can be said of Henry's religion is that it was not free from superstition: he was fearful of black magic. Sorcerers were prosecuted in the courts by his orders and his father's widow was punished by the loss of liberty and property for practising necromancy against him. This is far indeed from an affectation of piety.

The charge of cruelty rests presumably upon the killing of the prisoners after Agincourt. The English were rounding up and stripping their captives when a fresh French attack was thought to be threatened. To prevent their escape while his troops dealt with this new task, Henry ordered them to put to death all but the most valuable of the prisoners. The sight of the execution of this order caused the attackers to withdraw and the English army was able to retreat with the survivors to Calais. Not an attractive episode, but it is necessary to say that it was condemned neither by contemporaries nor by the laws of war. Examples of exactly similar actions by French, Portugese, German, Italian, and Burgundian

[1] For further discussion of this see D. Knowles, *The Religious Orders in England* (Cambridge, 1955), ii, chap. xiii.

[2] See E. F. Jacob, *The Fifteenth Century* (Oxford, 1961), pp. 93, 126–7.

[3] *The Brut*, ed. F. Brie (E.E.T.S., 1908), ii. 378: 'Now is it good time for all England prayeth for us. And in remembrance that God died on the Cross for us let every man make a cross on the earth, and kiss it, and in tokening that we will rather die on this earth than flee.'

commanders can be collected to show that such inhuman conduct was excused in the hard-pressed. Another instance of Henry's severity to attract modern condemnation was the massacre of the citizens of Caen in their own streets when the city was stormed in September 1417. But this was not by Henry's orders and he did his best to ensure that women and clerks were spared; the city had deliberately refused to yield and the civilians were a party to the decision to resist; it is difficult to see how the slaughter could have been prevented. Against these incidents must be set those in which Henry showed himself merciful, in the pardon of scores of Lollards who had been seduced into rebellion by their leaders in 1414, in the offer, made in 1415, of a conditional pardon to the principal traitor Oldcastle, and in the clumsy but well-meaning attempt to save the life of John Badby, the heretic tailor of Evesham in 1410. Henry was a strict disciplinarian and was unwilling to suffer opposition to his wishes. But he was not cruel and his conduct of war compares favourably with the political assassinations which disfigured the record of both parties to the feud of Burgundians and Armagnacs. Seldom has an army of occupation been kept under better control than that with which he overran and held most of northern France.

And with that judgement the French chroniclers agree.[1] What they emphasize as Henry's most notable quality was his respect for justice, and their admiration is ungrudging; it is not as if they thought him a beast but a just beast: their praise is warm. Above all else he was a just prince and the prince of justice 'both in relation to himself, for the sake of example, and in relation to others, according to equity and right; he gave support to none out of favour, nor did he suffer wrong to go unpunished out of regard for kinship'. 'The said King' wrote an enemy, 'was a great administrator of justice, who without respect for persons gave as good justice to the mean as to the great.' He was imperious and harsh; but men expected no less in time of war and they recognized that Henry's justice, however roughly applied, was fairly and indifferently at the disposal of the conquered. Nor did they blame him

[1] For the sources of the following opinions, see Wylie and Waugh, *The Reign of Henry V*, iii. 424–5.

for deceit; if he gained his ends by guile, they still admired him as an honourable opponent. He was an honest man, upright in his dealings, temperate of speech and action, brave, loyal, uncomplaining in adversity, God-fearing. The judgement is unanimous, and coming from his victims has greater force than when it came from his fellow-countrymen who agreed with it. He was, says one 'magnanimous, valiant in arms, prudent'; 'sober and truthful,' says another, 'he was incapable of anything vile or base'. His energy and unyielding resolution were, his opponents all realized, no greater than his constancy, great-heartedness, and love of virtue. This chorus of strikingly consistent testimony is formidable. If we accept it, Henry was a paragon and a hero, a Bayard and Solomon in one; and in face of such disinterested unanimity, I for one do not see how acceptance can be withheld. His faults arose from the excess of his qualities. That he was hard, domineering, and quick to ruthless action can scarcely be denied; anyone so single-minded and unsparing of himself could scarcely fail to be an inexorable driver of others; but there is plenty of evidence that he enjoyed the trust and affection of his followers —and deserved them. The worst that can be said of him, that he was 'set on purposes unworthy of a great and good man',[1] would have been derisively rejected by supporters and enemies alike. In seeking glory in conquest and crowning it by war against the infidel he was a faithful exponent of the chivalric ideal; the Christian knight could do nothing nobler.

Finally there is no justification for calling him a prig. His self-dedication in 1413 had nothing sanctimonious about it; and his merciful treatment of the humble Lollards rebuts the charge of bigotry. Henry remained something of the old Prince Hal; to the end he was the ardent and light-hearted companion of his captains and friends. The Privy Purse expenses of his cousin, the Earl of March, who was at court at intervals during the first two years of Henry's reign, testify to the far from gloomy company by which the youthful king was surrounded. His losses at cards, backgammon, raffles, and chess, losses large and frequent, conjure

[1] Ibid. 426.

up a very different picture;[1] and there are references to many other courtly diversions. Henry, like King David, played the harp, he had a great fondness for music and mumming; he had a taste for burgundy too; and he was as much a patron of poets and actors as he was of scholars and godly clerks.

What his peers thought of him comes through in some of their letters to him. I can only cite one example—from that brilliant soldier, the Earl of Salisbury; dated Argentan, 21 June 1421, it is too long to quote in full:[2]

If it like your Highness to know of tidings from these parts of your land, blessed be God, at the time of writing this, it stood in good plight and never so well as now; for, thanked be God, your liege people here dread never less your enemy than they do this day, and all captains here do well their diligence as well in sure keeping of their places as in stirring and annoying of your enemies. Liketh your Highness to wite that, the Saturday afore the date of this, I, your humble liege man, came home from a journey which I had made into Anjou and Maine [hostile country]; where as I had assembled with me great part of the captains of your land. And, blessed be God, we sped right well; for your people is greatly refreshed with this road; for they sayen in common, they were never more in such road. And we broughten home the fairest and greatest prey of beasts as all those said that saw them, that ever they saw; and also, thanked be God, we miss no man of thrift nor other to account at the said road.

That was not written to a spoil-sport. The greatest of the magnates recognized in him a prince worth fighting under; and when Henry died, though his dynasty had usurped the throne less than a quarter of a century before, his baby heir was recognized without murmur or hesitation as the rightful king.

It pleases lesser mortals to detect the Achilles' heel of the great ones that live in the world's eye; but by whatever standards he is judged Henry was superlatively gifted: his only weakness was the physical one from which he died. He was born to rule and to

[1] B.M. Egerton MS. Roll 8746. The account itemizes losses of £157. 3*s*. 2*d*. during the period 13 Sept. 1413—30 Apr. 1414: e.g., 'Item, in xiiii die Septembris perdebat apud loge de Wynsor apud Tolman iiii ma. vis. viii d.'

[2] T. Rymer, *Foedera*, x. 131.

conquer. The author of the *First English Life* did not, it seems to me, exaggerate when he wrote of him: 'of whose superior in all nobleness, manhood and virtue, to my pretence, it is not read nor heard amongst the princes of England since William of Normandy obtained the government of this realm'.[1] Take him all round and he was, I think, the greatest man that ever ruled England.

[1] *The First English Life*, p. 4.

PART TWO

LOLLARD KNIGHTS

Editor's Note

THE text which follows is derived from a set of lectures given by Mr. McFarlane on at least five separate occasions (1956, 1957, 1960, 1963, and 1966). In 1965 the lectures were called 'The origins of the Lollard Movement'; ten years later they had become 'The Lollard Knights'. The great part of the present text is based on the lectures of Trinity Term 1966 (lectures 1, 3, and 4 are specifically dated to days in April and May of that year). This was the last series which Mr. McFarlane gave. They therefore include his very latest thoughts on the subject. But the text printed here also contains some passages drawn from earlier recensions in order to complete the sequence. The lectures have been divided up into an introduction and six chapters which have been given the six sub-titles chosen by the author for his main divisions. Mr. McFarlane also prepared a paper on the 'Origins of the Lollard Movement' for the Tenth International Congress of Historians at Rome which should have been given on 8 September 1955 and he read single papers on the Lollard Knights to Worcester College History Society (10 May 1962), to the Canterbury and York Society (13 December 1962), and on other occasions.

Wherever possible the text has been left as it stood ready for the lecturer. Some minor modifications, however, have had to be made. Underlinings have been removed. References have been transferred from the text to the footnotes. Editorial additions and alterations have been kept to a minimum. It is clear that the author intended to publish on the Lollard Knights and had begun to work out (in tremendous detail) the critical apparatus for a history of the Trussell family. This has been put in Appendix A. Throughout the footnotes have been compiled in the first instance from the extensive materials which Mr. McFarlane had accumulated in his own collections.

J. R. L. Highfield

CHAPTER I

Introduction

It would be as well, perhaps, if I began by defining a little more precisely the scope and purpose of these chapters. It is very far from my intention to rehash what I have already written. The discovery of a number of new facts seems to me to make it necessary to reconsider the problem of Lollard origins and has led me to adopt views rather different from those which commended themselves to me ten or a dozen years ago, and very different from those long current among historians, especially political historians, of the later fourteenth century. The most recent statement of what may be fairly described as the established tradition will be found in Miss McKisack's volume in the *Oxford History of England*.[1] I will try to show how hopelessly this tradition of interpretation underrates the importance of Lollardy in high places throughout the reigns of Richard II and Henry IV and misconceives the attitude of members of the ruling classes—both lay and ecclesiastical—towards the sectaries and their powerful protectors. The evidence upon which a judgement must in any case be based is so slight that a few scraps of fresh information may be sufficient to give the whole subject a new look; and that, it seems to me, is what has happened. Some of it is far from being conclusive evidence, but it is evidence difficult to reconcile with our accepted notions and equally difficult to explain away. It has to be taken into account and it may involve a wholesale revision of our somewhat naïve ideas about the character of popular religion in fourteenth-century England.

The title should have made it clear that my concern will be with people rather than with ideas. This is not a search into the origins of the Lollards' beliefs—an attempt to trade afresh their intellectual ancestry. Rather its aim is to discover the

[1] M. McKisack, *The Fourteenth Century, 1307–1399* (Oxford, 1959), pp. 320–2.

circumstances in which the movement—one hesitates to call it a sect—arose, to explain how and why it spread and to identify the influences, whether personal or institutional, that fostered its early growth. And by 'early' I mean within the lifetime of the first generation Lollards, the period of rapid expansion which followed the dispersal of the Oxford leaders in 1382.

To date the birth of a popular heresy is often difficult. If Lollardy had been confined to university-trained theologians its beginnings would be easier to pinpoint; but, if not from the start, at any rate from an early stage, it was what I have called extramural, popular rather than narrowly academic, and for that reason largely unrecorded. Until it threatened the peace of the Establishment and therefore called for disciplinary action, its growth escaped the notice of the chroniclers; their silence makes it hard for us to know. Yet once the alarm had been sounded, those who clung to its tenets in defiance of authority naturally tried to conceal their activities from their episcopal persecutors; and in so far as they succeeded, they do so as much from us. The transition from the first kind of obscurity to the second, from the obscurity of neglect to the obscurity of the underground, began in 1382, when the teaching of Wycliffe was at last officially and publicly condemned, and the more prominent of his Oxford disciples were tried, humbled, and driven from the university. It is doubtful which obscurity is the greater. There is a sharp contrast between the vast bulk of the master's writings and the teaspoonful of ascertainable fact which survives as material for a history of the movement he inspired. The absence of any evidence connecting his retirement at Lutterworth with the active proselytizing of the Leicester group almost makes one doubt whether the movement was Wycliffe-inspired; but the doctrines he and they had in common are too many to permit such scepticism; the obvious explanation is that it was Wycliffe-inspired, but not Wycliffe-led. Of the two chroniclers who devote any prolonged attention to Lollardy, neither offers much in the way of hard dates, still less an intelligible narrative of the progress of heresy. The judicial records of those few diocesans who were conscientious disciplinarians and employed conscientious registrars can be of great use, but they are rare and seldom full. In any case most episcopal registers of the fourteenth century have been by now searched for evidence of Lollard trials and there is little prospect of fresh finds. It so happens that the only unprinted report of such a trial that I have found—William Swinderby's before Buckingham of Lincoln's judges in 1382[1]—destroys nearly as much as it contributes to our knowledge. For it shows that Knighton cannot even be trusted to report correctly events which occurred under the very noses of the canons of Leicester.[2] Buckingham's register makes it almost certain that the sermon on Palm Sunday 1382 which the chronicler ascribes in some detail to Mr. John Aston of Oxford was in fact preached by the local evangelist[3] Swinderby. As well as casting doubt upon Knighton's uncorroborated statements, that leaves Philip Repton as the only probable link between the Leicester heretics and the university. It is a high price to pay for the little the report offers to fill out our picture of William the Hermit. Can we even believe what Knighton has to tell us about that missionary's somewhat restless past? Probably not.

What then is left? Not very much. The archives of the royal government do, but only occasionally, throw up a morsel of helpful fact. As for the writings of the Lollards themselves, from the Bible translations to the numerous homilies and broadsheets, they are undated, often, though not quite always, undateable and generally anonymous. I shall have occasion to make use of devotional tracts the owner of which can be identified, as well as some of the authors, but such information is unhappily rare; when it exists it is invaluable. Until the presentments by local juries in 1414 revealed how numerous and how scattered were the pockets of Lollards implicated in Oldcastle's treason, inquiry is frustrated

[1] Lincoln Diocesan Record Office, Register (xii) of John Buckingham, fos 242ᵛ–243ᵛ, 9–14 June 1382.

[2] *Chronicon Henrici Knighton*, ed. J. R. Lumby (R.S., 1889, 1895), ii. 176–8; cf. ibid. 192–7 and Reg. Buckingham, fos. 242–4.

[3] Reg. Buckingham, fo. 242. William Swinderby, hermit, was chaplain of the chapel of St. John, Leicester (K. B. McFarlane, *John Wycliffe and the Beginning of English Nonconformity* [London, 1953], p. 104, and A. Gibbons, *Early Lincoln Wills 1280–1547* [Lincoln, 1888], p. 31).

at every turn by the fragility and discontinuity of the existing evidence. After reviewing it one feels inclined to think that it will probably never be possible—certainly not unless new material is found of a kind and quantity so far unsuspected—to discern the stages by which the movement came into being and took root; nor to name its principal adherents; nor to explain how a logical system of the most academic ingredients was so speedily vulgarized that within a couple of decades this gospel of the Schools had become widely diffused among the laity as well as the non-graduate clergy, right across the English midlands from Kent and East Anglia to the marches and mountains of central Wales. Perhaps all these things are irremediably hidden from us. But before the search is given up in despair, it would be well to make quite certain that the evidence we have is incapable of telling us any more. Considering how much it has been cited and interpreted this may seem unlikely. It rather depends whether we have asked it the questions it can answer. These may not be the ones we should prefer to ask.

Prospecting the familiar ground afresh, the desperate inquirer may think that he sees one not quite exhausted working. Most of its ore was brought to the surface in an article published in the *Scottish Historical Review* by the late Professor W. T. Waugh;[1] but here, if nowhere else, an abandoned mine may be worth reopening. As a result of Waugh's pioneering work one group of reputed Lollards has ever since been written off as supposititious: namely the influential lay sympathizers.

Both the St. Albans and the Leicester chroniclers declare that the heretic missionaries owed their success to the protection of certain misguided but powerful members of the lay nobility. Discretion may explain—though discretion was scarcely Walsingham's strong point—their failure to indicate who, apart from Lancaster, were the dukes and earls they had in mind, but they mention by name a handful of knights to whose activities from time to time they attach most of the blame. Their lists are not identical, though they partly overlap; altogether, including Sir John Cheyne who escaped notice until 1399, they provide us

[1] 'The Lollard Knights', *Scottish Historical Review*, xi (1913–14), 55–92.

with ten names. Waugh laboriously investigated the careers of these men, their birth, rank, employments, affiliations (incidentally, well over a decade before this technique began to be applied to eighteenth-century members of parliament). The result was an amount of evidence, which, if largely negative, seemed to rule out any possibility of dispute with his careful finding that there was little or nothing in the chroniclers' charges. To go over all his work again was as unpalatable a chore as it seemed unpromising; but having done it, I can now enjoy the relief of knowing that it was not in vain. There were many things, some of them of major importance, that Waugh overlooked; the tests he applied for detecting heresy were sometimes misconceived and far too rigid; his conclusion was not nearly as inevitable as he made it seem. It is not only possible, but to my mind clearly necessary, to treat the chroniclers' allegations with respect. What a fresh study of much obscure biographical detail can teach us is to wonder whether we have not been blinded by our preconceptions to the real nature of popular Lollardy in its early stages. It has convinced me that the apostles of heresy really did enjoy for something like thirty years the support and protection of a group of devout and influential laymen quite unconnected with the Duke of Lancaster. The evidence for this view and then its implications form the subject-matter of these chapters. I shall first try to correct and supplement Waugh's account of the 'Lollard knights', considering them merely as members of a group (if such they were) without trying to pin a charge of heresy upon any of them. As men who were prominent in the court and council of Richard II, they are worth examination on their own account quite apart from any suspicion of religious heterodoxy. Some sides of their careers Waugh unaccountably ignored; his treatment of their political affiliations is not very penetrating; nor is he very sound on their economic position. My first task will be to get all these aspects into better focus.

Secondly, I want to consider some new and some old evidence for concluding that these men—and a few others not mentioned by the chroniclers—were either Lollards themselves or willing to patronize and protect those that were. Not all this evidence is equally conclusive, though it includes a treatise by one of the suspects in which he admits that his opinions laid him open to a charge of Lollardy. Cumulatively it seems to me too weighty to be disregarded.

Lastly, there are what I have called the wider implications. If, until in the first months of Henry V's reign Arundel struck at Oldcastle, there existed an influential group of Lollard knights who were known to be Lollard knights and yet were molested by neither the spiritual nor the secular arm, a good many things follow. An immunity of thirty years enjoyed by men who waited upon the king at court and attended his Council at Westminster during which *de Haeretico Comburendo* passed into law, needs some explaining. It is curious how little this bothered those historians who, writing before Waugh, accepted the chroniclers' story without hesitation. If Waugh is to be repudiated, this difficulty needs to be faced. Its explanation, it seems to me, involves a fairly radical revision of our views about the character of late fourteenth-century religion in England. The Lollard knights then fall into place as the English exponents of that *devotio moderna* which followed a different course abroad; or perhaps rather as a sort of left-wing deviation from a larger norm. That, at any rate, is how the evidence compels me to see them.

Since all this will involve a great deal of detailed criticism and correction of Waugh's article, I had better go on record at once as a firm believer in his accuracy as a scholar and level-headedness as an interpreter of difficult and contentious evidence. His article is easily the most important contribution of this century to our knowledge and understanding of Lollardy. Though he opted in the end—from too great caution—for what seems to me the less likely alternative, he came very near to the correct solution of the problem and he saw at least some of the consequences that the correct solution would involve. His article deserves to be read.

As a biographer Waugh falls into two general errors. They are serious and often cause a distortion in his brief lives of the Lollard knights. They arise from his misunderstanding of two of the most prominent characteristics of late fourteenth-century English landed society, namely the retinue and the 'use'.

In the case of retinue Waugh has been deceived by an ambiguity in the contemporary usage of the word *retinencia*. No distinction was made between those who were enrolled under a captain in time of war and those who had been retained by him for life in *peace* and war by indenture; both were spoken of as members of his retinue, though the first were his subordinate companions-in-arms and the second his menial servants. Sometimes the former were described as members of his *comitiva*, but *retinencia* is just as often used. To take an example, all those who served directly under John of Gaunt in his great *chevauchée* of 1373–4 went to France in *retinencia sua*; but the majority of them were not bound by indenture to give him life-service and do not appear upon his private retinue-list. Their loyalties had a limited purpose and a limited duration. Their appearance in the lists printed in John of Gaunt's first *Register*[1] is no evidence of their close attachment to his interests. His genuine retainers—his 'meignie'—are those given under the title *Nomina militum et scutiferorum* at the beginning of his second *Register*.[2] This point needs to be laboured; the blurring of the distinction between the two types of retainer has caused Waugh and others to assign to Lancaster's retinue—and hence in politics to his so-called 'party' many knights and esquires whose permanent attachments lay elsewhere.[3] To go to Brittany or Calais in Lancaster's company is no evidence of political affiliation. His retinue was large enough in all conscience without these fortuitous accretions. Sir Thomas Latimer, in Waugh's words, appeared 'in the retinue of John of Gaunt' in 1373;[4] so did Sir Lewis Clifford both in that year and again in 1378;[5] but neither was, as far as we know at any time,[6]

[1] *John of Gaunt's Register, 1371–1376*, ed. S. Armitage Smith (Camden Soc., 3rd ser., 1911) xx. 31–5 (nos. 45–50).

[2] Ibid., *1379–1383*, ed. E. C. Lodge and R. Somerville Camden Soc., 3rd ser. 1937), lvi. 6–13.

[3] Waugh, op. cit., p. 89.

[4] Ibid., p. 71.

[5] Ibid., pp. 58–9.

[6] Clifford, described as 'nostre bien ame chivaler monsire Lowys de Clifford', was done a favour by the duke on 21 Mar. 1373 (*Register, 1371–6*, i. 125). On 13 Apr. that same year he, among others including the Black Prince and Sir John Clanvow, received a present of plate from Lancaster (ibid. ii. 192). And on 8 May 1374 Lancaster's receiver-general was ordered to pay him 100 marks (ibid., p. 224). But not all who enjoyed the ducal largesse were retainers. In 1378 when Clifford

one of Lancaster's indentured retainers; it was these latter who served him in peace as in war; that was the point of them—they were full-time menial servants, members of his household and drawing his fees.

Failure to understand the use has perhaps even more serious consequences. By the end of the third quarter of the fourteenth century the practice of granting legal seisin in one's lands to a group of defendants, kinsmen, and friends while retaining the use, management, and yield in one's own hand had become very common if not almost universal. An enfeoffment to use had so many advantages, not least, that it enabled a landowner to evade most of the feudal incidents to which his estate was liable as well as to will his lands to whom he would. To misunderstand a use when you see one can be a great source of error. In the first place it can make a great landowner appear to die a landless man. When the escheator took an *inquisitio post mortem* to discover what lands the dead man died possessed of the answer might be none; because he had conveyed the seisin to feoffees—members of a trust, an undying corporation which never suffered a minority and could not be given in marriage. Thereby the overlord lost wardship, marriage, and escheat; and the inquisitions *post mortem* cease to provide historians with a true list of the dead man's manors, rents, and advowsons. Waugh completely missed this point. On the one hand, using the inquisitions *post mortem*, he concluded that the majority of the Lollard knights were virtually landless and dependent upon the wages and annuities they received from their lords.[1] This was far from true. On the other

was about to serve once more with him in the French war, Lancaster nominated Sir Lewis one of his feoffees in his lands after his death (*Cal. Pat. Rolls, 1377–1381*, p. 262), but not all the feoffees were 'Lancastrians'. Like Sir Guy Brian and Sir Simon Burley (who were similarly absent from the 1379 list of Gaunt's retinue), Clifford is more likely to have been chosen to reinforce the Lancastrian servants with a sprinkling of influential courtiers. That the feoffees were not necessarily members of the duke's party is shown by the presence at their head of his recent opponent, William Courtenay, Bishop of London.

[1] Waugh, op. cit., p. 89. That Waugh did not grasp the significance of the use is demonstrated by his reference to Sturry's 'joint-ownership of the manors of Risinglass, Suffolk and Hickling, Norfolk, though his share cannot have yielded much' (ibid., p. 70 n. 3).

hand finding charters of enfeoffment to uses, he thought these were simple, outright alienations. When one of his knights enfeoffed his manors to uses Waugh assumed that he was being compelled by necessity to part with his capital; when one of them acted as a feoffee, Waugh thought he was becoming a part owner of the land and since it was usual to have a good many—sometimes more than a dozen—feoffees (in case some died), he concluded that each's share was correspondingly small. Both deductions were completely erroneous. They combined to persuade him that he could trust the evidence of the inquisitions *post mortem* and that his Lollard knights had no great landed resources. Of all his deductions this was the most vulnerable.

CHAPTER II

The Record of the 'Lollard Knights'

I BEGIN to review the careers of the ten named 'Lollard Knights' of the chronicles, disregarding for the moment the question of their religious beliefs or sympathies and concentrating on the evidence that tells us who they were and what they did. We derive seven names from Walsingham and six from Knighton. They may be classified as follows:

1. *Those common to both lists*:
   Sir Lewis Clifford
   Sir Richard Sturry
   Sir Thomas Latimer

2. *Those mentioned only by Knighton*:
   Sir John Trussell
   Sir John Peachey
   Sir Reynold Hilton

3. *Those mentioned only by Walsingham*:
   Sir William Nevill
   Sir John Clanvow
   Sir John Montagu

4. *Walsingham's afterthought*:
   Sir John Cheyne.

Next a not very important point: the dates at which these knights are mentioned in the chronicles. Walsingham recites their names on two occasions, in 1387 at the time of the Pattishall affair, and in 1395 when the Lollards petitioned Parliament.[1] It is a testimony to the accuracy of his reporting that the two knights in his first list who had died in the interval are omitted from his second: Sir William Nevill and Sir John Clanvow. Knighton's single list appears in his history under the year 1382.[2] It might therefore be possible to argue that the three knights peculiar to his account had ceased their association with the heretics by the time of which Walsingham was speaking. In support of that view is the fact that one of them, Sir John Peachey, had died in 1386. But as an argument this perhaps depends too heavily upon the assumption that Knighton is a reliable witness.[3] I have already given reason for doubting his accuracy as a reporter of what happened in 1382 at his own house of Leicester. He was wrong—and Walsingham again was right—about the identity of the Palm Sunday preacher.[4] It is on the face of it likely that Walsingham was better informed than he about the membership of the group of Lollard knights. The three names peculiar to Knighton's list belong to a totally different category from the rest. They must be regarded as resting under a lesser degree of suspicion than the other seven. I propose, therefore, to dismiss them briefly before turning to the chief suspects. If the latter could be cleared no one would bother about the three accessories; but that does not mean that there is nothing in Knighton's charges.

It is indeed uncertain whether one of his knights exists at all. No Sir Reynold Hilton is known for that period; and although it

[1] *Thomae Walsingham . . . Historia Anglicana*, ed. H. T. Riley (R.S., 1863–4), ii. 159 and 216. The same passage will be found with slight difference in *Chronicon Angliae*, ed. E. M. Thompson (R.S., 1874), p. 377, but whereas the *Chronicon* has 'et inter omnes major fatuus, Johannes Mountagu' the *Historia* changes this to 'et, inter caeteros major fatuus, Johannes Mountagu'. The Pattishall affair was a riot in London occasioned by the preaching of an Austin friar, called Peter Pattishall, who had been influenced by the Lollards, cf. A. Gwynn, *The English Austin Friars in the time of Wyclif* (Oxford, 1940), pp. 273–6.

[2] Knighton, ii. 181.

[3] He grouped too many incidents in which Wycliffe, Swinderby, and other Lollards were concerned within a single year for the accuracy of his dating to be accepted (*Knighton*, ii. 151–98). As Waugh noticed (op. cit., p. 87 n. 4) there are indications that Knighton's account was written a good many years after the events he describes.

[4] *Historia Anglicana*, ii. 53; *Chronicon Angliae*, p. 338.

is just conceivable that a man could be a knight and yet escape mention in the public records it is by no means likely. There was a Sir Robert Hilton, Sheriff of Yorkshire 1383–4 and 1386–7, commissioner and justice of the peace, altogether an active figure in the public life of his county during the 1380s and 1390s and a landowner in the district of Holderness.[1] There is nothing to connect him, as far as I can discover, with any of the other knights on our list. He seems to have been a Lancastrian; as the elder Sir Robert Hilton he is described as a 'king's knight' in the reign of Henry IV.[2] The only Reynold Hilton known to have been living

[1] For his tenure of the office of sheriff see *Calendar of Fine Rolls*, x. 7, 76, 152, and 208; for his commissions see *Cal. Pat. Rolls*, *passim*. There is a short account of the Hiltons of Swine in G. Poulson, *History and Antiquities of the Seignory of Holderness* (Hull, 1840–1), ii. 197–9, and there are biographies of two members of the family in *Parliamentary Representation of the County of York 1258–1832*, ed. A. Gooder (Yorks. Arch. Soc. Record ser., 91), i. 92–4 and 177–8. Whatever his affiliations may have been during Richard II's reign, such evidence as there is suggests that these were exclusively confined to the East Riding. His connections were with such local families as those of de la Pole, Hastings, Meaux, Sutton, and Constable of Halsham (*Cal. Close Rolls, 1377–81*, pp. 228–9, 245, and 247; *1389–92*, pp. 83–4; *1392–6*, pp. 378 and 503; *1396–9*, pp. 194 and 196).

[2] *Cal. Close Rolls, Henry IV*, ii. 326. The one fragile thread that joins him to any one of 'the Seven' leads not surprisingly to his fellow northerner. Nevill's wife was the step-daughter of Sir Brian Stapleton, K.G. of Carlton (near Snaith) and Wighill in the West Riding (*Complete Peerage*, 2nd edn., ed. V. Gibbs *et al.*, xii, pt. ii. 322–3). She is mentioned in his will (*Testamenta Eboracensia*, ed. J. Raine [Surtees Soc., 1836], i. 198–201). His heir at his death (25 July 1394) was his grandson Brian (Sir N. H. Nicolas, *The Controversy between Sir Richard Scrope and Sir Robert Grosvenor* [London, 1832], ii. 285–90; G. F. Beltz, *Memorials of the Order of the Garter* [London, 1841], pp. 77–89). On 14 Feb. 1397 the wardship and marriage of the younger Brian was obtained by Sir Robert Hilton (*Cal. Close Rolls, Henry IV*, ii. 326). Livery of the inheritance was granted to the heir on 2 Dec. 1407 (Ibid. iii. 302). In or before 1404 he had been married, presumably by his guardian, to Agnes, the daughter of Sir John Godard (cf. *Parl. Representation Yorks.* i. 143 and 176). Her mother, Constance, daughter and co-heir of Sir Thomas Sutton of Holderness, had been previously married to Sir Piers Mauley VI (*Complete Peerage*, viii. 568 and xii, pt. 1, p. 575). Agnes's father almost certainly died between 16 Feb. and 13 May 1392 (*Cal. Fine Rolls*, xi. 37 and 43–4) and her mother had married before 28 Aug. 1395 a third husband: Sir Robert Hilton (*Cal. Pat. Rolls, 1391–6*, pp. 654–5). There she is wrongly called Margaret, the name of her sister who had died on 10 Oct. 1391 (*Complete Peerage*, i. 102; *Test. Ebor.* i. 149–52). Poulson (op. cit. ii. 198 and 326) makes Hilton's wife Constance the daughter of Piers Mauley VI, but the commission of 28 Aug. 1395 cited above rules this out. Sir Robert Hilton's namesake, who was also his son and heir,

in Richard II's reign was not a knight but a clerk.[1] Since it was usual in that period to describe both priests and knights as 'sir' *dominus*, Knighton may simply have mistaken his rank. For Reynold Hilton, priest of the diocese of Lichfield, is a much more plausible suspect than Sir Robert the Yorkshire knight. For he was Controller of the Royal Wardrobe from the beginning of Richard II's reign until Michaelmas 1381.[2] He had, according to Tout, begun his official career as a clerk in the Black Prince's service.[3] After 1381 he had a somewhat chequered career as a clerical pluralist.[4] He was still alive in 1390. As a servant of the

received a substantial annuity from Henry IV soon after the Lancastrian usurpation (ibid. i. 12; *Feudal Aids*, ed. H. C. Maxwell Lyte [London, 1899–1920], vi. 546).

[1] Cf. Waugh, op. cit., p. 87.

[2] T. F. Tout, *Chapters in Medieval Administrative History* (Manchester, 1933), vi. 30 (1 July 1377–30 Sept. 1318).

[3] Ibid. iii. 329–30 and iv. 195–6. The inference was based on Hilton's absence from the royal service before Richard II's accession when he became Controller and on his association in office with those known to have been inherited from the Black Prince's service. It gains some necessary support from the prince's order, 4 June 1363, to pay him 50*s*. by way of imprest (*Register of the Black Prince*, ed. M. C. B. Dawes and H. C. Johnson [London, 1930–3], iv. 497).

[4] He had obtained the prebend of Hembury or Henbury in Westbury College on 15 Nov. 1375 (H. J. Wilkins, *Was John Wycliffe a Negligent Pluralist?* [London, 1915], p. 37). He exchanged it for that of Farndon-cum-Balderton in Lincoln Minster about 5 May 1379 (J. Le Neve, *Fasti Ecclesiae Anglicanae*, new edn., *Lincoln Diocese*, ed. H. P. F. King [London, 1962], p. 65). His prebend at Westbury is his first recorded benefice. On 31 Mar. 1378 the king had granted him the deanery of the royal free chapel at Holyhead (*Cal. Pat. Rolls, 1377–81*, p. 160). On 1 Apr. that year he was presented by the Crown to the church of Warton-in-Kendale, Lancashire (ibid., p. 168) and on 27 Feb. 1380 by the same patron to that of Bassingbourn, Cambridgeshire (ibid., p. 442). By 13 Feb. 1382 he had added prebends at Chichester (Henfield) and St. Asaph (Llanefydd, normally attached to the chancellorship) to that of Farndon-cum-Balderton and the rectory of Bassingbourn (ibid. *1381–5*, p. 96). In 1389 he exchanged the deanery of the king's free chapel of Tamworth for a prebend at St. Mary's-in-the-Castle, Leicester (ibid. *1388–92*, pp. 157 and 163). Neither the royal grant of Dunnington in York Minster (11 June 1380), nor that of the rich living of Meifod, diocese of St. Asaph (26 Feb. 1381) came off (Le Neve, op. cit., *Northern Province*, ed. B. Jones, [London, 1963], p. 46; *Welsh Dioceses*, ed. B. Jones [1965], p. 45 and n.). Hilton's efforts to obtain possession of the latter got him into trouble with both pope and king (*Calendar of Papal Letters*, ed. W. H. Bliss and J. A. Twemlow [London, 1902], iv. 427; *Cal. Close Rolls, 1381–5*, p. 22; *Cal. Pat. Rolls, 1385–9*, p. 93). For Dunnington see *The Diplomatic Correspondence of Richard II*, ed. E. Perroy (Camden Soc., 3rd ser. xlviii), p. 5 (no. 8 and n.).

Black Prince who became a household official of the prince's son, Reynold Hilton must have come into close contact with most of the principal subjects; but then so must many wholly innocent men. Reynold Hilton's guilt is not proven.

There is no visible sort of case for suspecting Sir John Trussell. Not much is known about him, though he had some property in Northamptonshire not very far from Knighton's abbey. He was the younger son of a cadet branch of a prominent Warwickshire family. His father was Sir Theobald and his elder brother was Sir Avery. The Trussells were closely associated with the service of the Beauchamp Earls of Warwick and in the first surviving receiver-general's account of Earl Thomas the Appellant (1396–7) we find both Sir John and Sir Avery in receipt of fees of 20 marks p.a. Sir John seems to have been of a turbulent nature; he was constantly in trouble and his friends were repeatedly forced to go surety for his good behaviour. His grandfather Sir William, *c.* 1280–*c.* 1346, was a deeply committed servant of Thomas and Henry of Lancaster until 1330.[1] Thereafter he was primarily a royal servant (as were the Earls of Lancaster too). His only connection, as far as we know, with the family under the patronage of which he had risen to wealth and prominence, was the sinecure stewardship of the honour of Leicester in Northamptonshire—the sort of retaining fee an influential royal agent might hope to collect from a great lay magnate.[2] His younger brother, however, Sir Edmund Trussell, who had been an adherent of Thomas of Lancaster from 1313 or earlier down to 1322 (though, unlike Sir William,[3] he made his peace with Thomas's enemies

[1] For the career of Sir William Trussell see Appendix A.

[2] He is found as steward of Lancaster's honour of Leicester in Northants. in 1337, with a deputy to do his work (R. Somerville, *Duchy of Lancaster* [London, 1953], i. 356) and he witnesses a release to the earl at London, 14 Sept. 1332 (*Cal. Close Rolls, 1330–3*, p. 598). He was paid £20 'ad voluntatem domini' in 1330–1, but this does not seem to have been an annual fee (P.R.O. D.L. 40 /1/11, fo. 48v).

[3] Pardoned as an adherent of Thomas of Lancaster 16 Oct. 1313, 1 Nov. 1318, and 9 Apr. 1324 (*Parliamentary Writs*, ed. F. Palgrave [London, 1827–34], ii, div. ii, appendix, 67, 128, 254 and div. iii. 1527–8; *Cal. Close Rolls, 1318–23*, pp. 421, 702, and cf. 628). On 20 Apr. 1328 John Mowbray granted him £20 p.a. for life from Melton Mowbray (ibid. *1327–30*, p. 379). He witnessed a Mowbray deed on 8 May

after Boroughbridge), remained a Lancastrian servant in Edward III's reign. By 1336 he was Steward of Earl Henry's household and he is mentioned as still holding that important and confidential office in the earl's will made a fortnight before death in September 1345.[1] Sir Edmund died in 1349, the year of Sir John's birth.[2]

Sir William's son, Sir Theobald, the father of the Lollard suspect, was his father's and his childless uncle's heir. He was often employed in his youth as his father's colleague or deputy[3] and on at least two occasions when he went to the French wars—in 1347 and 1356—it was under the captaincy of Henry of Grosmont the fourth Earl and first Duke of Lancaster.[4] There is no evidence that he was permanently retained by this lord or by his successor in the earldom and duchy, John of Gaunt. He sat at least four times for the county of Northampton in Parliament (three times between 1365 and 1368).[5] He died in 1369. The only odd thing about a somewhat ordinary life was his failure to marry his mistress until at least ten years after the birth of their eldest child.[6] Sir John his heir had therefore an elder brother, Sir Avery,

1328 (ibid., p. 385). At some date before 28 Apr 1341 his annuity had been reduced to 100*s*. and 'robes of the suit of knights' of Mowbray livery, and he was now receiving 20 marks p.a. from Lancaster's manor of Higham Ferrers (*Cal. Pat. Rolls, 1340–3*, p. 176). He witnessed a grant to the earl at Leicester, 23 July 1339 (Somerville, op. cit., p. 354).

[1] Lincoln Diocesan Archives, Register of Thomas Bek (vii), fo. 216[r] and [v] (will dated 8 Sept. 1345; the earl had died on the 22nd). The legacy to Sir Edmund Trussell does not appear in the summary of the will in A. Gibbons, *Early Lincoln Wills*, pp. 17–18.

[2] He was thought to be alive on 20 June 1349 (*Cal. Fine Rolls*, vi. 142), but was dead by that year according to Somerville, op. cit., p. 354. He may therefore have been a victim of plague, which returned that summer.

[3] *Cal. Pat. Rolls, 1334–8*, pp. 421; *Cal. Close Rolls, 1339–41*, pp. 196 and 262.

[4] Hon. G. Wrottesley, *Crecy and Calais* (1898), p. 131; 'Military Service performed by Staffordshire Tenants', *Collections for a History of Staffordshire*, Wm. Salt Arch. Soc., orig. ser. viii, pt. i. (1887), 101.

[5] Feb. 1351, Jan. 1365, May 1366, and May 1368. (*Members of Parliament, Returns*, pt. 1 [Parliaments of England, 1213–1702] [London, 1878], pp. 148, 175, 177, and 180.)

[6] This allegation was made by his granddaughter, Philippa Trussell, the wife of Alexander Bozon in a Chancery suit against her own mother between 1432 and 1442, the date of her mother's death. Though *ex parte* and highly suspect, the story conflicts with no known evidence about the children of Sir Theobald

and an elder sister, who were illegitimate and who were provided for at his expense by their father.[1] Sir Avery with the Warwickshire manor of Nuthurst made a great marriage and founded the Trussell family that survived at Nuthurst and elsewhere in Warwickshire into the seventeenth century.[2] The bastard sister was given various tenements. She did not marry.

Sir John inherited three groups of manors: the group near Leicester, the group near Northampton (including Gayton where Sir John died), and the group strung out in the Welland valley on either side of Market Harborough.[3]

Born in or about 1349 he was nearly or quite of age at his father's death.[4] The first thing he did which brought him into prominence

and makes sense of what would otherwise be puzzling about them. The bastard child Philippa named was her aunt, Agnes or Anne (P.R.O., C 1/11/139 and cf. C 1/11/263).

[1] For the sister see p. 153 n. 6 above, for the putative brother see p. 156 n. 3 below. Sir Theobald's widow, Katharine, presented to the living of Gayton, Northamptonshire, on 28 Apr. 1369, 3 July 1370, and 18 July 1373. There was not another recorded presentation until 1396 (G. Baker, *History and Antiquities of the County of Northampton* [London, 1822–41], ii. 279). Since she was the mother of the bastard daughter and survived her husband, John may have been her son. The lands held by Sir John in Leicestershire and Northamptonshire were assessed at £40 p.a. for the income tax of 1412 (*Feudal Aids*, vi. 495).

[2] *V.C.H. Warws.* iv. 100.

[3] In the north-west those of Littlethorpe, Peatling Magna, and Fleckney, all within a radius of less than ten miles of Leicester near the roads joining that town to Lutterworth, Northampton, and Market Harborough. To the East, on both sides of Market Harborough, were the manors inherited from Sir Edmund, John's great uncle: Hothorpe by Theldingworth on the Northamptonshire bank of the Welland some four miles up-stream from the town, and Westhall in East Carlton, Trussell's manors in Holt, Prestgrave, Drayton, and Bringhurst on the borders of Rutland and close to Rockingham. (For these see G. E. Farnham and A. Hamilton Thompson, 'The Manor, House and Chapel of Holt', *Trans. Leics. Arch. Soc.* 13, pt. ii [1924], 209–12; the same authors' 'History of the Manor of Withcote', *Associated Architectural Socs.' Reports and Papers*, 36 [1921], 173–4; and J. H. Hill, *The History of Market Harborough* [Leicester, 1875], pp. 67–8, 158, and 284). In the south-west the manors of Gayton (its new owner's favourite residence) and (after 1405) Flore were in the Nene Valley not far from Northampton and only just off Watling Street.

[4] He was described as twenty-four years and more in the inquisition following the death of William Hakluyt taken at Oakham, Rutland, on 14 Nov. 1373 (*Calendar of Inquisitions post mortem* [Rec. Comm., 1954], xiii, no. 262). It is not certain when he was knighted. The Leicester chronicler, writing in the 1390s, may have antedated it. It had happened by 26 Sept. 1387 (*Cal. Close Rolls, 1385–9,*

was to abduct—no doubt with her consent—a tenant-in-chief who was also a widow: Alice who had been the wife of Sir Hugh Despenser, a younger son of the baronial house. As Waugh noticed,[1] though it is not clear what importance he attached to it, the grandfather of her second husband had presided at the trials and executions of the grandfather and great-grandfather of her first. No doubt it made an interesting subject of conversation in the families concerned.

Alice was an heiress, the daughter of Sir John Hotham, the great-nephew and heir of the rich John Hotham, Bishop of Ely 1316–37.[2] Unfortunately for Trussell she had given a jointure in her manors (the most important were Solihull, Warwickshire, and Colleyweston in Northamptonshire)[3] to the landless Hugh Despenser and settled them on her children. So when she died in 1379 her second husband (who had omitted or failed to obtain a jointure in them for himself) lost them to his stepson Sir Hugh Despenser the younger. The possession of Solihull, 1374–9, may be an influential factor in bringing Sir John Trussell into contact with other Lollard knights.

He had a son John by Alice Hotham—unfortunately half-witted. So when he married again (his wife's name was Margaret but we do not know her family) he settled his own inheritance upon her in jointure with himself. Again he had bad luck. His and Margaret's only surviving issue was a girl, Philippa.[4]

Now about his personal affiliation to the service of a particular lord: there is nothing whatever to connect him with John of Gaunt. Though the latter as lord of the manor of Leicester was a powerful influence in the two counties where Trussell's manors lay, the records of the duchy never mention either Sir John or his brother Sir Avery. Where they turn up is in the retinue of Thomas Beauchamp, Earl of Warwick, the Appellant of 1387.

pp. 436–7) and could have happened long before that date. Chancery enrolments are very irregular in their recording of a man's status.

[1] Waugh, op. cit., p. 86 n. 8.

[2] Sir W. Dugdale, *The Antiquities of Warwickshire* (London, 1730), pp. 941–2; *Cal. Close Rolls, 1343–8*, p. 388; *V.C.H. Warws.* iv. 218.

[3] *Cal. Inq. p.m.*, xiv, no. 56. For Solihull see *V.C.H. Warws.* iv. 218–19.

[4] See above p. 153 n. 6.

The Beauchamp accounts do not begin until the financial year 1395–6 (Michaelmas to Michaelmas). By then both Trussells were retained for a fee of 20 marks p.a.[1] And they are still on the next receiver-general's account for the year of Warwick's arrest for treason 1396–7.[2]

One of the most serious gaps in our knowledge of the political history of Richard II's reign is the almost total absence of any record of the names of those servants, retainers for life and retainers *ad hoc*, who accompanied the Appellants against Robert de Vere in Oxfordshire in 1387 before following them to their confrontation with Richard in the Tower in the last days of the year. If the Trussells took any part in these events it is hardly likely to have been on the king's side. In 1395–7 Sir Avery seems to have been more prominent in Warwick's service than Sir John. In April 1397, for example, he was sent with a letter from their master to Henry, Earl of Derby, at Brecon, a tantalizing hint as to what was going on beneath the outward calm before Warwick's arrest on 12 July.[3] Another entry suggests that Sir Avery was a member of Warwick's council: he attended a meeting of councillors at Henley-in-Arden in June 1397.[3] The Trussells were certainly not on the king's side in this new crisis—though they seem to have been ready (as were so many others) to desert a lost cause both in 1397 and again in 1399. As a result they ceased to be feed by Richard Beauchamp who succeeded his father as Earl of Warwick in 1401.[4] If they took service with someone else the evidence does not survive.

The only other incidents in Sir John's career which call for notice are those which suggest a strain of lawlessness in his character. The abduction of an heiress was too common to be regarded seriously and Trussell's of Alice Hotham was punished by a fine of 100*s*.[5] But his imprisonment in the Tower before June 1378 (and despite his brother's and stepson's efforts to bail him he was still there and strictly confined in September)

[1] Beauchamp Accounts, P.R.O., SC 6/1123/5 m. 1 d.

[2] B.M. Egerton Roll 8769, m. 1 d.

[3] Ibid., m. 3 d.

[4] *Complete Peerage*, xii, pt. 2. 378; and cf. B.M. Egerton Roll 8770.

[5] *Cal. Pat. Rolls*, *1374–7*, pp. 34–5.

requires some explanation.[1] The offence is merely described as trespasses against the king and his ministers in Rockingham Forest. If these were forest offences they must have been unusually serious to merit solitary confinement in the Tower of London for some months at least.

The next occasion may refer to some more political misdemeanour but the evidence is compatible with some kind of local feud or riot. On 3 April 1398 Sir John was subpoenaed before the Council at Westminster 'in order to declare what shall be laid before him by the council at his coming'.[2] This was followed by a number of recognizances to keep the peace towards certain of his neighbours. It may have something to do with the seizure and distribution between the courtiers of the Beauchamp estates.

The last incident of this sort that calls for mention is in a different class. Not only was John Trussell the aggrieved party but it was the only occasion apart from his alleged Lollard sympathies when he can be said to have hit the headlines: by being mentioned in the chronicles, and much more resoundingly than in Knighton's list. Fortunately the records are even fuller than the chronicles and describe the whole incident in great detail. We need not go into every detail but some circumstances provide valuable light on the Trussells in church.

The incident occurred in two parts on Easter Day 1417 when Sir John was about sixty-eight.[3] It took place after High Mass in the morning and at Vespers in the afternoon in the church of St. Dunstan-in-the-East behind Thames Street in the City of London. The chroniclers allege and the records confirm[4] that the origin of the trouble lay in a quarrel between Lady Trussell and the wife of Lord Strange of Knockin, a Welsh border landowner.

[1] *Cal. Close Rolls, 1377–81*, pp. 200, 215.

[2] Ibid. *1396–9*, p. 277; cf. p. 497.

[3] *The Register of Henry Chichele, Archbishop of Canterbury, 1414–1443*, ed. E. F. Jacob (Oxford, 1943–7), iv. 169–75.

[4] *Historical Collections of a Citizen of London*, ed. J. Gairdner (Camden Soc. N.S. [1876]), pp. 115–16; *The Great Chronicle*, ed. A. H. Thomas and I. D. Thornley (London, 1938), p. 96. J. Stow, *The Annales of England*, continued by E. Howes (London, 1631), p. 352; cf. *Cal. Close Rolls, Henry V*, i. 393, 447, and 458.

We are not told what about. In the morning Lord Strange abused Sir John, calling him a lewd knave and various other dishonourable epithets. Sir John told him he lied in his throat. Strange went home to dinner vowing violence. So three aldermen waited on him in his inn and got him to promise to do Sir John no harm. Then they extracted the same promise from his enemy. They do not seem to have been sure of the outcome since after dinner they accompanied Trussell back to Vespers. When he was deep in prayer either just before or after the sermon (this is not clear) in came Lord Strange accompanied by a dozen Shropshire esquires and yeomen armed with swords and daggers. These were followed by Lady Strange and an esquire. She cried out, 'Hearst thou, Trussell, thou shalt abide this bargain though boughtst never none so dear.' Her esquire seized Sir John by the throat and flung him to the ground. Then Lord Strange moved in to the kill, shouting 'Stick him, slay him'. A London citizen and some of Trussell's servants went to the fallen knight's aid. All, being unarmed, were wounded, the citizen being killed. Trussell tried to defend himself with his staff, but received sword wounds on the left elbow and wrist.

This affair caused a great stir. The ecclesiastical authorities excommunicated the assailants and compelled them to do elaborate penance.[1] Lady Strange was made to give £10 to the polluted church, her husband £5. Trussell recovered 1,000 marks damages and costs in the King's Bench. Though he had not turned the other cheek in the verbal battle at High Mass he had avoided all provocation at Vespers.

That is virtually the last we hear of him. He died aged about seventy-five on 21 March 1424. When his first wife's descendants by Hugh Despenser died out in 1408 he tried to recover parts of the Hotham inheritance for his feeble-minded son. This merely involved him in vexatious litigation. His widow lived on until 1442. Waugh gets almost every fact wrong.[2] What are we to make of them? Well, in the first place, Trussell's lands lay not merely near Knighton's Leicester, but also in the very tracks

[1] *Reg. Chichele*, iv. 174–5.

[2] Waugh, op. cit., pp. 86–7.

that William Swinderby is said to have travelled as a preacher, when he visited Market Harborough.

On the other hand, secondly, his record hardly seems to fit our normal idea of a Lollard sympathizer: the evidence of lawlessness, the membership of a lordly meinie, the preoccupation with the affairs of the world such as land-grubbing and land-grabbing. Waugh, if he had thought Trussell worth serious investigation, would have dismissed the charge of Lollardy on this ground. Other evidence about other knights of proved Lollard sympathies must make us question this line of argument.

There remains the knight's demeanour in St. Dunstan's on Easter Day. No hint of unorthodoxy here—unless there be something suspicious in his very show of devoutness 'at the preaching time' as one chronicler described it. But if every one who went to church twice on Easter Day and was punctual in his devotions is to be branded a Lollard, our problem would be greatly simplified. For the moment we can merely take note of the lawlessness, worldly objectives, and the devout appearance and compare them with the behaviour of other more certain heretics. As far as Trussell is concerned the verdict is once again: not proven.

With regard to Sir John Peachey, Waugh missed the one really significant fact. He was a minor at the time of his father's death in 1376, having been born in either 1360 or 1361;[1] and on 1 March 1376 Edward III granted the wardship of his lands and the marriage of his person to Sir Richard Sturry.[2] Unfortunately we do not know the surname of the wife Katherine to whom Sturry married him. But it is a point of some moment that during the first four or five years of Richard II's reign, the young John Peachey was a ward of one of the chief suspects. The chances that Katherine Peachey was a kinswoman or connection of his guardian are high. Sir John Peachey's lands, including his principal manor of Hampton-in-Arden,[3] were during the same period enjoyed by Sturry, and these, as Waugh noticed, lie close to the

[1] *Cal. Inq. p.m.* xiv, no. 278.

[2] *Cal. Pat. Rolls, 1374–7*, p. 250.

[3] *V.C.H. Warws.* iv. 83 (Hampton-in-Arden); and cf. vi. 80 (Dunchurch); iii. 120–1 (Honiley); v. 48 (Fenny Compton); and v. 221 (Wormleighton).

town of which Sir John Trussell was lord *iure uxoris* at that time, namely Solihull. A faint justification for the inclusion of at least Peachey in Knighton's list can therefore be made out.

So much for these three minor figures who were ignored by Walsingham. They may have given aid and comfort to the Lollards, but we know too little about them to say. But it is worth remembering that Warwickshire was one of the areas visited by Swinderby in 1382 after Leicester got tired of him and that in 1415 there were enough sympathizers in the county for Oldcastle to take refuge there. With such slight reservations we must write off this trio. The ten little nigger boys are reduced to Walsingham's seven—of whom three are also mentioned by Knighton. By contrast these seven were for long prominent in national as well as local affairs. It is to them that my remarks will in future apply.

The most obvious thing about them is their compactness as a group. Of very widely scattered geographical origins and of widely different inherited blood and property, their public careers and employments had brought them into intimate association over a long period. Their names occur together in scores of private instruments, as witnesses, feoffees, mainpernors, and executors. There is clear and plentiful evidence that ties of friendship and mutual trust existed between them. The court was their common ground, but it cannot wholly explain their intimacy. As Waugh, who grasped this fact and stated it fairly though he was reluctant to draw the obvious conclusion, realized: 'the striking point is that the chroniclers, with several scores of king's knights to choose from, should pick out as fellow heretics some half-dozen who as a fact were particularly intimate.' Even among the inner circle of household knights this is true. The knights of the king's Chamber at any one time seem to have numbered sixteen. Tout has collected the names of twenty-six who are known to have served Richard II in this capacity;[1] four of these were so-called 'Lollard knights': Clanvow, Clifford, Nevill, and Sturry; only one of the remaining twenty-two is found associating as closely with them as they with one another, and he was Sir Philip

[1] T. F. Tout, *Chapters*, iv. 344–6.

de la Vache, Sir Lewis Clifford's son-in-law and heir, the exception in fact that proves the rule. There are reasons to which I shall refer later for thinking that la Vache is one of those who should have been on the chroniclers' lists;[1] we must add him to ours. Lollard or not, he belongs to the group we are considering.

Since they were friends and business associates it is natural that they should have possessed certain marked characteristics in common. Some of these they shared with a good many of their contemporaries. For instance, that they should have been career-soldiers who had seen much campaigning in Edward III's wars is to be expected of members of their class, born as they were in the quarter-century 1325–50. What is less usual but still not uncommon is that they all belonged to that distinct branch of fighting-men who were retainers in the narrow sense, retained by their lords for peace as well as for war, in particular that they were menial servants of the royal house.

They were not a territorial group: they did not come from a single locality nor were they bound together by dependence on the patronage of a single great landowner. Their social origins were gentle but varied. They were slightly separated in age. Unfortunately the fighting-men of the fourteenth century usually made themselves out to be considerably younger than they really were, not merely before the escheator's inquisition but even when giving evidence in such a matter requiring a long memory as the dispute between Scrope and Grosvenor in the court of chivalry. We do not know the exact birthday of any one of our seven knights, though in the case of Latimer the month and year, September 1341, are pretty certain.[2] However, a fairly close approximation is possible for the other six.

Sturry was the oldest, having been born in the later 1320s. His nearest contemporary was Clifford whose birth came soon after 1330. Then there is a gap of roughly a decade and the births of Latimer, Nevill, and Clanvow follow in or about 1341. Then

[1] See below, p. 185.

[2] *Cal. Inq. p.m.* xi, no. 378. The proof of age says that he was born and baptized at Braybrooke on Monday, the feast of the Exaltation of the Cross, 15 Edward III; but 14 Sept. 1341 was a Friday.

another decade until 1351 when Montagu was born and soon afterwards Cheyne.

There is nothing surprising in the discovery that the better their birth and connections the more rapid their rise. Nevill, as the brother of John, Lord Nevill of Raby (d. 1388), and Alexander, Archbishop of York (1374–88), became Admiral of the North in 1372 when he was only thirty-one.[1] Montagu, the eldest son of a peer, though not yet heir-presumptive to the earldom he ultimately inherited, was knighted in 1369[2] after already distinguishing himself as a soldier by the age of eighteen. Latimer, of a less important family achieved the same rank in his early twenties. The diversity of their geographical origins is typical. The Nevills were a County Durham family whose interests were almost entirely north of the Trent;[3] Latimer's not very extensive lands were in the east midlands; while the Montagus' belonged to the south and south-west.

The other four—Clanvow, Clifford, Sturry, and Cheyne—with some help from connection and some from marriage, sprang from the lesser gentry and made their way more slowly by their wits. Clanvow was the only one who inherited a modest estate;[4] the other three seem to have started as landless gentlemen, cadets of families similar to the Clanvows. Lewis Clifford is stated by Waugh and by other historians to have been a brother of Lord Clifford, head of the great and ancient Westmorland family. This is due to an error of Froissart's.[5] In fact John of Gaunt's *Register* provides evidence to disprove it.[6] Lewis Clifford, far from being of north-country baronial family was a cadet of the Cliffords of Devonshire, such small fry that their pedigree is difficult to trace. Thanks in part to Sir Lewis's additions to the estates of the family, the descendants of his brother became Lords Cliffords of Chudleigh in the seventeenth century. Sir

[1] *Cal. Close Rolls, 1369–74*, p. 428.

[2] Jean Froissart, *Chroniques*, ed. K. de Lettenhove (Brussels, 1876), viii. 344, 346; *Cal. Pat. Rolls, 1381–5*, p. 362.

[3] For those of Ralph, second Lord Nevill, father of William, see *Complete Peerage*, ix. 499–501.

[4] See Appendix B.

[5] Froissart, x. 394.

[6] *John of Gaunt's Register, 1371–6*, i. 124–5 (no. 293).

John Clanvow's ancestors were Welsh, close neighbours of the Oldcastles in the upper valley of the Wye in Herefordshire. His father was an esquire of Edward III's household in 1349 and this official connection may have helped him at the beginning of his career.[1] Sturry who came from Kent was similarly[2]—but probably not so closely—related to a royal official: Sir William Sturry, Marshal of the Household 1338–40. Such official connections were invaluable and even the noble Montagu owed something of his ability to win Richard II's friendship to the fact that his father and namesake was Steward of that king's household from 1381 to 1387. Sir John Cheyne's origins have long puzzled historians and the fact that there were two other Sir John Cheynes active in Richard II's reign has added to the confusion.[3] There were in fact half a dozen well-established families of the name in various parts of the country. Sir John settled himself on the land in Gloucestershire and Lincolnshire, but he was a cadet of the family of Drayton Beauchamp in Buckinghamshire—a not unimportant fact in the light of that family's adherence to Lollardy well into the fifteenth century.[4] John Cheyne of Drayton Beauchamp is found in a document of 1437 described as kinsman and heir male of our Sir John Cheyne.[5] The heraldic evidence supports this relationship.[6]

[1] See Appendix B.

[2] The origins of Sir Richard Sturry of Barnwell (Northamptonshire), Bolsover (Derbyshire), Lee, Lewisham, Blackheath, Bromley, and East Greenwich (Kent) etc., are unknown. His acquisition of considerable property in Kent, which went to his heirs, suggests a connection with the parish of Sturry, Kent. On the other hand his interests were by no means confined to Kent. He married as her second husband Alice, daughter of Sir John Blount and heir of her mother, Elizabeth, daughter and heir of Simon Furneaux of Kilve (alive 1384); Richard d. *s.p.* in 1395, Alice similarly in 1414. Her first husband had been Sir Richard Stafford junior or 'le fitz', born *c.* 1330, died 1370/4, without issue.

[3] Sir John Cheyne of Isenhampstead Chenies (Buckinghamshire), M.P. for Bedfordshire in 1372 and Sir John Cheyne of Herefordshire and Shropshire, who was the Earl of March's knight and died in 1398.

[4] On 10 Aug. 1394 our Sir John Cheyne appointed Roger Cheyne as his attorney (*Cal. Pat. Rolls, 1391–6*, pp. 486, 562, and 638). This connects him with the Cheynes of Drayton Beauchamp.

[5] Magdalen College, Oxford, Hickling 105 (Macray 286) and 98 (301). John Cheyne of Drayton Beauchamp then claimed to be his kinsman.

[6] Sir John Cheyne's coat of arms was 'checky a fesse fretty' with a crest of an

By what avenues they reached the service of Richard II is of more importance. Taking them in order of age:

1. Sturry began as a yeoman in the household of Edward III, from 1349 to 1363, then served as esquire,[1] and finally from 1366 as knight[2] 'who stays continually by the king's side in his service'[3] —that is to say a knight of the Chamber. He was in fact one of the small number of Chamber knights of the old king who continued in that office under Edward's grandson. In view of Walsingham's famous story about Sturry at the Black Prince's death-bed,[4] rendered improbable by the knight's subsequent high favour with Joan, Princess of Wales,[5] it should be mentioned that the surviving registers of the Black Prince show Sturry receiving various small rewards at the prince's hands in 1353 in association with various of the prince's yeomen.[6] The fact that he passed straight from Edward III's Chamber to Richard II's suggests that his links with the Black Prince's service were closer than Walsingham's puzzling report would allow.

2. Sir Lewis Clifford as a Devonian very properly began his career in the duchy of Cornwall which then as now included Dartmoor and other lands in Devon. On 5 Aug. 1364 he was as the Black Prince's esquire granted £40 p.a. for life from the revenues

oak tree (Magdalen College, Oxford, Hickling 81 [239], dated 12 June 1395). According to Papworth these arms were those of the Cheynes of Chesham Bois (Buckinghamshire); cf. J. W. Papworth, *An Ordinary of British Armorials*, new edn. (London, 1961), p. 791. But that family did not exist in 1395. The ancestor of the Cheynes of Chesham Bois was Roger Cheyne (*c.* 1362–1414) of Drayton Beauchamp, son of William and grandson of Thomas. His son John was an infant. The descendants of Thomas Cheyne who acquired Chesham Bois after 1423 and became Viscounts Newhaven in 1681 bore 'checky or and azure, a fesse gules fretted argent'. Thomas Cheyne's great-grandson inherited Drayton Beauchamp in 1468.

[1] *Cal. Close Rolls, 1360–4*, pp. 346–7; king's yeoman, 20 Dec. 1353 (*Cal. Pat. Rolls, 1350–4*, p. 532); 1 Sept. 1361 (ibid., *1361–4*, p. 57); 24 Dec. 1361 (ibid., p. 137); 9 Oct. 1363 (ibid., p. 400).

[2] Cf. *Cal. Pat. Rolls, 1364–7*, p. 312, grant of 12 Oct. 1366, 'before he had taken the order of knighthood'.

[3] *Cal. Fine Rolls*, vii. 261 (16 June 1363).

[4] Walsingham, *Chronicon Angliae*, p. 87.

[5] He was, for instance, her executor on 2 Dec. 1385 (*Cal. Pat. Rolls, 1385–9*, p. 65).

[6] *Black Prince's Register*, iv. 101, 161, 168; iii. 115.

of Cornwall;[1] he had already been in his service since at the latest 1360.[2] He was never retained by the Duke of Lancaster; but as a favourite knight of Gaunt's elder brother he received (as did others like John Clanvow) presents of plate and other courtesies from the duke.[3] His master was the Black Prince[4] and then after the latter's death he served first his widow and then his son.

3. Sir William Nevill may have been made a knight of Edward III's household in Dec. 1376 but it is more likely that the annuity he was then granted[5] was for service in the household of the new Prince of Wales. This annuity was confirmed for life in October 1378,[6] but the first definite reference to Nevill as a knight of the Chamber comes in 1381.[7] He held this office until his death.

4. Sir John Clanvow is first found as a knight bachelor in the service of Humphrey Bohun, Earl of Hereford in January 1373, when he received a life-annuity of £40. With the earl's death (16 January 1373) he passed into the service of Edward III.[8] On 15 June of that year, the day on which Clanvow's annuity from the Bohun estates was confirmed by the king, Edward granted him an additional £50 p.a. for life.[9] Thenceforward he is found in close association with other members of the court. Among the narrower circle of the knights in whom we are interested, his friendship with Sir William Nevill soon became particularly close. The first time that I have noticed them mentioned together was in 1376 when they were both among the mainpernors of William, Lord Latimer, accused in the Good Parliament.[10] They alone of the seven appear in that list but Sir Philip de la Vache is there, as is also Sir John Montagu, the father of the

[1] Ibid. ii. 208, 210, and 214.

[2] Ibid. iv. 389; cf. also pp. 514 and 394.

[3] *John of Gaunt's Register, 1371–6*, i. 124–5 (no. 293), and ibid. ii. 192 (no. 1342); 223–4 (no. 1429).

[4] On 1 Sept. 1368 his annuity from the Black Prince was increased to 100 marks p.a. from Cornwall (*Cal. Pat. Rolls, 1377–81*, pp. 157–8) and sometime before his death the prince also granted him £100 p.a. for life (ibid.). His knighthood seems to have dated from this time.

[5] *Cal. Pat. Rolls, 1374–7*, p. 389 (10 Dec.).

[6] Ibid. *1377–81*, p. 277.

[7] Ibid. *1381–5*, p. 54.

[8] Ibid. *1370–4*, pp. 303 and 325.

[9] Ibid. p. 301.

[10] *Rot. Parl.* ii. 326–7.

Lollard knight, and Sir William Beauchamp,[1] who is another suspect whom I shall have occasion to discuss later; suspect or not he was a close friend of our men; he repeatedly turns up in their company, in particular in matters affecting his and their estates. He was a councillor of the Black Prince and head of Richard II's Chamber from 1378 to the end of 1380 or the beginning of 1381.[2] The really intimate association between Clanvow and Nevill began in 1378[3] and continued until their deaths. Clanvow like Nevill was attached to Richard II's household from the start[4] and like him in 1381 received a large life annuity as a knight of the Chamber.[5]

5. Thomas Latimer, perhaps because from the year he came of age (1362)[6] he was the head of a landed family with local responsibilities,[7] or possibly because for some reason he did not commend himself to Richard II personally, was the least intimately connected of the seven with the royal service. But he *was* connected and, what is perhaps more important, he did not stand apart from the other six in their private activities. The chief difference is that while the others once more became Richard's trusted councillors and envoys after 1389, Latimer did not. His connection

[1] See below, pp. 214–15.

[2] Tout, *Chapters*, iii. 353, 356; iv. 333.

[3] On 26 Jan. 1378 he was retained to serve under Lancaster (Nicolas, *The Controversy between . . . Scrope and . . . Grosvenor*, ii. 437). According to Waugh (op. cit., p. 75) he shared with Sturry, Sir Philip de la Vache, and Sir William Nevill the command of 120 men. On 25 Mar. 1380 he, Sir William Beauchamp, Sir William Nevill, and Sir Lewis Clifford were executors of the will of the Earl of Huntingdon, proved on 12 July 1382 (*Cal. Pat. Rolls, 1381–5*, p. 153) and connected with the winding-up of Richard Lyons's lands in London, 23 Aug. 1382 (ibid., p. 164; *Calendar of Select Pleas and Memoranda Rolls, 1381–1412*, ed. A. H. Thomas (London, 1932), pp. 103–4).

[4] His £50 p.a. was continued by Richard II (*Cal. Close Rolls, 1377–81*, pp. 71 and 280).

[5] 100 marks p.a. for life, as the king's knight, from the issues of Haverford when his friend Sir William Nevill was granted the same (*Cal. Pat. Rolls, 1381–5*, p. 8).

[6] Cf. *Cal. Close Rolls, 1360–4*, p. 371. He had been born in Sept. 1341 (*Cal. Inq. p.m.* xi, no. 378).

[7] He inherited lands in Northamptonshire, Rutland, Somerset, Nottinghamshire, and Leicestershire and married Anne, the widow of John Beysin of Ashley, Staffordshire. (Cf. *Complete Peerage*, vii. 454–6.)

with the court ended, as far as we know, with the death of Richard's mother—or soon after. It is one of the common characteristics of the Lollard knights that they all made themselves scarce during the crisis of 1387–9 and to a man avoided the fate of their fellow-members of the Chamber, Sir Simon Burley, Sir John Beauchamp of Holt, and Sir James Berners. Sir Thomas Latimer did not return to the king's service after the deluge had subsided: the others did and were promoted for their loyalty. Latimer *may* have been a member of the Black Prince's ménage; he certainly saw his first campaigns in Gascony and Spain, 1365–70, in the prince's retinue;[1] but his service may have been of the freelance variety, as it was with Gaunt in 1373–4[2] and on the Breton expedition of 1377–8.[3] Practically the only evidence, apart from his association with known knights of the household, for his connection with the court is the order to him, together with Richard Sturry and Lewis Clifford and some others, to remain about the Princess of Wales's person (12 June 1385)[4] instead of accompanying the king against the Scots. Unlike Sturry and Clifford, Latimer was not one of Joan's executors when she died later that year. But that he was one of her attendants is certain; and that he came to her service from her husband's is at least likely.

6. John Montagu's connection with the court was hereditary. His grandfather William, first Earl of Salisbury, beginning as a yeoman of the royal household, owed his advancement and wealth to Edward III's gratitude for the part he played in Mortimer's overthrow in 1330.[5] The earl's younger son, our man's father, Sir John Montagu, was by 1354 a knight in the Black Prince's household, a training which prepared him to be Steward of Richard's from 1381 to the end of 1386.[6] His career overlapped

[1] For 1365–7 (Gascony and Spain) see Sir W. Dugdale, *The Baronage of England* (London, 1675–6), ii. 33; for 1369, T. Rymer and R. Sanderson, *Foedera*, ed A. Clarke, F. Holbrooke, and J. Caley (London, 1816–69), iii, pt. 2. 857.

[2] *John of Gaunt's Register, 1371–6*, i. 34 (no. 50, undated).

[3] T. Carte, *Catalogue des Rolles Gascons*, . . . (London, 1743), ii. 124 and Waugh, op. cit., p. 71 n. 5.

[4] *Cal. Close Rolls, 1381–5*, p. 553; T. Rymer, *Foedera* (1704–35), vii. 474.

[5] *Cal. Pat. Rolls, 1324–7*, p. 169; *Complete Peerage*, xi. 385–6, ix. 82.

[6] *Cal. Pat. Rolls, 1381–5*, pp. 97, 560; ibid., *1385–9*, pp. 207–324; and Tout, *Chapters*, vi. 44.

that of his son and namesake by many years; it is difficult to disentangle the two Sir Johns, but there is no doubt which was accused of Lollardy. Walsingham's reference to Shenley, Hertfordshire, as the scene of the knight's iconoclasm[1] makes it clear that the son is meant, since Sir John the younger acquired Shenley by his marriage between 1381 and 1383 with a London merchant's daughter.[2] The death of his cousin in 1382 made his ultimate succession to the earldom of Salisbury probable since his uncle had no other children; his father's death in 1390 brought him a peerage. But the elder Sir John's survival (he was not an old man) inevitably caused the son to be somewhat overshadowed; in the 1380s the latter was only to a limited extent his own master; his wife's not very valuable dower lands were his sole support. At this date he was the only one of the seven knights to have a father living and an inheritance not yet his to enjoy. But it was during this period of waiting that he attracted the king's notice, established friendly relations with our group of courtiers, and laid the foundation of his later success as a royal favourite. It was not so much his own comparative youth as his father's continued prominence that stood in the way of his career. After a brilliant start as a soldier in 1369[3] and his appointment as a king's knight on or before 1383,[4] nothing much happened to him until the 1390s. In spite of his superior rank and connections he did not equal Clifford or Sturry in importance until the last years of the reign.

7. Finally, Sir John Cheyne: though not mentioned by Walsingham among the other suspects and even in 1399 only as an enemy of the Church,[5] not as a Lollard, he had long been a member of the group—for some time indeed before 1383, the year in which he is first described as having been retained as a

[1] *Historia Anglicana*, ii. 159.

[2] For Shenley cf. *Cal. Close Rolls, 1385–9*, pp. 634–5; for Maud, relict of John, son of Andrew Aubrey and widow of Sir Alan Buxhall, daughter of Adam Francis, Mayor of London, see *Complete Peerage*, xi. 392–3.

[3] He was knighted on the field of Bourdeilles by the Earl of Cambridge (Froissart, vii. 344, 346).

[4] *Cal. Pat. Rolls, 1381–5*, p. 362.

[5] *Johannis de Trokelowe et Henrici de Blaneford . . . Chronica et Annales . . .*, ed. H. T. Riley (R.S., 1866), pp. 290–1.

knight in Richard's service. He was then rather more than thirty years of age. It is possible to trace his career back for about a decade before this. He was already a knight in 1378.[1] The first evidence of military service dates from the same year when he sailed in Gaunt's expedition to Brittany in the retinue of Sir William Beauchamp and Sir Lewis Clifford;[2] it looks as if he was even then attached to Richard II's household. But whereas the other six knights were old campaigners with a long record of fighting in the armies of Edward III or his captains, it looks as if Cheyne's experience as a soldier was in 1378 of recent date and short duration. One explanation of this might be his age: he was born too late by a year or two to have taken much share in the Black Prince's campaigns before 1370. Another may have been the accident of his birth: a landless younger son of no great family and little influence. But according to Walsingham who might have heard the tale from Cheyne's native Buckinghamshire, the reason was that the knight had begun life as a clerk and was a renegade deacon.[3] If Walsingham's allegation has any substance, this episode in his career must have been over by November 1373 when he had made an extremely advantageous marriage with the daughter of one peer who was the widow of another.[4] Soon afterwards in August 1374 he was described as a king's esquire on the Patent Roll.[5] Waugh absurdly tries to identify

[1] *Cal. Pat. Rolls, 1377–81*, p. 312 (4 Mar.).

[2] Waugh, op. cit., p. 82 n. 2.

[3] *Historia Anglicana*, ii. 266.

[4] This was Margaret, daughter of William, Lord Deincourt (d. 1378/80); she had married Cheyne by 14 Nov. 1373 (*Cal. Fine Rolls*, viii. 219), having previously been married to Robert, Lord Tiptoft (d. 13 Apr. 1372). (*Abstracts of Inquisitiones post mortem . . . Nottinghamshire 1350–1436*, ed. L. S. S. Train [Thoroton Soc., Record ser.] xii [1952]. 59.) Dugdale says that Margaret's dower consisted of the manors of Langar, Nottinghamshire and Oxindon, Gloucester, with the advowsons of Barrow and Langar, and that she died in 3 Richard II or before (Dugdale, *Baronage*, ii. 40 and i. 388). He subsequently married Margaret, daughter and heiress of Edward Lovetoft (*Cal. Fine Rolls*, xii. 297–8) by 15 Oct. 1389 (*Cal. Pat. Rolls, 1388–92*, p. 118 and ibid., *1391–6*, p. 632); she was still alive in 1438. By her he had issue Sir John Cheyne, died 1420 (*Cal. Fine Rolls*, xiv. 333), and Edward Cheyne, died 1415 (cf. *Cal. Pat. Rolls, 1416–22*, p. 26), who married 'Elizabeth' before 1403. After Sir John Cheyne's death Margaret Lovetoft married William Herle esq. (*Cal. Close Rolls, Henry V*, ii. 178–9).

[5] *Cal. Pat. Rolls, 1370–4*, p. 492.

him with a namesake who was a clerk in Gaunt's administration until 1383.[1] John Cheyne's marriage had made him a considerable, though temporary, landowner in his wife's dower, he had been knighted for at least six years before 1383 and had been employed abroad on military as well as diplomatic business; it is inconceivable that he was at the same time parson of Hanbury and receiver of the Lancastrian manor of Tutbury; and absurd to suppose that he, a king's esquire and then knight, a courtier and the husband of a lady of noble birth, would have been consistently described in Gaunt's chancery as plain 'John Cheyne, clerk'. If he was ever a deacon, it must have been before 1373 and not after. That he was a man of some formal education seems to be indicated by his frequent employment by both Richard II and Henry IV on embassies to the Roman *curia*.[2] There is no evidence to suggest a period of university study as in the case of the Herefordshire esquire and heretic, Walter Brute. It is not clear to what or to whom Cheyne owed his first introduction to the royal household, but his marriage had greatly increased his consequence and was closely followed by his earliest mention as a king's esquire. So he too passed from Edward III's household to become Richard's knight. He was later to forfeit Richard's regard and to win Bolingbroke's by getting himself involved in the downfall of Thomas of Woodstock. For some time after Gloucester's arrest in 1397 Cheyne also underwent imprisonment.[3] Though he escaped death, his health was affected by the rigours of his captivity. Waugh needlessly complicates this period of his career by crediting him with all the actions of a namesake, Sir John

[1] Waugh, op. cit., pp. 81–2.

[2] Thus he went to the King of the Romans in 1381 (E. Perroy, *L'Angleterre et le Grand Schisme* [Paris, 1933], p. 154 n.); and to the Pope in 1390 (ibid., p. 318; Waugh, op. cit., p. 83; Perroy, *Diplomatic Correspondence*, pp. 220–1 [15 June–13 Dec.], and in autumn 1399 (sent by Henry IV: Walsingham, *Historia Anglicana*, ii. 242); to France in 1404 (*Royal and Historical Letters*, ed. F. C. Hingeston [R.S., 1860], i, pp. 224, 279, and 306; Sir N. H. Nicolas, *Proceedings and Ordinances of the Privy Council of England* [London, 1824], i, 167, 241; Waugh, op. cit., p. 85; *Foedera*, viii. 446, 452, and 479; *Reg. Chichele*, i, pp. xxvii–xxviij); and to France in 1410 and 1411 (Waugh, op. cit., p. 85).

[3] *A Chronicle of London from 1089 to 1483*, ed. Sir N. H. Nicolas and E. Tyrrell (London, 1827), p. 81 (Waugh, op. cit., p. 83).

Cheyne of Shropshire, who was the Earl of March's knight and died in 1398.[1] Our Sir John Cheyne has also been confused with another namesake who was M.P. for Bedfordshire in 1372.[1] The only parliaments he is known to have been returned to (as knight of the shire for Gloucester) were those of 1390, 1393, 1394, and 1399.[2]

To sum up: all seven knights were attached to the court by the early 1380s; three (Sturry, Clanvow, and Cheyne) and possibly a fourth (Nevill) had been retained by Edward III. One (Clifford) was an old servant and companion-in-arms of the Black Prince; while Sturry had been and Latimer may have been; all these three were particularly trusted by Joan of Kent and were left with her in 1385. Only one (Montagu) and the most aristocratic had no discoverable menial experience before becoming a king's knight to Richard. Clanvow alone is known to have begun his career outside the household of a member of the royal family. None can be traced to the service of the Duke of Lancaster; where the Lollard knights are concerned we have no justification in talking of that King Charles's head, 'the Lancastrian faction'. On the other hand it would be equally foolish to think of them as opposed to John of Gaunt: they were the servants of Edward III and his successive heirs. When Walsingham denounced the protectors of the heretics, he was attacking—though he omitted to say so—some of the men most prominent at court. All seven, together with their two colleagues in the Chamber who were also their friends (Sir William Beauchamp and Sir Philip de la Vache) escaped the resentment of the Merciless Parliament which brought others in that office to the block. Their immunity—whatever its reason—deserves to be noted. For all but Latimer it was the prelude to greater favour and greater power after the king regained his independence in 1389.

Since they were courtiers, it is hardly remarkable that they prospered. In the 1370s and 1380s Latimer and Clanvow alone

[1] See above, p. 163 n. 3.

[2] *Members of Parliament, Returns*, pt. i. 237, 244, 247, 258, and cf. J. S. Roskell, *The Commons and their Speakers in English Parliaments 1376–1523* [Manchester, 1965], pp. 353–4.

enjoyed some inherited wealth and consequence, but all earned their share of the prizes of service, becoming in time considerable landowners. To enumerate all their employments and rewards before 1387 and after 1389 would be tedious. They are by no means all set out by Waugh. I shall content myself with calling attention to some of the features he either ignores or underestimates or occasionally misinterprets.

For one thing he was not very much interested in their marriages—and indeed not quite all of them were significant. But, considering the advantages to be gained by marriage, the ties of kinship which it could create or strengthen as well as the short cut it might provide to lands and influence, it would be very surprising if these seven career-soldiers turned courtiers had neither sought nor enjoyed its prizes. Marriage either with an heiress or a dowager was the beginning of worldly wisdom. Six of the seven showed themselves to be wise. The exception was Clanvow.

And Clanvow may not have been an exception. There is no evidence that he had a wife. But a landowner who remained a bachelor was such an exceptional figure in medieval society that it is hard to believe that Clanvow did not marry. Sir Thomas Clanvow, who was his heir, may well have been his son; he was the right age; but we do not know.[1]

The curious thing about the marriages of the other six is that those already related to the higher nobility (Montagu, Latimer, and Nevill) married outside it and that those who were least well born found wives among the peerage. Something must be said about each of them. I will try not to enter into more detail than is necessary.

1. I have already mentioned that John Cheyne was unheard of before his marriage; it was a sufficiently notable one to give him his start in life. His first wife, whom he married without a licence and to the indignation of her kin was Margaret, daughter of William, Lord Deincourt, and widow of Robert, Lord Tiptoft (d. 1372).[2] The Deincourts were accused shortly afterwards of having assaulted and injured him at Langar in Nottinghamshire

[1] See above, p. 169.

[2] Ibid., n. 4

one of the manors the marriage brought him.[1] Margaret Cheyne died about 1377 and Sir John promptly married another Margaret, daughter and heiress of Edward Lovetoft a Lincolnshire esquire; she, unlike the dowager, gave him offspring; he had to wait a long time for her inheritance. But no one can say that Sir John failed to take advantage of the opportunities that marriage then offered.

2. Sir Thomas Latimer, who had less need to,[2] also married a dowager who gave him no heir. She was Anne, widow of John Beysin of Ashley, Staffordshire. Her maiden name is unknown. I mention her chiefly because she is a link in the chain of evidence for her husband's (and incidentally her own) Lollard sympathies. But she did also bring him the life enjoyment of quite a valuable collection of dower lands in Staffordshire and Shropshire.[3]

3. Sir Lewis Clifford's marriage, which took place between 1370 and 1372, was very like Cheyne's first but even more distinguished. His wife was Eleanor, daughter of John, Lord Mowbray of Axholme, by his wife Joan of Lancaster. She too had the advantage of a peeress's jointure. Her first husband had been Roger, Lord de la Warr (d. 1370).[4] Eleanor was not merely of royal descent and with many important connections (she was for example the aunt of Thomas Mowbray, the Appellant Earl of Nottingham, afterwards Duke of Norfolk),[5] but her family had screwed an unusually

[1] *Cal. Pat. Rolls, 1370–4*, p. 492, ibid., *1374–7*, p. 63.

[2] He was the third of four known sons of Sir Warin Latimer and his wife, Catherine, widow of Robert Brewes and daughter of John de la Warr (*Complete Peerage*, vii. 452–4).

[3] John Beysin of Ashley, Staffordshire, had given his wife Anne a jointure in two-thirds of the manor of Broseley, Shropshire; she had one-third of Broseley, one-third of Langnor manor, one-third of Milnehope manor, and other thirds in dower, etc. (Cf. *Cal. Close Rolls, Henry IV*, i. 550–1, etc.) She was therefore quite a catch.

[4] For his will, dated Wakerley, 28 Apr. 1368, proved at Lincoln on 5 Oct. 1370 and at Lambeth on 19 Oct. 1370, cf. Register of Whittlesey (Cant.), fos. 116^{v}–117. His widow was granted for life with remainder to his heirs all his vestments, books, and other chapel furniture, all his silver plate (*vasa*) and all his wardrobe 'cum libris meis de Gallico'; she was left freely an enamelled cup and all his jewels and paternosters; she was a residuary legatee of one-third of his goods.

[5] She was the granddaughter of Henry, Earl of Lancaster (?1281–1345); niece of Henry, Duke of Lancaster (?1300–61), Blanche, Lady Wake (d. 1357), Mary, Lady Percy (d. 1362), Maud, Countess of Ulster, and Eleanor, Countess of Arundel (d. 1373); first cousin of Maud, Duchess of Bavaria (d. 1362), Blanche,

large jointure for her out of the de la Warr estates—including the valuable lordship of Manchester. On 12 February 1373 Sir Lewis Clifford did a particularly profitable stroke of business with John de la Warr, his wife's stepson, her first husband's heir. He exchanged her jointure—which would have reverted to the de la Warrs at her death—for a grant of the castle and lordship of Ewyas Harold in Herefordshire and other lands to himself and Eleanor jointly, together with a lump sum down of 500 marks.[1] He thereby made sure of the enjoyment of these lands for his life should his wife die. Perhaps she was delicate. Anyhow die she did; in June 1387 he bought the de la Warrs out of Ewyas Harold entirely.[2] His marriage had greatly enhanced his importance as well as his revenues. His son and heir Lewis was descended from Henry III.

4. Sir Richard Sturry's marriage followed the same pattern. He, like the other career-soldiers and political adventurers, treated a dowager from the nobility as a stepping-stone in his progress. His wife was Alice, daughter and heiress of Sir John Blount and widow of Richard Stafford[3] (d. in or before 1374). Stafford was the son and heir of Richard, Lord Stafford,[4] who has unaccountably

Duchess of Lancaster (d. 1369), Elizabeth, Countess of Clarence (d. 1363), Henry, Earl of Northumberland (d. 1408), Sir Thomas Percy (afterwards Earl of Worcester), Henry, Lord Beaumont (d. 1369), Richard, Earl of Arundel (d. 1397), John, Lord Maltravers (d. 1479), Thomas, Bishop of Ely, afterwards Archbishop of York and Canterbury (d. 1414), Joan, Countess of Hereford (d. 1419), and Alice, Countess of Kent (d. 1416). She was the sister of John, Lord Mowbray (d. 1368) and the aunt of two successive Earls of Nottingham. This may have had something to do with her husband's K.G. in 1377.

[1] *Cal. Pat. Rolls, 1370–4*, pp. 246–7; *Complete Peerage*, iv. 147.

[2] *Cal. Pat. Rolls, 1385–9*, p. 310; cf. ibid. *1391–6*, p. 227 (after the death of young Lewis (?) 20 Feb. 1393, when he enfeoffed John Montagu, Philip la Vache, Thomas Latimer, and John Cheyne with it).

[3] *Miscellanea Genealogica et Heraldica*, 3rd ser., iii. 273; cf. *Cal. Pat. Rolls, 1381–5*, p. 532. She founded a chantry at Hampton Lovett in 1414 for the souls of Sir John Blount and Elizabeth his wife, her father and mother, and for Richard Stafford and Richard Stur(r)y her two husbands (T. Nash, *Collections for the History of Worcestershire* (1781–2, 1799), i. 536 and 540). In 1393 she had settled the manor on her second husband, Sir Richard Stur(r)y, with remainders to Elizabeth Blount, Walter Blount, and John, son of Walter Blount (cf. Feet of Fines, Divers. Cos., 56/250, quoted in *Complete Peerage*, ix. 332).

[4] Cf. *Cal. Pap. Pets.* i. 507 and cf. p. 179, *Cal. Pap. Letts.* iii. 352.

been omitted from the *Complete Peerage*. He was summoned to the Lords in 1370[1] and died in 1380.[2] The younger brother of Ralph the first Earl of Stafford, he had for many years been one of the most important members of the Black Prince's Council and administration.[3] Thereafter he became a political figure of great influence, being a member of the first two minority Councils of Richard II's reign.[4] Sturry married Alice Stafford in 1374,[5] almost certainly by Edward III's gift. She brought her husband at least one valuable manor, that of Hampton Lovett, Worcestershire.[6] Both Clifford's and Sturry's marriages—and to some extent Latimer's—gave them territorial links with the area where Cheyne and Clanvow had their lands, the area, incidentally, to which Swinderby travelled after 1382.

5. I have already mentioned John Montagu's marriage. His wife (he married her between 1381 and 1383) was Maud, daughter of Adam Frances, a wealthy mercer and Mayor of London. She had had two husbands before, the first Sir Alan Buxhall, K.G., the Constable of the Tower, who violated the choir of Westminster Abbey in 1378, and the second John Aubrey a prominent London citizen and grocer-sheriff.[7] She had been well provided for by her father and both her previous husbands; until he inherited his own family estates, Montagu resided at her manor of Shenley.

[1] *Reports . . ., touching the Dignity of a Peer of the Realm* (1820–9), ii. 495.

[2] *Cal. Pat. Rolls, 1377–81*, p. 539; and cf. *Cal. Fine Rolls*, ix. 258.

[3] Ibid. vi. 394; *Cal. Pat. Rolls, 1345–8*, p. 308; *Black Prince's Register*, i. 48; ibid. iii. 11.

[4] N. B. Lewis, 'The "Continual Council" in the Early Years of Richard II, 1377–1380', *E.H.R.* 41 (1926), 248.

[5] She was unmarried on 10 and 28 Mar. 1374 (*Cal. Pat. Rolls, 1370–4*, pp. 415 and 479).

[6] The father presented to the living of Hampton Lovett in 1332; Alice Stur(r)y, Lady of Hampton Lovett presented in 1396 and 1412 (Nash, *Worcestershire*, i. 540). She and her husband Richard Stafford had been seized in Hampton Lovett in 1370 (*V.C.H. Worcs.*, iii. 154). Also she and her first husband had been possessed before 1370 (Feet of Fines, Divers. Cos., Mich. 44 Ed. III no. 60, Chant. Cert. 25 no. 20, in *V.C.H. Rutland*, ii. 28). In 1393 she and Sir Richard Stur(r)y settled it on themselves and the heirs of their bodies with remainder to Elizabeth le Blount for life, etc. (Feet of Fines, Divers. Cos., Trin. 17 Richard II: ibid.)

[7] *Complete Peerage*, xi. 392–3; Beltz, *Garter*, pp. 188–92; A. H. Cooke, *The Early History of Mapledurham* (Oxford, 1925), pp. 35–6.

6. Sir William Nevill married before Michaelmas 1366, Elizabeth,[1] daughter and co-heiress of Sir Stephen le Waleys (d. 1347), and step-daughter of Sir Brian Stapledon (d. 1394). She brought him lands in Yorkshire.[2] The chief interest of this marriage is that there are other reasons for suspecting her step-father of Lollard sympathies. Sir Brian Stapledon, K.G., is another possible Lollard knight omitted from the chroniclers' lists.

Thus Clifford and Cheyne seemingly owed their first advancement to the fortunes and connections of their wives; while Sturry, Latimer, and Montagu each derived considerable benefit from union with a dowager. By the time they were mentioned by the chroniclers all but Clanvow were joined by ties of kinship with the higher nobility.

[1] T. Madox, *Formulare Anglicanum* (London, 1702), pp. 427–8; *Wills and Inventories* . . ., ed. J. Raine (Surtees Soc.) (2) i (1835), 38–42.

[2] e.g. Burghwallis (cf. *Cal. Close Rolls, 1389–92*, p. 399). For the manors of Braham in Spofforth, Hartlington in Burnsall, and certain other lands in Braham, Follifoot in Spofforth, and Upper Durnsforth in Aldborough, all in Yorks., formerly belonging to William Hartlington cf. *Cal. Close Rolls, 1369–74*, p. 7.

CHAPTER III

Aspects of the Careers of the Seven

WE know something about the origins of the Seven, their coming-together in the service of Richard II, and their marriages. I want now to touch briefly upon a number of aspects of their careers which may help us to realize more precisely—as precisely as we can—what sort of people they were.

First, a little more about their military records. It is necessary to emphasize these if only for the reason that Lollard teaching was pacifist. The twelve *Conclusions* of 1395[1] summarize very well what may be taken to have been their belief's some decade after Wycliffe's death. The tenth Conclusion says 'that man-slaughter by battle . . . is express contrarious to the New Testament' on account of Christ's teaching to man 'to love and have mercy on his enemies and not for to slay them'; and in the twelfth Conclusion the 'armourers' are included with the goldsmiths among the crafts 'not needful to man' which should be 'destroyed for the increase of virtue'.

By 1395—and indeed in most cases long before—the majority of the Seven had ceased to pursue an active military career. Two were dead, Clanvow on 17 October 1391 and Nevill of grief two days later near Constantinople.[2] In 1390 they are said by the Westminster chronicler (whose court connection makes him well informed about their doings) to have obtained Richard II's permission to join the French in an attack on Tunis.[3] So at that time they do not seem to have disapproved of fighting, at any rate against the heathen. The other five are not known to have done

[1] Printed in *E.H.R.* xxii (1907), 292–304 and in *Rogeri Dymmok Liber*, ed. H. S. Cronin (1922).

[2] *Polychronicon Ranulphi Higden*, ed. J. R. Lumby (R.S., 1865–6), ix. 261–2.

[3] Ibid., p. 234.

much fighting after 1395, though Montagu accompanied Richard to Ireland in 1399 and was to lose his life in an insurrection intended to restore his old master to the throne, in January 1400. And in 1397 or 1398 he succeeded his uncle not only in his earldom but also in his Garter stall at Windsor. This was due, no doubt, as a reward for his services in the Parliament of 1397 and need not have been deserved by his martial successes. But the Garter was a military order and it was still given, regardless of rank, to the best fighting knights of the day. It was rather a delayed recognition of his prowess under Edmund Langley in 1369; but in 1391–2 he had campaigned against the heathen Slav in Prussia.[1]

The others at least had no recent and no future military service to their credits. Two of them were in any case old men in 1395. Sturry was over sixty-five and Clifford not much under. Sturry's was the longer record, Clifford's perhaps the more distinguished. Sturry was serving at sea in 1347.[2] He was captured by the French in 1359 or 60;[3] Edward III gave him £50 towards his ransom.[3] His bravery in a sea-battle is noticed by his friend Froissart.[4] The expedition of 1378 is the last in which he is known to have served.[5] Clifford was already a soldier when he was taken prisoner near Calais in 1351.[6] He fought in Spain in 1367 and in France in 1373–4.[7] Again the Breton expedition of 1378 is his last known appearance in arms. He received the Garter soon after Richard's accession in 1377; but the fact that sometime between 1385 and 1396 he was elected (with a number of prominent English lords and captains, but alone of the Seven) to the order of the Passion is perhaps stronger evidence of his martial reputation.[8] This international order of crusaders had been founded by a French

[1] *Complete Peerage*, xi. 391.

[2] P.R.O., E 101/391/9, fo. 7ᵛ.

[3] P.R.O., E 101/393/11, fos. 71ᵛ and 104ᵛ.

[4] Froissart, iii. 206.

[5] Waugh, op. cit., p. 59 n. 1.

[6] At the battle of St. George (Nicolas, *The Controversy between ... Scrope and ... Grosvenor*, i. 183) when according to his own account he was first armed. The battle according to Froissart (v. 297, 302) took place on Whit Monday 1352, near Ardres in Picardy. E. M. Thompson writes, 'he is obviously wrong in the year; but he is probably right in the day, which would be the 6th June [1351]', *Chronicon Galfridi le Baker de Swynebroke* (Oxford, 1889), p. 284.

[7] Nicolas, op. cit. ii. 428.

[8] M. V. Clarke, *Fourteenth Century Studies* (Oxford, 1937), p. 288 n. 2.

visionary, Philippe de Mezières, to replace the old crusading military orders and to recover the kingdom of Jerusalem. It did not do very much, but its objects were singularly out of harmony with Lollard professions. As for Thomas Latimer, the evidence for his war service falls between 1366 and 1378.[1] No one could accuse any of them of being knights of Venus rather than of Mars.

Two further points in connection with this war-service may be mentioned:

A good deal of it was almost certainly profitable; but we have no means of knowing what these knights cleared by way of profit. We know the names of two prisoners taken by Montagu on his first campaign;[2] we hear of successful actions by Sturry and others of the group. Clanvow and Nevill were in the army of Sir Robert Knollys which invaded northern France in 1370;[3] it achieved nothing but it is said to have been notable for the ransoms exacted and the plunder taken. That goes for Lancaster's march of 1373–4 also. Its want of strategic results, and high mortality from disease, has caused it to be regarded by English historians as a disastrous fiasco. But there is quite a lot of evidence of those who took part in it collecting not inconsiderable 'gains of war'. Clifford, Clanvow, and Latimer took part in it. This military service must be regarded as a source of far from negligible profit as well as of reputation.

Secondly, war was, to some extent, a source of what one must call for want of a better word 'education'. It made these English knights less insular: it involved them in prolonged residence in France and Spain; in the courtesies that passed between the fighting-men of opposing armies; in the launching of joint enterprises that took Clanvow and Nevill to Barbary, Montagu to fight beside the Teutonic knights east of Danzig, and Clifford to join the order of the Passion. They belonged to the international chivalrous class and spoke its lingua franca.

[1] Cf. Dugdale, *Baronage* ii. 33; T. Carte, *Catalogue des Rolles Gascons* (London, 1743), ii. 124; and Waugh, op. cit., p. 71 n. 5.

[2] Captain Ernaudons and Bernadès de Batefol in 1369 (Froissart, vii. 349).

[3] *Scrope* v. *Grosvenor*, ii. 437.

And that brings me to my next point: their diplomatic experience, their knowledge of foreign courts and their practices. Sir Richard Sturry's was particularly varied. Though it is probable that he was employed in embassies abroad from his early days as a chamberer to Edward III (since it was one of the normal duties of the post) the earliest evidence in the accounts shows him visiting the Low Countries several times on the king's behalf in 1368 and 1370–1.[1] More important was his visit in the early months of 1377 with Geoffrey Chaucer to the French court.[2] He had been sent in 1370 to accompany Charles the Bad of Navarre back to his French lands, and in the following year it was as ambassador to the Duke of Brittany that he was involved in a naval battle off the Breton coast.[3] It seems that he was on terms of intimacy with Duke John since the latter, sometime between 1372 and 1381, granted him a life annuity of £60 from his English county of Richmond.[4] Under Richard II his employment was continued; he escaped the Peasants' Revolt because he was treating for peace in France;[5] he was there again in the following year and frequently between 1389 and 1394 during Richard II's negotiations for a final peace with the French.[6] He died before the king's second marriage achieved his object. Sturry was one of a group of experts regularly employed to treat with the French. In his later years he was joined in this work first by Clanvow whose earliest recorded mission was in 1385[7] but who was fully occupied in diplomacy, as usual accompanied by Nevill in the last year or so before their departure to Barbary, and next by Clifford whose official part in bringing about the king's French marriage began

[1] L. Mirot and E. Déprez, 'Les ambassades anglaises pendant la guerre de cent ans', *Bibl. de l'École des Chartes*, 60 (1899), 185 (no. 270), 187 (no. 296), and cf. Waugh, op. cit., pp. 64, 65 and n. 2.

[2] Froissart, viii. 383, 473.

[3] *Foedera*, vi. 661; Froissart, viii. 93.

[4] *Cal. Fine Rolls*, ix. 274–5.

[5] *Foedera*, vii. 308–9; cf. Mirot and Déprez, op. cit., p. 204 (no. 402); Waugh, op. cit., p. 66 and n. 7.

[6] Waugh, op. cit., p. 77 n. 1; *Foedera*, vii. 667; Rot. Franc. 13 Ric. II, mm. 3, 6, in Waugh, p. 67 nn. 9 and 10; Mirot and Déprez, p. 211 (no. 517); Perroy, *Diplomatic Correspondence*, p. 247.

[7] *Foedera*, vii. 466; cf. *Cal. Pat. Rolls, 1381–5*, p. 575; *Proc. and Ord.* i. 8; *Scrope* v. *Grosvenor*, ii. 437–8; Mirot and Déprez, p. 59.

in 1391 and was continued until the treaty of 1396.[1] Sir John Cheyne's diplomatic work took him further afield, to the King of the Romans, in connection with Richard's first marriage in 1381, and to Pope Boniface IX in 1390 and yet again, at Henry IV's orders, in the autumn of 1399 (to persuade the Pope that the usurpation was justified).[2] From 1406 to 1408 he was once more employed on a delicate mission with Bishop Chichele of St. David's to persuade Gregory XII to forgive the murder of Archbishop Scrope and to discuss the healing of the Schism. For this purpose they visited the Clementine Pope Benedict XIII at Marseilles.[3] Cheyne was also employed by Henry IV in negotiating with the French; missions are recorded in 1404, 1406, 1410, and 1411.[4] He alone of the Seven (not many of them survived and he was younger) had an even more active diplomatic career under the Lancastrian king than before 1399. Sir John Montagu was sent by Richard in 1398–9 to dissuade the French king from marrying a princess of France to the exiled Bolingbroke, but otherwise no missions are recorded for him.[5] He seems, however, to have had unusually close relations with the French court; it is probable that he, like Clifford, paid private visits to friends in France. We shall see what came of it in a moment. Once more Thomas Latimer reveals his lack of similarity to his friends by having, as far as we know, no diplomatic employments—and no private contacts with foreign courts.

[1] Clifford had been a member of the Council since 29 Jan. 1392 (J. F. Baldwin, *King's Council* [Oxford, 1913], p. 492). This Council had sent a peace mission to France as early as 12 Feb. 1392 (ibid., p. 493); cf. also Froissart, xiv. 284, 288; H. Moranvillé, 'Conférences entre la France et l'Angleterre 1388–1393', *Bibl. de l'École des Chartes*, 50 (1899), 359, 369–70; *Foedera*, vii. 738–9; *Polychronicon*, ix. 280; P.R.O., E 364/27 m.B. d; Froissart, xv. 164, 194.

[2] Mirot and Déprez, op. cit., pp. 202–3 (no. 440); P.R.O., E 364/24/m.A; Perroy, *L'Angleterre et le grand schisme*, p. 318; *Diplomatic Correspondence*, p. 220; Walsingham, *Historia Anglicana*, ii. 242.

[3] *Foedera*, viii. 479; P.R.O., E. 364/42/m.C; L. Muratori, *Scriptores rerum Italicarum* (Milan, 1723–51), iii, pt. 2. 8000 (B); MS. Cotton Cleopatra E. II, fos. 262v–263; cf. N. Valois, *La France et le grand schisme d'occident* (Paris, 1896–1902), iii. 569 n. 2.

[4] *Royal and Historical Letters*, i. 226, 279; *Foedera*, viii. 351; *Proc. and Ord.* i. 222–3; *Foedera*, viii. 452–3; ibid. 636, 694–6.

[5] Ibid. 52; Froissart, xvi. 143–51; P.R.O., E 403, Mich. 22 Ric. II.

This skeleton survey of the embassies undertaken by six of the Seven, as well as their membership of the court, prepares one for the discovery that, career-soldiers though they were, they were cultivated men. John Montagu's distinction as a poet is the best known evidence of this. Though doubtless as a man of his position is bound to be overpraised, there is too much evidence of the estimation in which his 'ballads, songs, rondels and lays' were held for his achievement to be entirely discarded. The trouble is that his poems, written it seems in French, are wholly lost. But Christine de Pisan if not Creton, was an exacting critic and her praise is high.[1] The fact that she sent her son to live in Montagu's household is better than praise, for she had many patrons among the French nobility who would have taken him. There is no doubt about Montagu's patronage of poets or of his francophile tastes; that was one of the things which commended him to Richard's favour. Lewis Clifford is not known as a poet, but as the friend of poets. We know from this fact that he had been in France in 1385 until early 1386. For it was then that he brought a poem addressed by the French poet, Eustache Deschamps, to Geoffrey Chaucer. He is himself mentioned in the poem.[2] It was to Clifford's son-in-law Sir Philip de la Vache that Chaucer addressed his poem *Truth: Balade de bon conseyl*[3] in which the poet plays on the knight's name: 'thou Vache'.[4] It is possible that

[1] Quoted in J. H. Wylie, *History of England under Henry the Fourth* (London, 1884–98), i. 100 n. 2.

[2] Chaucer, *Complete Works*, ed. Skeat (Oxford, 1894–1900), i, introd., pp. lvi–lvii; *Canterbury Tales*, ed. J. M. Manly (n.p., 1929), pp. 22, 36, 40–1; cf. A. Brusendorff, *The Chaucer Tradition* (Copenhagen, 1925), appendix C, 'Chaucer and Deschamps', pp. 485–93. Deschamps mentions Clifford as 'l'amoureux-Cliffort' (*Œuvres Complètes de Eustache Deschamps*, ed. Marquis de Queux de Saint-Hilaire and G. Raynaud (Paris, 1878–1903), iii. 375–6). Froissart called him 'moult appert et vaillant chevalier' (Froissart, xiv. 110) and mentions him as having been present at St. Ingelvert (1390) and on embassies. (For 1393, cf. *Expeditions . . . made by Henry, Earl of Derby*, ed. L. Toulmin Smith [Camden Soc., 2nd ser., 1894), p. 278.) Clifford and Deschamps met for a second time in 1393. (*Proc. and Ord.* i. 45; Deschamps, *Œuvres*, vii. 311 and i. 67. Cf. J. L. Lowes, 'The Prologue to *The Legend of Good Women* considered in its Chronological Relations', *Publications of the Modern Language Association of America*, 20 (1905), 753–864.)

[3] Chaucer, *Works*, ed. Skeat, i. 390–1.

[4] M. Rickert, 'Thou Vache', *Modern Philology*, xi (1913–14), 209–25; de la Vache was retained as *custos* of Calais Castle for three years on 7 Apr. 1388, with

Clifford was godfather to Chaucer's son the 'little Lewis' for whom the treatise on the Astrolabe was written in 1391.[1] I have already mentioned how Sturry and Chaucer, if not already acquainted, had been on embassy together in 1377.[2] The close connection between Chaucer and two more of the Seven is brought out in a deed of 1 May 1380 enrolled on the Close Roll.[3] Chaucer, in what circumstances we do not know, had been guilty, though a married man, of the rape of a lady called Cecily Champaigne, the adult but apparently spinster daughter of a London citizen. The deed is a release by Cecily of all her rights of action against Chaucer in return for a fairly liberal gift of money. This intimate transaction was witnessed by Sir William Beauchamp, Sir John Clanvow, Sir William Nevill, John Philipot, and Richard Morrell, another citizen. Chaucerians have naturally tried to minimize this not very creditable incident in the poet's life and to suggest that rape was only a legal synonym for abduction. But the lawyers have disposed of that argument in 'The Strange Case of Geoffrey Chaucer and Cecilia Chaumpaigne' by P. R. Watts,[4] and 'Chaucer's Escapade' by T. F. T. Plucknett.[5] The chief interest of this link for us is that the famous poem 'the Cuckoo and the Nightingale', which used to be attributed to Chaucer and is one of the finest pieces written in this period, is attributed by one of the best manuscripts (Ff. 1.6.C.U.L.) to a Clanvow. It is printed by Skeat in his edition of Chaucer.[6] Its correct title is 'The Book of Cupid, God of Love', and the first line 'The God of Love a! *benedicite*!' Furnivall, that somewhat

10 horse and foot, 20 men-at-arms, 10 horse archers, and 10 foot archers (*Chaucer's World*, ed. E. Rickert (London, 1948), pp. 291–2, where his will is translated (ibid., pp. 404–7)).

1 Brusendorff, op. cit., pp. 175–7, quoting Lydgate, *Fall of Princes* which is earlier than Camb. Univ. Dd. 3. 53 fo. 27. G. L. Kittredge thinks little Lewis was Lewis Clifford (d. 22 Oct. 1391): cf. 'Lewis Chaucer or Lewis Clifford', *Modern Philology*, xiv (1916–17), 513–18; x (1912–13), 203–5; and cf. *Chaucer Life Records*, ed. M. M. Crow and C. C. Olson (Oxford, 1966), p. 545 and n. 1.

2 See p. 180 n. 2.

3 *Cal. Close Rolls, 1377–81*, p. 374.

4 *Law Quarterly Review*, 63 (Oct. 1947), 491–515; *Chaucer Life Records*, pp. 343–7 and especially p. 346 n. 1.

5 *Law Quart. Rev.* 64 (Jan. 1948), 33–6.

6 Chaucer, *Works*, ed. Skeat, vii (1897), 347–60.

hasty and eccentric scholar, pointed out that this description of Cupid as the god of Love was imitated from Hoccleve's Letter of Cupid *dei Amoris* which ends:

> The yere of grace Ioyful and Iocunde
> A thousand and foure houndred and secounde.[1]

Therefore Clanvow must have written it after 1402. The possibility that Hoccleve copied Clanvow or the much more reasonable view that Cupid's status was a commonplace anyway never occurred to Furnivall. The 'Cuckoo and the Nightingale' was therefore assigned to Thomas Clanvow, Sir John's heir. He also was a courtier and it is possible that he wrote the poem. But the friend of Chaucer has a rather better claim and this is reinforced by the slightly old-fashioned metrical character: it is Chaucerian rather than post-Chaucerian and not much like the post-Chaucerian Hoccleve. But the point cannot be pressed too far. For our purpose it is enough to record that at least one of the Seven was a poet of some accomplishment and that three were close friends of Chaucer while Sturry must have known him well. Finally it must be recalled that Sturry at least was the intimate of another literary figure, Froissart, who praises his courtesy highly and used his influence to get an interview with the king in order to present him with a finely illuminated copy of a book. 'The King asked me what the book treated of: I replied "Of love". He was pleased with the answer and dipped into several places reading parts aloud for he read and spoke French perfectly well.'[2] The 'ancient and valiant knight' Sir Richard Sturry appears more than once in the pages of Froissart.[3] Finally, the wills of various members of the court in Richard II's reign mention legacies of books to the knights as do the wills of their friends; not all the books were of an improving character. If these were Lollards, they shared many of the wordly tastes for which the court at all times, and not least under Richard II, was famous. But not all their books were light reading. If Sturry possessed a copy of the

[1] Chaucer, *Works*, pp. lvii–lix; *Hoccleve's Works*, ed. F. J. Furnivall (E.E.T.S., E.S. lxi) (1892), p. 92.

[2] Froissart, xv. 167.

[3] Ibid. xv. 157, 167, and cf. p. 387; iii. 206; v. 193; vi. 384; and cf. 1, pt. 1. 421.

'Romance of the Rose',[1] the Duchess of York in 1393 left Sir Lewis Clifford her book of 'vices and virtues'.[2] Sir Philip de la Vache whom Chaucer apostrophized mentioned no book in his will, but his widow (d. 1422) bequeathed 'a book of English cleped "Pore Caytife"', a huge collection of devotional tracts long wrongly attributed to Wycliffe, as well as a commentary on St. Matthew's Gospel.[3] There is nothing Lollard or surprising in this, but at least it shows evidence of serious-minded as well as courtly reading. The literacy of the group was exceptional; its character accords more with their worldly careers than their reputed Lollard sympathies. Waugh overlooked this strong confirmation of his argument that these seven were not Lollards, that they were if anything anti-clericals who were worldlings. Such they may appear to have been. But the evidence in favour of the chroniclers' charges remains to be considered.

[1] *British Museum, Catalogue of MSS . . . old Royal and King's Collections*, ed. Sir G. F. Warner and J. R. Gilson (London, 1921), ii. 328 (19 B. XIII).

[2] Will dated 6 Dec. 1392, proved 6 Jan. 1393 (Prerogative Court of Canterbury, Rous, fos. 49v–50).

[3] Prerogative Court of Canterbury, Marche, fo. 128v (25 Apr. 1407, proved 22 June 1408), printed in translation by Rickert in *Chaucer's World*, pp. 404–7.

CHAPTER IV

Employments, Rewards, and Landed Wealth

BEFORE beginning to deal with the evidence for the accuracy of the chroniclers' suspicions, it still remains for me to say something, though very little, about the material rewards that came to the knights from their years of service under the Crown. Edward III and his sons had certainly done nothing to moderate the traditional openhandedness—the largesse—with which it was customary and indeed wise for a prince to repay those who served him well. Their liberality has often been picked out for scholarly condemnation. One example of what such largesse might involve should be enough: when William Montagu in 1337 received his earldom from Edward III, he was at the same time given, to himself and the heirs male of his body, an annuity of 1,000 marks; this was to be paid in cash at the Exchequer until such time as it or any part of it was exchanged for lands of equivalent value at the king's disposal.[1] If Richard II was not strikingly his father's son, he was so at least in his readiness to distribute lands and annuities to his friends. The knights of his Chamber flourished.

In the first place their membership of the royal household entitled them to the customary allowances and fees. They were retained for life and paid an annuity; this varied in amount, but the evidence suggests that a knight of the Chamber enjoyed a life annuity of at least 100 marks. That amount was settled upon both Clanvow and Nevill, for example, on 5 May 1381.[2] But the annuities enjoyed by Clifford and Sturry give a better idea of

[1] *Reports . . . touching the Dignity of a Peer*, v. 33, and *Complete Peerage*, xi. 387, note b.

[2] *Cal. Pat. Rolls, 1381–5*, p. 8 (5 May); *Cal. Close Rolls, 1377–81*, p. 452.

what might be earned by an active and trusted Chamber knight. By 1360 Clifford was receiving £20 p.a. for life, as the Black Prince's yeoman;[1] this was increased to £40 p.a. in 1364 when he was promoted esquire,[2] and to 100 marks on knighthood in 1368.[3] At some time unknown the prince gave him an additional £100 for life[3] and when Clifford was appointed a councillor in 1389 Richard paid him at the rate of 100 marks p.a. as long as he served.[4] This made a total of 500 marks p.a., equivalent to a small baronial landed income. As we shall see, it was probably worth more than that and was supplemented from other sources.

Sturry as Edward III's yeoman had in 1353 a life annuity of only 10 marks;[5] increased with his rank it had grown to 100 marks in 1370.[6] He received another 100 marks p.a. for life from Joan of Kent in 1384[7] and as a royal councillor from 20 August 1389[8] until his death he received 10*s*. a day wages. It is not surprising that he attended regularly; what remain of the council-minutes for that period record 159 consecutive days on which he sat during 1392–3. It only needs to be added that the embassies on which these knights served were well remunerated. And Sturry, we know, also had an annuity of £60 from the Duke of Brittany.[9] We only know that because the duke made peace with France and lost his English lands in 1381; the royal confirmation is our only evidence for it. How many of these knights were in receipt of similar fees from other magnates we shall never know. But the Duke of York in 1412 granted Sir John Cheyne the manor and hundred of Barton by Bristol for life, which was by no means a negligible retaining fee.[10]

The grant of office, particularly office that could be performed by deputy, was a less direct but often valuable method of rewarding service. Sturry, once more, did particularly well in this

[1] *Black Prince's Register*, iv. 389; cf. also pp. 394 and 514.

[2] Ibid. ii. 208, 210, and 214.

[3] *Cal. Pat. Rolls, 1377–81*, pp. 157–8.

[4] Baldwin, King's Council, p. 133.

[5] *Cal. Pat. Rolls, 1350–4*, p. 532 (20 Dec.).

[6] Ibid. *1367–70*, p. 409 (14 Apr. It had been £50 from 12 Oct. 1366).

[7] Ibid. *1381–5*, p. 453.

[8] *Proc. and Ord.* i. 6.

[9] *Cal. Fine Rolls*, x. 34.

[10] *Cal. Pat. Rolls, 1408–13*, p. 451 and cf. *Cal. Close Rolls, Henry V*, i. 257–8.

respect. Near the beginning of his career in 1363 and again in 1372 he procured the office of king's escheator in Ireland merely in order to exchange it for something more useful and on the second occasion of greater permanent value.[1] Having obtained the custody of Bamburgh castle during pleasure he in 1376 converted this into a life tenancy only to exchange it in 1379 for an annuity of £100.[2] But his activities in South Wales were more interesting and paid even better. On 19 March 1376 on the eve of the Good Parliament he was appointed keeper and surveyor of the Despenser lordship of Glamorgan during the non-age of the heir (he was then under three years of age and the minority lasted until 1394) 'with full power of providing and disposing for the good rule thereof'.[3] It is clear evidence of his importance that Richard II confirmed his grandfather's grant by signet on 22 June, the first day of his reign.[4] This was no sinecure, but his wage was 100 marks per annum; the 'full power' which he exercised over this rich lordship the size of a county makes him a forerunner of those great exploiters of the king's landed resources John Milewater under Edward IV and Sir Reynold Bray under Henry VII. It also gave him an influential position in the affairs of the March. In 1384 he expanded his field into central Wales, when Joan of Kent granted him for her life the post of constable and keeper of the castle and town of Aberystwyth; it was confirmed for his life by Richard II three weeks later.[5] Sturry became Justice of Cardigan in 1387[6] and of South Wales in 1391[7] during pleasure; in each case the office could be performed by deputy. None of the others received as much as he did, and I do not propose to enumerate every office they engrossed, but one general point is worth emphasizing: the great concentration of power in their hands in one area: Wales and the Marches, particularly in

[1] *Cal. Fine Rolls*, vii. 258 (16 June), viii. 171 (26 May).

[2] *Cal. Pat. Rolls, 1374–7*, p. 347 (6 Oct. 1376); exchanged on 10 Mar. 1379 (ibid., *1377–81*, pp. 337–8.

[3] Ibid. *1374–7*, p. 251 (19 Mar.).

[4] Ibid. *1377–81*, p. 6.

[5] Ibid. *1381–5*, p. 453 (30 June, 26 July).

[6] Ibid. *1385–9*, p. 307 (24 May).

[7] Ibid. *1388–92*, p. 400 (5 May).

the south. In 1378 Joan of Kent committed the custody of Cardigan castle for life to Lewis Clifford.[1] In 1381 Clanvow received that of Haverford together with the stewardship of its lordship for life from Richard II;[2] Nevill's and his annuities were to be paid out of its profits. Next year he was made keeper of the forests of Snowdon and Merioneth (the latter only in reversion).[3] Finally Sir William Beauchamp farmed the lands of the Hastings, Earls of Pembrokeshire, for £400 p.a. from Michaelmas 1377 until he was deprived of them somewhat mysteriously in the Parliament of January 1390;[4] shortly afterwards he made good his claim by entail to the lordship of Bergavenny.[5] Thus during much of Richard II's reign his Chamber-knights were well entrenched in this area. Had the Mortimer lands been under his control as they were after the coming-of-age of the Earl of March in 1394 he would have had nothing to fear there from his enemies. But between 1381 and 1394 the Mortimer lands were being administered by the late earl's feoffees headed by Arundel and Gloucester, while the Bohun lordship of Brecon was in the hands of Henry Earl of Derby; that did something to redress the balance and obliged Richard to rely upon Chester and North Wales when it came to civil war in the autumn of 1387. That is by the way; but our knights did not lose by their share in the maintenance of the royal influence in the south.

The grant of the king's rights of wardship and marriage remained an acceptable form of reward to his servants. Sturry received far more there than any of his companions; I have already mentioned the case of Sir John Peachey in 1376; it is unnecessary to recite the others.

A less obvious favour which the king could confer upon a subject was the lease of estates either temporarily or permanently in his hands at an uneconomic rent. This was facilitated by the practice of fixing the rent in accordance with an obsolete valuation known as an extent—always well below the actual yield and

[1] Ibid. *1381–5*, p. 185 (confirmation dated 29 Oct. 1382).

[2] Ibid. *1377–81*, p. 627.

[3] Ibid. *1381–5*, p. 104.

[4] On the death of John Hastings, Earl of Pembroke, on 30 or 31 Dec. 1389, his earldom reverted to the Crown (*Complete Peerage*, x. 396).

[5] Ibid. i. 24–6.

sometimes as little as a half of what it was worth. To have lands committed on condition that the amount at which they were 'extended' was paid into the Exchequer *per annum* was a disguised way of conferring a benefit. It is not surprising to find that most courtiers and other royal servants and favourites farmed the greater part of the land belonging to the Crown 'for the extent'. If an annuity for life had been granted at the Exchequer, it was the ambition of the holder to exchange it for lands equivocally described as 'of equal value' in order to enjoy the difference between the extent and the actual yield; with luck the value of the annuity could not only be doubled but a stake in the country could be acquired with the territorial and political consequence that only land could give. Sir Richard Sturry in 1376 exchanged his life-annuity of 100 marks as a Chamber-knight for the manor of Bolsover, Derbyshire[1] and the life-annuity of £60 from the Duke of Brittany in 1384 for the Lincolnshire manor of Wicks near Boston;[2] this was extended at £80 p.a. so he had to pay a £20 rent for it. Sir Lewis Clifford similarly exchanged 215 marks p.a. of the 250 marks p.a. he had received from the Black Prince for the manors of Princes Risborough, Buckinghamshire, and Mere, Wiltshire in 1377 and 1381 respectively;[3] in 1404 another Prince of Wales reversed this arrangement but for twenty-seven years Clifford had almost certainly enjoyed great financial and other advantages from it; he did not, as Waugh mistakenly believed, lose everything in 1404; he merely reverted to the receipt of his annuities in cash, a hardship no doubt but not ruin.

An interesting feature of the land-acquisitions of these knights is the extent to which they invested in monastic land: the English manors and appropriated rectories belonging to monasteries within the dominions of the French king, generally known as alien priories. Taken into the king's hands for the duration of the war, these offered, in a period notable for the scarcity of good land in the market, an opportunity for investors well enough

[1] *Cal. Pat. Rolls, 1374–7*, p. 372; cf. ibid. *1377–81*, p. 121.

[2] *Cal. Fine Rolls*, x. 34 (23 Feb.).

[3] *Cal. Pat. Rolls, 1377–81*, pp. 157–8 and 159; cf. *Cal. Close Rolls, 1381–5*, p. 26.

placed to secure them by their influence at court. The first step was to obtain their custody for the duration of the war from the king at an artificially low rent; the second to negotiate with the mother-house in Normandy or elsewhere to buy out its interest; since the French houses saw no prospect of recovering possession (they had been deprived on and off since 1295 and were justified in rating their chances low) they were willing to take a small price as the value of their reversion and be glad to get anything at all. As a result courtiers were heavy buyers of alien priory land. This needs to be emphasized since Professor Knowles has convinced himself that there was practically no disendowment from this cause and that therefore the suppression of the alien priories was no precedent for the Tudor dissolution.[1] Several of the Seven were owners of monastic lands on quite a considerable scale. In 1379, for example, Sir John Cheyne obtained the alien priory of Beckford in Gloucestershire at a rent which was later cancelled;[2] this consisted of three manors in Gloucestershire and one in Lincolnshire. Ten years later in 1389 he got permission to obtain the custody from the Norman priory of St. Barbe for his own life, that of his wife, and that of his eldest son; it remained in the family until 1438.[3] He acquired lands in Gloucestershire in or shortly before 1387 belonging to the abbey of Beaubec[4] and between 1400 and 1402 he converted his annuity of 100 marks from Henry IV into the custody of the lands of Newent priory (extended at 150 marks p.a.) in Gloucestershire and Herefordshire.[5] Since these included three appropriated rectories, one has the spectacle of Sir John Cheyne as a lay rector long before the Reformation. Both Sir Lewis Clifford and Sir Richard Sturry made similarly large investments in monastic land, the former in

[1] M. D. Knowles, *The Religious Orders in England* (Cambridge, 1955), ii. 164.

[2] Cf. *Cal. Fine Rolls*, ix. 167, 238–9, and 240; D. J. A. Matthew, *Norman Monasteries and their English Possessions* (Oxford, 1962), pp. 112–14; *Proc. and Ord.* i. 195; cf. *Cal. Pat. Rolls, 1381–5*, p. 312; ibid., *1388–92*, p. 118; ibid., *1391–6*, p. 632.

[3] *Cal. Inq. p.m.* (Record Commission), iv. 55 and 182 (16 Henry VI no. 27); *Cal. Close Rolls, Henry V*, ii. 178–9; and cf. *Cal. Pap. Letts.* iv. 328.

[4] Cf. *Cal. Fine Rolls*, x. 175.

[5] *Cal. Pat. Rolls, 1399–1401*, p. 200; cf. p. 205, *Proc. and Ord.* i. 195 (Jan. 1403) and *Rot. Parl.* iii. 653.

four manors in Norfolk and elsewhere in 1390,[1] the latter when he acquired the keeping of two Kentish priories in 1373 and 1388 that rounded off the considerable estates he purchased in his home county.[2] Sir John Clanvow in 1381 tried to do the same sort of thing on an even larger scale with the lands of the Norman abbey of Lyre but his plan seems to have fallen through;[3] while Sir John Montagu, either father or son, held the alien priory of Hayling from 1382 to 1394.[4]

To argue that all owners of alien priory lands were Lollards would be as absurd as to assert that all sixteenth-century purchasers of monastic property were Protestants; but at least each had something substantial to lose by reaction. These courtiers had a vested interest in disendowment at a time when Lollard petitions were recommending the government to use the lands of the possessioners for the creation of new soldiers' fiefs. They had incidentally also—where they had not bought out the mother-house—a vested interest in the prolongation of the war. Lollards or not, they were compelled to endure a conflict between interest and creed.

And that at last brings us to the question of their patronage of heresy. What were their relations with the heretic preachers? Were they themselves in any sense Lollards?

Waugh was prepared to admit the possibility that Sir Thomas

[1] *Cal. Pat. Rolls, 1388–92*, p. 306. The manors were Monks Toft, Norfolk; Warmington, Warwickshire; Spetisbury, Dorset; and Aston Tirrold, Berkshire, obtained from the Abbot and convent of Préaux, Normandy, paying £80 p.a. during the war with France; on 6 Dec. following he and his son Lewis were rebated the £80 p.a. in survivorship (ibid., p. 355).

[2] Ibid. *1370–4*, p. 366 (Thurlegh); *Cal. Fine Rolls, 1383–91*, p. 211 (Greenwich with Lewisham).

[3] On 20 Nov. 1381 he and Ralph Maylock, proctor of the abbey of Lyre in England obtained the right to farm the abbey's English lands from 14 Apr. 1381 for the duration of the war, for £120 p.a. (*Cal. Fine Rolls*, ix. 274). Lyre owned Hinckley, Leicestershire, worth £34 p.a. in 1540; Livers Ocle (in Ocle Pychard, Herefordshire), worth £7 in 1535; Llangua, Monmouthshire, worth £2 p.a. in 1535; and Wareham, Dorset, worth £20 p.a. in 1291. (M. D. Knowles and R. N. Hadcock, *Medieval Religious Houses* [London, 1953], pp. 85, 86, and 91.) No more is heard of this. (But cf. also Reg. Buckingham xii B, fos. 44, 44^{v}, and 50^{v} [1385].)

[4] *Cal. Fine Rolls*, ix. 285, 295 (30 Mar. 1382).

Latimer was rightly accused: 'if any of the knights—was guilty of heresy, Latimer was the man'; and again 'except perhaps in the case of Latimer, [the chroniclers] were mistaken in ascribing to the knights'[1] any sympathy with Lollardy. The reason for his hesitating to dismiss the charge against Latimer was that on 2 May 1388—he wrongly dates the incident in 1387—a messenger was sent to Sir Thomas ordering him to come before the council 'cum certis libris et quaternis in custodia sua existentibus de erronea et perversa doctrina fidei catholice ut dicitur'.[2] Waugh thought that Latimer, who was a J.P.,[3] might have seized them from Lollards in the neighbourhood; but if that were the case it is singularly loosely expressed. The ordinary meaning of the words implies that the books and quires he was alleged (no more) to possess were his own. If that were all the evidence against Latimer, it would be enough to justify the conclusion that he had been delated to the council during the session of the Merciless Parliament and sent for cross-examination. This fits the account given by the Westminster Chronicle that shortly before 20 March 1388 'in pleno parliamento magnus rumor exuberavit de Lollardis' and their preachings and their English books 'quasi per totam Angliam'.[4] It fits also the evidence cited by H. G. Richardson[5] of the government's drive against the Nottinghamshire Lollards that year. A short-lived campaign by the victorious Appellants against a heresy favoured by the knights of Richard's Chamber and household flared up and quickly died away. But fortunately that does not exhaust the evidence against Latimer. Some I shall withhold until I come to deal with the wills of all the Lollards considered together. But the register of Bishop Buckingham of Lincoln and a cartulary made for a member of the Griffin family,[6]

[1] Waugh, op. cit., pp. 72 and 91.

[2] F. Devon, *Issues of the Exchequer* (London, 1837), p. 236; Waugh, p. 71, nn. 9 and 10.

[3] J.P., Northamptonshire (14 Dec. 1381, 8 Mar. and 21 Dec. 1382, 15 Mar. 1383 (*Cal. Pat. Rolls, 1381–5*, pp. 84, 141, 246–7, and 254)).

[4] Higden, *Polychronicon*, ix. 171.

[5] H. G. Richardson, 'Heresy and the Lay Power under Richard II', *E.H.R.* li (1936), 171.

[6] Griffin Cartulary I (u u) (Northamptonshire Record Society): see especially fos. xliii^{v}–xliv (from Assize Roll, Northamptonshire 12 Richard II (1388–9)).

descendants of Latimer's sister and ultimate heir,[1] now in the Northamptonshire Record Office, provide a good many facts to substantiate the council's anxiety in 1388. The Griffin Cartulary contains the record of a suit brought by Thomas Latimer against William Sligh, vicar of Blakesley, Northamptonshire, at that time rural dean of Brackley, at the County Assizes. From this we learn that it was ordered by the common council of the lord king that those believing, holding, or preaching heresies and errors against the truth of the Catholic faith should be proceeded against by the Ordinaries.[2] The initiative in 1388 came from the council. Though no such general directive has been preserved, a number of letters patent beginning with one to the Bishop of Worcester on 29 May and enrolled on the Patent Roll provide evidence that bishops were being individually stirred into activity by the government. No letter to Buckingham of Lincoln was enrolled but evidently one was sent. When the bishop, therefore, was informed that one John Wodard of Knebworth, junior, chaplain, staying in the village of Chipping Warden, Northamptonshire, was guilty of preaching divers errors and heresies in the diocese,[3] he sent a mandate to the rural dean citing Wodard to appear before him or his commissaries Thomas Brandon the subdean and John Bottlesham the future Bishop of Rochester, at Sleaford on 18 December 1388 to answer for his misdeeds.[4] On Tuesday 8 December Sligh, accompanied by a chaplain and a second man, appeared at Chipping Warden to serve the bishop's summons.[4] Now Chipping Warden was a small market town, the lord of which was Sir Thomas Latimer, and one of his privileges was that of holding a weekly market on Tuesdays. Since Sligh's attempt to serve the writ led to disorder and since he

[1] His sister Elizabeth married Thomas Griffin, whose son and heir, Richard Griffin, married Anne, daughter of Richard Chamberlain. Their son and heir John Griffin, died without issue in Feb. 1445 and was succeeded by the descendants of his younger brother, Nicholas (d. 12 Oct. 1435), and Margaret, daughter of Sir John Pilkington.

[2] Griffin Cartulary I (u u), fo. xliv.

[3] A royal serjeant-at-arms, who had been sent to him to get him to come to the Council with all his heretic books and quires in his possession, was paid 13*s*. 4*d*. on 2 May 1388 (Devon, *Issues*, p. 236).

[4] Griffin Cartulary I (u u), fo. xliv.

repeated the attempt on the six Tuesdays following (according to Latimer) it seems probable that Wodard used the assemblage on market-days as an opportunity for spreading the word to the people. Sligh's appearance, Latimer alleged, led to such debates and insults that many inhabitants of the town dared not display their wares and he, as the owner of the market, lost his profits. He averred that John Warner, John Butcher, John Brackley, and the constable had in particular been frightened off. Sligh replied that he had done no more than cite the accused to appear. Appear he did not as Buckingham declared in a letter denouncing the heretics of Chipping Warden addressed to his archdeacons from Sleaford on 20 December.[1] And after the seven citations by Sligh had failed to produce any effect, the bishop invoked the lay power. He sent into Chancery a certificate of Wodard's contumacy and the names of forty-one men and four women whom he had led into error. On 8 March 1389 the king ordered the Sheriff of Northamptonshire to arrest the chaplain and his forty-five supporters and put them at the disposal of the bishop.[2] Two days later on 10 March Buckingham once more cited John Wodard to trial before him.[3] And there the record ends. The absence of any mention of Latimer as among the heretic's protectors does not detract from the significance of the episode. On the contrary his immunity when the fact of his protection was obvious reveals how little the Lollard knights had to fear. He felt so secure that he did not hesitate to bring an action against the bishop's summoner before the king's justices on assize; and this less than a year after he himself had been cross-examined before the council for his possession of Lollard books. Apart from matters connected with his will, there is nothing more that is new to be said about Latimer's dealings with Lollardy. But it is necessary to bear in mind the continued existence of heresy at Braybrooke, Latimer's place of residence, throughout the first quarter of the fifteenth century. Its rector Robert Hook, a notorious Lollard, was presented either by Latimer or his widow to the living before 14 July 1402 (Latimer himself died on 14 September

[1] Reg. Buckingham, fo. 347. [2] *Cal. Close Rolls, 1385–9*, pp. 667–8.
[3] Reg. Buckingham, fo. 357v.

1401);[1] he first brought himself to the notice of the authorities as a heretic in 1405 but little was done to molest him; a jury in 1414 presented him as a well-known preacher of heresy and he appeared before Archbishop Chichele in St. Paul's chapter-house on 18 October 1414 and abjured his false opinions.[2] But once more on 6 June 1425 he was charged with having continued the practices which he had abjured; he was lucky to escape with the penalty of reading a recantation at Paul's Cross and finding security in Chancery for his future good behaviour.[3] The leniency with which Hook was treated has significance to which I shall return. Doubtless it was he who in 1407 provided two Czech scholars at Braybrooke with a copy of Wycliffe's *De Dominio* which they there transcribed for despatch to Prague.[4] And in 1414 Hook was not alone to be presented by the anti-Lollard jurors. One of his parishioners, Thomas Ile, was delated as both a writer and distributor of Lollard tracts. There is every reason to regard Sir Thomas Latimer as having done everything the chroniclers complained of to lend countenance to the heretic missionaries and to enable them to pervert his tenants. It was probably Latimer who provided Knighton with his lurid picture of the Lollard knight who forced his humbler neighbours to come and listen to the wandering preacher, even in the parish church itself, and stood by armed with his sword to protect the heretic from their hostility.[5] This may be highly coloured but it is essentially true.

[1] Cf. J. Bridges, *History and Antiquities of Northamptonshire* (Oxford, 1791), ii. 13.

[2] *Reg. Chichele*, iii. 105–7.

[3] Ibid., pp. 105–12.

[4] *De Dominio Divino*, ed. R. L. Poole (1890), p. 249 n. and p. x.

[5] *Knighton*, ii. 181.

CHAPTER V

The Lollardy of Nevill and Clanvow

WILLIAM NEVILL and John Clanvow, the Castor and Pollux of the Lollard movement, have attracted a good deal less notice than Latimer, their almost exact contemporary, were omitted from Knighton's list altogether, and have been pronounced by Waugh 'not guilty of the reproach of heresy' along with Sir John Cheyne of Beckford.[1] Fifty years old at the time of their deaths together in Greece in October 1391, it was only after the revival of the king's personal rule in 1389 that they had begun to draw level with Sturry and Clifford in political influence. In the earlier part of the reign, though Chamber-knights much used in government business, they had been overshadowed by their seniors. Yet it is to this period before 1388 to which Knighton's allusions refer, that the one piece of evidence for Nevill's Lollard contacts belongs. 'The cases of Sir John Clanvow and Sir William Nevill', Waugh remarked, 'naturally fall together.' If that is true then they stand together also. Guilt by association may be a dangerous principle for a court of law; and the historian may prefer not to invoke it too often. But well-founded suspicion, though not legal proof, cannot be treated by the historian as a jury must treat it. In history and law the burden of proof falls differently. [Innocent until proved guilty in law; I propose, quite frankly, to apply the principle of guilt by association where it appears to be justified.] If ever this could be safely done it would be in the case of these devoted friends who did so much in each other's company and were even united in death. But in fact it is not necessary, since there is independent evidence against each—though naturally it is all the stronger for the confirmation.

[1] Waugh, op. cit., pp. 87–8.

That against Nevill is best considered first, since it only needs to be treated briefly. It has been in print since 1921 in a place no less obvious than the *Calendar of Close Rolls*. I could afford to comment more ironically upon the blindness of other scholars had I not overlooked its significance myself. One hardly expects to find anything new at this date there. However there it is and Waugh at least is free from blame; had he known it, he might still have thought it immaterial.

As befitted a Nevill, Sir William received most marks of the royal favour by the grant of offices in the north of England. It was there that he was admiral in 1372.[1] On 9 June 1381 he was appointed justice of the forest north of the Trent;[2] a valuable but not arduous office which he exchanged in January 1387 for lands in Devon and Cornwall extended at 200 marks a year.[3] And before 28 February 1382 he had become constable of Nottingham castle.[4] In that capacity he was gaoler to two of his colleagues, Sir Simon Burley and another Chamber-knight Sir William Elmham, when they were awaiting trial by the Merciless Parliament in February 1388;[5] presumably he made them comfortable. It was as constable of Nottingham castle that he revealed his connection with that prominent heretic Master Nicholas Hereford, in 1387.[6] Hitherto, on the strength of Walsingham's testimony, Montagu has been regarded as Master Nicholas's only patron among the Seven. His association with Nevill also is fresh evidence for the coherence of the group.

In January 1387 Archbishop Courtenay learnt that Hereford, who had long been excommunicated for contumacy—in particular his refusal to appear when summoned—was somewhere in the north midlands. On his signification of this to Chancery in accordance with the procedure laid down in the Parliament of May 1382, commissions were issued on 17 January ordering various gentlemen in the counties of Nottingham, Leicester, and Derby to arrest Hereford and to keep him in prison until he had

[1] *Cal. Close Rolls, 1369–74*, p. 428.

[2] *Cal. Fine Rolls*, ix. 257.

[3] *Cal. Pat. Rolls, 1385–9*, p. 267 (9 Jan.).

[4] *Cal. Close Rolls, 1381–5*, p. 39.

[5] Ibid. *1385–9*, p. 394.

[6] Ibid., p. 208 (1 Feb.).

satisfied Holy Church.[1] In the Nottinghamshire commission, but not in the other two, the mayor of the county town was included; so Courtenay seems to have had a good idea where the heretic was most likely to be found. Within a few days Master Nicholas had been caught by the civic authorities of Nottingham and lodged in the town gaol. It is not without interest that the town was then in the diocese and province of York and that the Ordinary was Sir William Nevill's brother, Alexander, another of the king's courtiers. Courtenay was using the lay arm to penetrate the ecclesiastical defences of the northern province.

Hereford's arrest was immediately followed by the receipt of a petition from Sir William[2] and this in its turn led to the issue on 1 February of a royal letter close to the mayor and bailiffs.[2] The petition stated the fact of the arrest and asked that the prisoner should be committed to Nevill's keeping in Nottingham castle 'because of the honesty of his person', a strange description of a notorious excommunicate of long standing and clear evidence of Nevill's partiality. The petitioner offered to go bail for Hereford and to keep him safe so that he should not walk abroad to preach errors or distribute tracts contrary to the Church's faith. The royal letters granted his request. Nothing more is known of Hereford's adventures until, a few months after Nevill's death, there is evidence that he had made his submission;[3] but this interval was probably filled by the residence at Montagu's manor of Shenley described by Walsingham[4] and some years in Courtenay's prison according to Knighton.[5] Full of uncertainties as Hereford's career is, this episode at least is valuable for the evidence of Nevill's desire to befriend him.

Sir John Clanvow's distinction lies in the fact that he alone of the suspects can be proved to have taken notice of the accusation of Lollardy brought against him. He did not admit its truth, but only that it had been made. When so many of the Lollards' tracts were anonymous, it is something to be able to read one,

[1] *Cal. Pat. Rolls, 1385–9*, p. 316.

[2] *Cal. Close Rolls, 1385–9*, p. 208; and see above p. 198 n. 6.

[3] *Cal. Pat. Rolls, 1391–6*, p. 8.

[4] Walsingham, *Historia Anglicana*, ii. 159–60.

[5] *Knighton*, ii. 174.

the author of which is not merely a name, if that, but a public figure whose career can be traced in considerable detail. The evidence is contained in a manuscript belonging to University College, Oxford.[1]

First something should be said about the manuscript and its compiler. The greater part of it, at any rate, was written in or soon after 1400 and consists of twenty-five separate items. Some of these are copies of various official records and one is a will made on 6 July 1399 which was proved on 20 November following. There are a couple of skeleton chronicles, the later of which notes Henry IV's accession. But the greater part of the volume[2]—seventeen items—is taken up with short devotional and homiletic pieces, mostly in English. A few are assigned to a named author; thus 'a treatise that Richard Hermit made to a good ancress that he loved'[3] or 'a good meditation the which St. Anselm made',[4] one of St. Bernard's letters and an excerpt from his writings. The majority are anonymous, though a good number are traceable to the hand of the fourteenth-century mystic, Richard Rolle of Hampole, the Richard the Hermit to which the treatise is ascribed. Whoever made this collection was evidently strongly under the influence of the contemporary English mystical tradition. One other affiliation is interesting in view of Wycliffe's one-time alliance with the Austin Friars; the manuscript contains 'a good sermon by John Gregory, Austin friar of Newport' in Monmouthshire, a house and an author otherwise unknown to fame.[5]

Who was the compiler? There are two possible candidates. The documents copied into the volume include grants in favour of (*a*) 'dominus W.C. clericus'[6] or 'capellanus' and (*b*) 'dominus J.B. de N. capellanus'.[7] The latter was for example, granted a pension of £20 a year on 22 July 1398 by the Prior and convent of Lanthony by Gloucester. I have been unable to identify him,

[1] H. O. Coxe, *Catalogus Codicum MSS. qui in collegiis . . . Oxoniensibus . . . adservantur* (Oxford, 1852), i. 28–9; given to University College by Mr. Thomas Walker, Master.

[2] University College MS. (Coxe) 97, fos. 85^{r}–171^{r}.

[3] Ibid., fos. 133^{r}–153^{r}.

[4] Ibid., fos. 155^{v}–158^{v}.

[5] Ibid., fos. 162^{v}–170^{r}.

[6] Fos. 171^{r}–172^{r}.

[7] Fos. 172^{v}–173^{v}.

but while there is a chance that he was the compiler, 'W.C.' appears more often and is so far to be preferred. In one document he receives a furred livery robe from the Abbot and convent of 'A.' (10 April 1400), while on 15 October 1392 he was presented to the parish of 'P.' in the diocese of Worcester by none other than Sir William Beauchamp.[1] The latter describes W.C., chaplain, as his clerk. Since in 1396 the rector of Pirton, Worcestershire, patron Sir William Beauchamp, was William Counter,[2] we know the identity of W.C. As further confirmation among the executors of the will in this University College manuscript will be found the name of Sir William Counter, priest. As Beauchamp's clerk in 1392 he was in a position to have access to the original homily which we must now consider.

This is entitled:[3] 'this treatise next following made Sir John Clanvow knight the last voyage that he made over the great sea [the usual name for the Mediterranean] in which he died, of whose soul Jesu have mercy.' This last pious ejaculation indicates that Clanvow was known personally to the compiler or to the patron for whom he was writing (the inclusion of the various odd documents suggests that the collection was for his own use). There is in any case no reason to doubt the ascription of the treatise to Clanvow, nor the date at which it was said to have been composed. As the only known statement of his religious views attributed by a contemporary to one of the Lollard knights it deserves to be closely studied; from it alone can be derived some sort of picture of what they stood for. It is a pity that it should turn out to contain so much dreary cant, but that in itself is significant. What else, in any event, would we expect?

Let me try briefly to summarize its contents. The treatise is between 9,000 and 10,000 words in length;[4] its principal subject, to which it returns from every digression, is set out in the opening words:

The gospel telleth that in a time when our lord Jesu Christ was here

[1] Fos. 174^{v}–175^{r}. [2] Nash, *Worcestershire*, ii. 259.

[3] University College MS. (Coxe) 97, fo. 114^{r}. The text which follows has been put into modernized spelling.

[4] University College MS. (Coxe) 97, fos. 114^{r}–124^{v}.

upon earth, a man came to him and asked him if that few men shoulden be saved. And Christ answered and said: the gate is wide and the way is broad that leadeth to loss [in its original meaning of 'perdition']; and many go-en in that way; and how strait is the gate and the way narrow that leadeth to the life; and few finden that way.

The two ways provide the text for this layman's sermon. Man can choose between the pain of hell and the bliss of heaven; he had better choose soon 'for we been every day going full fast towards another place' and none knows when his time will come; those who that day are found in the broad way cannot be saved from the pain of hell. The bliss of heaven is commended: 'that joy of this world is passing and soon i-done and fulli-meddled with dread and with many other diseases and travails. But the joy of heaven is more and more and no dread ne travail ne diseases therein ne lacking of nothing that heart may desire and thereto it lasteth without end'. The prudent will therefore seek the narrow way. If they do not, then they are reminded that 'the pain of hell is greater than any heart can think and shall never have end. And he that is there shall never die, but ever liven among the fiends in darkness and in torment without end.'

What are the precepts for finding the narrow way? Be meek, fear God, and shun all manner of evil: particularly 'the ways of the fiend, the lust of their flesh or liking of the world', for these are baubles for fools. For everlasting life keep God's commandments, for 'the dread of God is the beginning of wisdom'. Recklessness in the keeping of these leads straight to the broad way; and so on with a profuse citation of scriptural authority to prove how foolish as well as wrong it was to do evil and right to do good: 'And if we do not thus we been fools, though we getten us never so much worship and ease or richesse of this world.' The devil, the world, and the flesh are disposed of in turn. The fiend 'will put to us that it is no need to us for to dread God so sore, for God is full of mercy'; the flesh will persuade us that its denial cannot from weakness be borne;

and the world will put to us that it is not profitable . . . and that all wise and worshipful men of this world travailen for to geten hem eases and lusts and worship . . . in this world. And if that we diden otherwise men would blamen us and scornen us and set right naught by us. And therefore it is wisdom and worship [for] a man to conform him to the world. And also that he must be surer of his livelihood after his estate the whiles that he liveth: these been the skills of the world.

The folly of this too is demonstrated by further citations from scripture and a loving enumeration of the seven deadly sins leads to the praise of the *via media*: 'Coveting to have too muchel of the world is a vice';

and the mean between these two is a great virtue; and that is: for to travail truely for that that men needeth, and, if men getten more over that, for to help therewith their needy brethren and neighbours. And eek it is a great sin for to mistrust in the mercy of God: and it is a great sin for to sin the more for trust of God's mercy; and that the mean of these two is a great virtue; and that is for to leaven evil for dread of God and for to do good for the love of God. And therefore thus our belief shall teachen us the mean way, that is virtue, between the extremities that been vices.

There is much more in praise of measure in the treatment of the flesh also: 'we must keep our flesh in right rule as men keep a sick man . . . hoping to bring him to health'—by help of the spirit. The world is selected for particularly bitter denunciation: 'the foul stinking muck of this false failing world'. Even, despite Sir William Nevill, St. James's denunciation of those who make friends in this world is greeted with approval; 'they that setten their trust in this world been all deceived'. Naturally the treasures of this world are likewise dismissed as 'false and passing and unsavoury'. At this point Clanvow breaks into abuse of his own class:

For the world hold them worshipful that been great warriors and fighters and that destroyen and winned many lands and wasten and given much good [i.e. wealth] to them that have enough and that dispenden outrageously in meat, in drink, in clothing, in building, and in living in ease, sloth and many other sins . . . And of such folk men maken books and songs and readen and singen of them for to hold the mind of their deeds the longer here upon earth.

And in this the world is deceived. Drunkenness, dicing, swearing, and lechery are next disposed of; and especially the temptation of evil company (this gives rise to a long and detailed description of the way a fowler makes use of a 'watch-bird' as he calls a decoy); the 'watch birds' of the fiend are those that the world calls 'good fellows'. There is rather a fine piece of eloquence on what is likely to happen to those

> that will waste the goods that God hath sent them in pride of the world and in lusts of their flesh. And go-en to the tavern and to the bordel and play-en at the dice, waking long a-nights and swearing fast and drinking and jangling [chattering] too much, scorning, backbiting, japing, glozing [flattering], boasting, lying, fighting and being bawds for their fellows and living all in sin and in vanity; they be hold good fellows!

The ten commandments of the old dispensation are then recited and glossed and then the two commandments of the new: the love of God and the love of thy neighbour: 'And in these two commandments hangeth all the law and the prophets'—which leads easily to a brief account of the Incarnation and the Redemption and so back to the grisly pains of hell and the narrow way to Heaven.

Well, that should be enough to show what a farrago of pulpit commonplaces this treatise was. But its competence and the way the argument is worked out is not amateurish; it is skilled professional work. Had it come to us from the pen of a recluse or a revivalist preaching friar, its wholesale rejection of all that 'this wretched world' holds worshipful, of the sins of the flesh, of swearing, drinking, gaming, and slaying, would have excited little comment. But the author of this censorious, puritanical, and pacifist tirade was after all a fifty-year-old warrior and courtier who, until the journey on which he died, was one of Richard II's trusted councillors. That is the striking thing about it. Clanvow is revealed as a moralist of the most sanctimonious type, a reminder that the rule of the saints has an ancestry far older than the break with Rome under the Tudors. The literate laity were taking the clergy's words out of their mouths. The lay party, whatever its doctrinal position, based its religion upon the sinfulness of the flesh and 'the foul stinking muck of this false failing world'. It was also strictly biblical in character. The treatise is a mosaic of scriptural quotations; there is nothing that I can see from any other source; the nearest it comes to the fathers of the Church is the epistles of the New Testament. Clanvow relies exclusively on the authority of Holy Writ; his religion is Bible Christianity.

Here at least he wrote nothing recognizably either Wycliffite or even Lollard, using that adjective to cover Swinderby's sermons and those of the later popular preachers against image-worship and pilgrimage, the effectiveness of the clerk in sin to perform the sacraments, and the payment of the tithe to negligent pastors. The only trace of Lollardy is in the silences. Clanvow says nothing in favour of confession, pilgrimage, the veneration of the saints, the effectiveness of the sacraments, nothing at all about the priesthood. He ignores the Church as an institution altogether. He was a lay preacher and he has assumed to himself at least as much of the clergy's functions. That was what aroused the Church's resentment against the 'lay party'. Men such as Clanvow were implicitly suggesting that the layman had no need of an intermediary between himself and his God.

That Clanvow was aware of the resentment is shown by a passage that I have omitted from my summary of his treatise. He has been scorned and abused. But he goes out of his way to accept for himself and those who thought like him the popular name by which the heretics were known. At the point where he denounces the warriors and fighters who spend 'outrageously in meat, in drink, in clothing, in building and in living in ease', and commends those who live meekly in this world 'and ben out of such forsaid riot, noise and strife and liven simply and usen to eaten and drinken in measure and to clothen them meekly and suffren patiently wrongs that other folks doen and sayen to them and holden them apaid with little good of this world', he breaks off to remark:

Such folk the world scorneth and holdeth them lollers and losels [good-for-nothings] fools and shameful wretches. But surely God holdeth them most wise and most worshipful . . . And therefore take we savour in those things . . . and reck we never though the world scorn us or hold us wretches. For the world scorned Christ and held him a fool . . . And therefore follow we his traces and suffer we patiently the scorns of the world as he did.

In this passage Clanvow is aware that he is speaking for a despised minority and he wasn't ashamed to own himself one of those that the world called 'Lollers'. In this context it is worth recalling a famous scene in the *Canterbury Tales*. In the interlude between the Man of Law's Tale and the Shipman's the Host is rebuked by the Parson for his blasphemy

> What eyleth the man, so sinfully to swere?

And

> Our hoste answerde, O Iankin, be ye there?
> I smelle a loller in the wind.[1]

Chaucer was the friend of Clanvow and his friends. Without going so far as to suggest that the Parson was intended as a portrait of a Lollard priest—though the idea is not new—I see in this passage at least the poet making mild fun of men with whom he was on terms of some intimacy. Though where Lollardy and Cecily Champaigne found accommodation together is a nice problem; but no nicer than that of how the same hand produced the treatise on the strait gate as well as the Cuckoo and the Nightingale. Yet unless our picture of Lollardy can find room for both then it can be no proper likeness. It was nothing like so simple and straightforward as Protestant historians with literal minds believed. The fundamental weakness of Waugh's thesis is that it is far too logical.

[1] Chaucer, *Works*, ed. Skeat, iv. 165 (ll. 1171–3).

CHAPTER VI

Lollard Wills

WITH the consideration of the 'Lollard wills' we reach the crux of our subject—and its most baffling problem. Hitherto, although the evidence may be thought to have lacked body, what little there was pointed unmistakably to one conclusion. That Latimer, Montagu, and Nevill befriended Lollard missionaries and that Clanvow confessed in so many words that he and those who thought like him were branded as 'Lollers' by the worldly-wise: these are facts that do not admit of question. Not so the evidence now to be reviewed. Everything about it, except its very solid existence, is doubtful. Its interpretation is beset by difficulties; it is not merely possible, but almost necessary, to object to any theory on the ground that it fails to take some inconvenient but quite solid fact into account. No simple explanation is adequate, no complex one easy to devise. All the same this evidence by itself leaves—in me at any rate—a settled conviction that no theory which would see the knights dying, whatever their previous record, as faithful and unquestioning sons of Holy Church, is for long seriously tenable. And when it is approached in the light of the facts dealt with in my last two lectures it loses what little credibility it ever had. But proof—Oh dear no, there's no proof.

The wills of only three of the seven knights have been preserved; in all three cases in copies proved and registered in the court of the Archbishop of Canterbury. They are those of Latimer (made 13 September 1401),[1] Clifford (made 17 September 1404),[2] and Cheyne (made 1 November 1413),[3] in each case shortly

[1] Prerogative Court of Canterbury, Marche, fos. 12–12ᵛ.

[2] Ibid., fo. 7: printed in Dugdale, *Baronage*, i. 341–2; proved 5 Dec. 1404 (*Testamenta Vetusta*, ed. N. H. Nicolas [London, 1826], i. 164 f.).

[3] Reg. Arundel (Cant.), ii. fo. 203ᵛ.

before death. The absence of wills for the other four is a little mysterious since their possession of chattels in more than one diocese meant that the right of probate belonged to the court of the metropolitan, and the Canterbury registers, those at Lambeth, Canterbury, and Somerset House, are for this date pretty complete. The deaths of Nevill and Clanvow in Greece and the lynching of Montagu at Cirencester in 1400 after he had refused, it is said (Walsingham), the sacraments of the Church,[1] might be thought a sufficient explanation for the absence of wills in their cases, but that leaves Sturry's silence unaccounted for. If they made no wills, we should still expect the archbishop's court to provide for their intestacies; it did not. Since they had much to leave they are unlikely to have set out for the Mediterranean or upon a hazardous conspiracy without taking the most obvious precaution against the consequences of disaster. That they had conscientious objections to the makings of wills seems improbable, it is easier to believe that those they made were for some reason or reasons either not proved or not registered in the obvious court.[2] That is not a very satisfactory explanation, but it was a thing which could and did happen; Nevill's will is not among the York registers, nor is Clanvow's at Hereford.

However, we may be thankful for having three out of seven. Between these three documents there exist striking points of resemblance both of matter and language. It is in itself a fact of great significance that all the surviving wills of our seven suspects are alike and at the same time unusual; this can hardly be dismissed as the result of chance. That they should be Clifford's, Latimer's, and Cheyne's is in itself useful: it helps to bridge the gaps between the generations, shows—as other things do also—that Latimer's *comparative* isolation from the court did not weaken the bonds that existed between him and the others, and once more suggests that Cheyne's omission from Walsingham's list of Lollard knights was a mere oversight. There is another link between

[1] *Historia Anglicana*, ii. 244.

[2] Lyndwood suggests that wills might or might not be registered (*Provinciale* [*seu Constitutiones Angliae*] [Oxford, 1679], Lib. iii, tit. xiii c 'Adeo quorundam', gloss 'insinuationes hujusmodi', p. 181 and n.v. I owe this reference to Mr. J. L. Barton).

the three wills apart from content and language. The responsibility of overseeing the execution of Latimer's will is shared between the widow and Sir Lewis Clifford; the overseers of Clifford's will were Sir John Cheyne, Sir Philip de la Vache, and Sir *Thomas* Clanvow. Waugh thinks that the significance of the resemblances between the wills is 'somewhat diminished' by this evidence of the ties of friendship between the testators. But it is precisely in what they shared that the significance lies.

In the first place all three wills are written in English. This is very unusual, but not unheard of at that date. Enough depends upon how rare it was to justify a brief statistical survey. After 1383 wills within the Canterbury jurisdiction could be proved either before the archbishop's own court—in which case they were copied into his register now at Lambeth—or before his commissary's in the City of London, usually known as the Prerogative Court of Canterbury, the registers of which are now preserved at Somerset House. During a vacancy the Prior of Christ Church, Canterbury, enjoyed the archbishop's jurisdiction *sede vacante*. There was no hard distinction between what could be proved at Lambeth and what in the Prerogative Court, though at the beginning of the fifteenth century the socially important showed a preference for Lambeth. No English wills were proved *sede vacante* in 1396 and 1414, the only vacancies that matter for our purpose. The earliest English will proved in the Prerogative Court is dated 1395[1] and there are only sixteen before the death of Henry V. A good few of these were wills of London citizens. The earliest testament (Sir William Heron's will for lands is dated 1404)[2] at Lambeth is that of Sir William Beauchamp

[1] Prerogative Court of Canterbury (hereinafter P.C.C.) Rous, 4, fos. 29^v–31^v. It is that of Alice, Lady West (15 July), and is printed in *The Fifty Earliest English Wills in the Court of Probate, 1387–1439*, ed. F. J. Furnivall (E.E.T.S.), lxxviii (1882), 4–10.

[2] *Testamenta Eboracensia*, ed. J. Raine, iii (1864), 25–7 (30 Oct., proved 12 Dec.). The term 'testament' was applied by civilians to an instrument executed with all requisite formalities and, in particular, containing the institution of an heir. An instrument which lacked these formalities could take effect only as a codicil. The canonists adopted the same distinction in principle, but preferred, since their rules were laxer, to describe the informal disposition as an 'ultima voluntas'. In England the appointment of executors was equated with the civilian

(1408, proved 1411)[1] and there are two others between it and 1422: Sir John Cheyne's and that of Edward Cheyne, Sir John's son.[2] To give an idea of their frequency: there are 108 wills in Archbishop Chichele's register between 1414 and 1422; only one, Edward Cheyne's, is in English. After 1422 the vernacular gradually becomes commoner; but it is interesting that three of the first nineteen testators to receive probate at the Archbishop of Canterbury's two courts should be persons otherwise suspect of Lollardy and two more their relations or friends. The existence of as many who used the common tongue without betraying any evidence of contact with heresy makes it impossible to argue that an early English will should be treated prima facie as a Lollard's will. It depends upon the contents and the phrases employed.

What our three wills possess in common and share with certain others are:

(*a*) Extravagant emphasis upon the testator's own unworthiness,

(*b*) Strongly contemptuous language towards the body, and

(*c*) Strict injunctions against funeral pomp.

Some traces of all these characteristics can be found in a good many late medieval wills, especially those of ecclesiastics, but the language in which they are expressed is usually conventional, perfunctory, and brief, without either the vehemence or the vividness of those we are considering. Thus it was usual but not obligatory for a bishop to refer to himself as the unworthy minister of his church, to discourage excessive feasting and display at his burial and even, on occasion, to direct that his corpse should be laid to rest either beneath the feet of the celebrant of mass at

institution and the canonical distinction between a testament and a will was that a testament contained an appointment of executors and a will did not. In practice it was quite common for persons of substance to make a testament disposing of their chattels and a separate will disposing of their lands since the executors had nothing to do with any disposition of freehold unless it was actually devised to them. (I owe this valuable note to Mr. J. L. Barton [Ed.].)

1 Reg. Arundel (Cant.), ii, fo. 155^{v}; cf. *Genealogist*, v (1881), 214.

2 Reg. Arundel (Cant.), ii, fo. 203^{v}; cf. *Genealogist*, v (1881), 326; *Reg. Chichele*, ii. 45–9.

the high altar of his church or in some even less conspicuous corner, for instance under the doorstep at the west end. We notice once more the Lollard knights' tendency to ape their ecclesiastical superiors, here indeed to exaggerate their conventions to the point of caricature. Clifford's and Latimer's wills have been printed,[1] Cheyne's is less accessible[2] so I shall quote from it.

(*a*) Unworthiness: 'I John Cheyne false traitor to my lord God and to his blessed mother our Lady St Mary and to all the holy company of Heaven make and ordain my testament and my last will in this manner: at the beginning I most unworthy and God's traitor recommend me, wretched and sinful wholly to the grace and to the great mercy of the blissful Trinity.'

(*b*) Contempt for the earthly body: 'my wretched stinking carrion to be buried without the chapel new made within the churchyard of the church of Beckford, my head joining to the wall under the window of the east end of the same chapel'.

(*c*) Absence of funeral pomp: 'I pray and charge my surveyors [i.e. overseers] and mine executors as they will answer before God and as all mine whole trust in this matter is in them that on my stinking carrion be neither laid cloth of gold ne of silk but russet cloth price the yard fifteen pence; and one taper at mine head and one other at my feet . . . Do my executors all things which owen duty to be done in such case without any more cost save (alms) to poor men.' £7 worth of groats and pence are to be dealt on the day of the funeral to poor needy men there present 'to pray for my soul'.

God's traitor, stinking carrion, cheap russet cloth, two tapers, and poor needy men: these in conjunction are the things which set these three wills apart from those of the ordinary run of men. And they fit with notable ease the sentiments and even the language of Clanvow's homily. Clanvow, if he had made a will and we had it, would, we feel have found such a one very much to his taste. We begin to feel that we are not far from an

[1] Dugdale, *Baronage*, i. 341–2; *The Ancestor* (July 1904), x. 19–20.

[2] It is in Reg. Arundel ii, fo. 203v (cf. *Genealogist*, v (1881), 326). The spelling has been modernized.

understanding of these laymen's religion. But were these testators canting or recanting? Waugh assumes the latter to be the likelier view: 'they would hardly', he puts it, 'have used this remorseful language unless they had some special load on their souls'. Certainly treason towards God is consonant with such an interpretation, but why should not that treason have been committed before they underwent a religious conversion, when they were young? Again, Walsingham's account of Clifford's abjuration of Lollardy in 1402, when the knight is said to have informed against his friends and teachers, certainly favours the theory of recantation.[1] But Walsingham's unsupported and slightly 'fishy' story—the views Clifford is made to ascribe to the Lollards are wilder than usual—is shaken, if not disproved, by Clifford's choice of executors. Sir John Cheyne's appearance as an overseer can be explained on the assumption that he too had recanted, but can those of Sir John Oldcastle and Richard Colefox esquire at the head of the executors named in the will? They have been omitted in Dugdale's transcript but they are known to have acted. Oldcastle needs no identification; his association with the Clanvows and his executorship for Clifford are the only known links between Lollardy's military leader in 1414 and the pioneers; but it is enough to undermine our faith in Clifford's recantation. Richard Colefox, a Kentish esquire, was one of those who were prominent in Oldcastle's abortive rising.[2] Like Clifford he began his career as a retainer of a Prince of Wales, though his master was the future Henry V.[3] He and Clifford are first found in association on 6 September 1401 when he was executor, and Clifford overseer, of the will of Agnes, Lady Arundel, widow of Archbishop Arundel's nephew Sir William. Sir Philip de la Vache was another overseer.[4] If Clifford recanted in 1402 he continued to keep rather bad company and left his affairs to be settled by

[1] *Historia Anglicana*, ii. 253, cf. 'Annales Henrici Quarti' in *Trokelowe, Chronica et Annales*, ed. H. T. Riley (R.S., 1866), p. 347. Waugh's translation 'leaders' is unsatisfactory (op. cit., p. 56).

[2] Cf. *Cal. Close Rolls, Henry V*, i. 176–7.

[3] Cf. *Cal. Pat. Rolls, 1422–9*, p. 77, confirming letters of Prince Henry, dated Kennington, 15 Feb. 1402.

[4] Reg. Arundel (Cant.), i, fos. 183–183ᵛ.

persistent heretics. One cannot be sure, but canting seems much the likelier answer. Such a wholesale victory for the true faith as the recantation of three former Lollard knights would seem too good a story for the chronicler to have missed it. The sentiments expressed in these wills—particularly the macabre loathing of the flesh—were, as Clanvow's treatise confirms, the marks of a sect. The wills embody, we may conclude, the attitude of believing rather than repentant Lollards. Their Lollardy lay in the repentance.

Are there any more such wills or any that seem to have been influenced by the same spirit? There are a few which without corresponding with them in every particular show that their makers had imbibed most of their notions. Take first the wills of those who are otherwise known to have been associated with the Seven:

The earliest in date is that of Robert Folkingham, 6 July 1399. This is the will of which William Counter was executor, which is transcribed in University College MS. 97.[1] It is in English and it has two out of the three characteristics: 'Also I bequeath my wretched sinful body to buryen here in earth abiding the dreadful doom of God', and there is the provision for two tapers of wax and a modest funeral ceremony. Little is known of Robert Folkingham. He was Treasurer of Calais in 1393[2] and 1394[3] and he may have been related to a group of royal clerks, one of whom was his namesake, prominent in the Chancery of Richard II. It is just possible that he and Robert Folkingham of the Chancery[4] were one and the same man, since married clerks were then not uncommon. The will shows the testator to have had a wife and a daughter. It is written in his own hand and the legacies include his

[1] Fos. 170–1.

[2] 4 Oct. 1393; cf. *Cal. Pat. Rolls, 1391–6*, p. 369 (revocation of protection granted 24 Sept. 1393).

[3] Ibid.; cf. *Cal. Close Rolls, 1392–6*, p. 237.

[4] For him see ibid. *1388–92*, p. 559; ibid. *1392–6*, p. 237; *Cal. Pat. Rolls, 1381–5*, p. 231; *Cal. Close Rolls, 1381–5*, p. 97, where he is referred to as clerk and parson of Tilbury, Essex; ibid. *1388–92*, p. 356, he exchanges the living of Ashen, Sussex, for that of Sherborne St. John, Hampshire, on 16 Dec. 1390 (cf. also ibid., pp. 14 and 356, ibid. *1381–5*, p. 231).

armour. The only obvious link with William Counter is Calais; Sir William Beauchamp had been its Captain until he was succeeded by the Earl of Nottingham in 1391.

Secondly, Dame Anne Latimer, the widow of Sir Thomas, who made her will on 14 July 1402 and was dead by the following October. Of the three overseers of her will Sir Lewis Clifford was one and Robert Hook the Lollard parson of Braybrooke was another. Her will is in English, witnessed by Hook, and she offers God 'so poor a present as my wretched soul'.[1]

Thirdly, Edward Cheyne esquire, second son of Sir John (his elder brother died intestate) whose will, made 2 July 1415, was proved on 18 October following. This is a pure 'Lollard will'.[2] 'I most unworthy recommend (me) wretched and sinful to the mercy and grace of God the blissful Trinity and my stinking carrion to be buried in the Church hawe of Beckford beside my father . . . that on my stinking carrion be neither laid cloth of gold neither of silk but a russet cloth', etc. He clearly shared all his father's views.

Fourthly, Dame Alice Sturry, Sir Richard's widow, on the other hand made a French will on 3 May 1414, proved 15 November following.[3] The Lollard influence if perceptible at all can only be detected in her desire for an absence of pomp at her funeral. She obviously shared the taste of her father's friends to that extent, but the right conclusion is that probably that was as far as she went in the direction of Lollardy, at any rate by the time of her death nearly twenty years after her husband.

Fifthly, Joan Beauchamp, Lady Bergavenny, the widow of Sir William Beauchamp. The latter's will, though in English, has none of the other Lollard features, but his widow's has some.[4] Joan was a Fitzalan, the daughter of the Earl of Arundel who perished on the scaffold in 1397; she survived her husband by a quarter of a century and was one of those wealthy and strong-willed dowagers for which the period was notable. She leaves

[1] *The Ancestor*, x. 21; P.C.C. 3 Marche, fo. 18v. The third overseer was Philip Repton, Abbot of Leicester. Her executors were Robert Lechlade, parson of Kynmerton, Thomas Wakelyn, Henry Slayer, parson of Chipping Warden, and John Pulton.

[2] *Reg. Chichele*, ii. 45–9. [3] Ibid. 7–10. [4] Ibid. 534–9.

'my simple and wretched body to be buried' beside her 'worthy lord' without 'pomp or vainglory' though she has no objection to cloth of gold and 'all the worship that ought to be done unto a woman of mine estate'; and she declares herself 'a meek daughter of holy church full in the Christian faith'. She like Dame Alice Sturry is a marginal case; but it is interesting to notice that as late as 1435 the influence of Sir William's friends could still be traced in his widow's testament. No heretic, she had retained something of their attitude to the world and the flesh. In that she was by no means exceptional; the puritanism, rather than the false doctrine, of the Lollards was long-lived.

Sixthly, Sir Brian Stapleton who died in 1394 is selected by Waugh as an example of someone 'under no suspicion of heresy' who speaks of his soul as well as his body as 'caitiff';[1] this argument is weakened by the discovery that Sir Brian was in fact the father-in-law of Sir William Nevill.

Seventhly, William Stourton, member of an ancient Wiltshire family and the father of John, the first Lord Stourton (*c.* 1399–1462), was M.P. for Somerset, Dorset, and Wiltshire six times at least in Henry IV's reign, and was elected Speaker in 1413.[2] Illness prevented him from serving and he died that autumn. Stourton was perhaps a lawyer;[3] he is found in association with John Montagu, Earl of Salisbury,[4] Sir Thomas Latimer,[5] and Sir John Cheyne,[6] as well as Sir William Beauchamp. He made a will three years before his death on 20 July 1410 which though in Latin refers to the simple burial of his 'putrid body, naked as it came into the world except for a linen cloth' in the Carthusian cloister at Witham; he leaves Archbishop Arundel a gold cup.[7]

[1] *Test. Ebor.* i (1836), p. 198.

[2] Roskell, *The Commons and their Speakers*, pp. 363–4.

[3] He served on the bench with Thomas Brooke, 29 Apr. 1401 (*Cal. Close Rolls, Henry IV*, i. 388), J.P. for Wiltshire, 8 Mar. 1381 (*Cal. Pat. Rolls, 1381–5*, p. 141); for Dorset (ibid. *1388–92*, pp. 139, 342); and attorney for Sir John Grey, 25 May 1408 (ibid. *1405–8*, p. 437); cf. also Roskell, op. cit., pp. 363–4 and 'William Stourton of Stourton', *Proc. Dorset Nat. Hist. and Arch. Soc.* 82 (1960), 155–66.

[4] He was his tenant at Othery (Somerset).

[5] Ibid. *1399–1401*, p. 207 (20 Feb. 1400).

[6] *Cal. Close Rolls, Henry IV*, i. 118 (12 Jan. 1400).

[7] P.C.C. Marche, fo. 216.

Eighthly, Sir Thomas Broke of Holditch, Dorset, who sat in Parliament for Somerset or Dorset thirteen times or more between 1386 and 1413;[1] his son and heir, another Sir Thomas, was at least four times an M.P. in the decade 1417–27, after the father's death.[2] Now the interest of the Brokes is that on 20 February 1410 the father arranged with Sir John Oldcastle the marriage of the son with Joan Braybrooke the only daughter and heiress of Oldcastle's wife Lady Cobham.[3] The younger Thomas Broke took part in his father-in-law's rebellion and spent some part of 1414 in irons in the Tower before his release under Henry V's amnesty.[4] The wills of the two Brokes strikingly confirm their connections with Lollardy. The father's dated 1 June 1415 and proved 5 February 1418, is in English:[5] 'I wretched sinner Thomas Broke . . . praying [God] . . . of his high endless mercy vouchsafe to receive my wretched unclean soul . . . and my will is that my body be buried in the church haw of the parish-church of Thorncombe as men goith over into the church . . . right as they must step on men . . . And neither hutch [coffin] ne lead to be laid in but a great cloth to heal [cover] my foul carrion and of torches both three and three tapers.' There is much about poor men clothed in russet. Sir Thomas the son echoed the phrases when he made his will on 12 February 1439. He too is a 'wretched sinner' his 'true repentance and continual for thinking' is referred to and his funeral is to be simple and attended by poor men (in white).[6]

[1] *Members of Parliament, Returns*, pt. i (England), 1213–1702, pp. 229, 232, 242, 250, 253, 256, 259, 263, 266, 272, 275, 278 (Dorset).

[2] Ibid., pp. 290, 298, 303, 314.

[3] J. H. Wylie, *History of England under Henry the Fourth*, iii (London, 1896), 294; cf. J. C. Wedgwood, *History of Parliament, Biographies 1439–1509* (London, 1936), p. 115.

[4] Cf. *Cal. Close Rolls, Henry V*, i. 116 (8 Feb. 1414, when he was in the Tower); and ibid., p. 428, which shows three of his friends entering into a recognizance for £1,000 on his behalf on 13 July 1417 on 'condition that Thomas Broke, esq., shall make or lead no unlawful assemblies and shall not adhere to John Oldcastle late lord of Cobham for annulment or violation of the rights of Holy Mother Church or secretly or openly by himself or by others maintain or aid him in his heretical opinions'.

[5] P.C.C. Marche, pt. 2, fo. 316v–317 in *Fifty Wills*, pp. 26–8; R. R. Sharpe, *Calendar of Wills Proved and Enrolled in the Court of Husting, London*, pt. ii, *1358–1688* (London, 1890), p.v. n. 2.

[6] P.C.C. Luffenam, fo. 217v: in *Fifty Wills*, pp. 129–31.

Finally, Sir Gerard Braybrooke, nephew of Robert, Bishop of London, and uncle of Thomas Broke the younger's wife, who died in 1429, made a will noticeably full of Lollard cant phrases on 12 March 1428.[1] He calls himself a 'wretch' refers to his wretched body twice, wants a plain funeral with twelve poor men in russet. He too protests that he dies 'in full belief as holy church teacheth or ought to teach'. His father Sir Gerard Braybrooke, the bishop's brother, was frequently to be met with in the company of the Lollard knights; he was a distant cousin of Joan of Kent.

So far the test works well; those whose wills we should expect to find tainted by Lollard influence come up to expectation. It remains to consider the cases that disconcertingly do not. These are not cases where we should expect to find Lollardy but do not, rather those that use Lollard phrases and yet cannot be Lollard. Putting aside those wills that merely express exaggerated contrition—such as the Black Prince's[2] and John of Gaunt's[3] and those of clerks who merely refer to their own unworthiness to hold their benefices or to the fact that they are miserable sinners, there still remain a few cases, some of them very awkward.

Philip Repton, who abjured Lollardy in 1382, became Abbot of Leicester in 1394 and ruled as Bishop of Lincoln from 1405 to 1420. In 1420 he took the most unusual step—indeed unprecedented as far as I know in late medieval England—of resigning his see. He died in 1424. His will is undated but was made after his resignation. In Latin, it contains all three of the Lollard characteristics: his own sinfulness, his putrid body to be food for worms, the pompless funeral.[4] On the strength of a somewhat doubtful source, William Thorpe the Lollard's graphic description of his own trial before Archbishop Arundel in 1407, Repton has generally been described as a determined persecutor of Lollards. But there is no evidence of harsh persecutions by him and some evidence of his gentleness towards the heretics in his diocese. Take the case of Robert Hook, the parson of Braybrooke whose confession of

[1] *Reg. Chichele*, ii. 409–14.

[2] *Testamenta Vetusta*, i. 12–13; cf. J. Nichols, *Collections of all the Wills . . . of the Kings and Queens of England* (1780), pp. 66–77.

[3] *Test. Ebor.* i. 223–39.

[4] *Reg. Chichele*, ii. 285–7.

penitence in 1425 is in Chichele's register.[1] He says that in 1405 he appeared before Repton 'in open audience' in the town of Northampton for having the previous Good Friday (1404) neglected the accustomed worship in his church and sown 'both error and heresy'. Repton ordered him to do penance in Lincoln cathedral and when he failed to appear pronounced him accursed. That seems to have been the end of it, and Hook remained rector of Braybrooke. In 1414 a jury presented him to the king as 'a common Lollard' and the archbishop now hauled him before convocation at St. Paul's to do penance as Repton had ordained. But it was not until 1425 that Hook was at last brought to heel by Chichele.[2] Again John Barton who appeared before convocation in 1416 had been excommunicated and then forgotten by Repton six or seven years before.[3] This hardly looks like zeal on Repton's part. And there may have been a reason of a rather unexpected kind: because Hook and Repton were not strangers to one another and Repton had not broken all that thoroughly with his old associates. I mentioned that Sir Lewis Clifford and Robert Hook were two of the three overseers of Anne Latimer's will in 1402; the third was Philip Repton.[4] His lifelong revulsion against the heresies of his youth remains to be demonstrated.

Repton in his last years as Abbot of Leicester was the spiritual director of the Lancastrian patron of his house Henry IV, the friend of Archbishop Arundel and the enactor of *De Heretico Comburendo*. He made an English will—the first royal testament in the vernacular—on 21 January 1409, of which the Primate was an executor. 'I Henry sinful wretch by the grace of God King of England and of France and lord of Ireland . . . bequeath . . . my sinful soul the which had never be[en] worthy to be man but through [God's] . . . mercy . . . which life I have mispended.'[5] Open-mindedness can scarcely go so far as to entertain the possibility that King Henry was a Lollard. But if anyone wished to, he could point to the presence of Lollards among Henry's and

[1] *Reg. Chichele*, iii. 110–12.

[2] Ibid. 105–12.

[3] Ibid. iv. 168–9.

[4] See above, p. 214.

[5] Nichols, *Collection of all the Wills . . . of the Kings and Queens of England*, pp. 203–7.

still more his heir's servants, and to the fact that according to Capgrave, in 1404 Archbishop Arundel had to rebuke the courtiers at Coventry for turning their backs on the sacrament when it was being carried through the streets.[1] And after all Henry was Gaunt's son. But what explanation can be offered of the next case?

This is that of Thomas Arundel of Canterbury himself, in a will made on 12 February 1414. It is in Latin.[2] He begins by calling himself not merely a miserable sinner and an unworthy minister but 'a most miserable and most unworthy sinner' and 'a most useless and most lukewarm minister'. He orders the most lowly burial for his 'foetid and putrid cadaver' and he reverts to his sins once more in the course of his will. Does anyone think that Arundel was a secret Lollard? Must we therefore conclude that the Lollard wills are a false clue, that the coincidences to which I have drawn attention were pure coincidences and no more? The answers to both these questions, it seems to me, must be 'no'. Arundel was not a Lollard; but the coincidences were not pure and simple

I can offer nothing to account for the terms of Arundel's will. Nothing else in his life prepares one for this outspoken confession of his own unworthiness, but it is difficult to believe that he was unaware that he was using the language favoured by the Lollard knights. Yet such language was never used (apparently) before the date of his tenure of the throne of Canterbury. In the Lambeth registers of his three predecessors Whittlesey, Sudbury, and Courtenay (1368–96), there are 169 wills; not one contains any sign of loathing for the flesh and only three—and those of ecclesiastics—have even a perfunctory reference to unworthiness; occasional injunctions against excessive pomp and in favour of plainness and simplicity are pointers to what was to come. And barring Lollards, known or suspect, that still remains true of the wills in Arundel's own register. In adopting such language Arundel had only, as far as we know, the precedents I have cited. His motives are inexplicable.

[1] J. Capgrave, *Chronicle of England*, ed. F. C. Hingeston (R.S., 1858), p. 288.

[2] *Sede Vacante Wills*, ed. C. E. Woodruff (Kent Arch. Soc., Records Branch), iii (1914), 81–2.

But at least Arundel's action suggests that the influences which helped to form the Lollards' convictions on these points were not confined to them; that their excesses of sentiment, the revivalist streak which their wills display, came from exaggerating one aspect of contemporary religion; it was not something that others did not feel. They formed not so much a distinct sect as a group of extremists; if not a lunatic fringe, at least a fringe; to some of the charms of which Arundel, but no other bishop save Repton, was susceptible. The wills proved not only in London and Lambeth, but also the great series at York, Lincoln, and Norwich show how exceptional such wills were. That the sentiments attracted so many Lollards and their friends and so few others cannot be dismissed statistically. Their significance is overwhelming.

CHAPTER VII

Conclusions

THERE is one point that apparently did not occur to Waugh—nor, I think, to any other scholar, but which is material to the solution of our dilemma. When two quite independent chroniclers tell the same or similar stories, it may be inferred that they are not drawing upon private sources of information unknown to the world at large. What is shared by Walsingham and Knighton is likely to be common knowledge. It is far more likely to be inaccurate but widespread hearsay than secret truths concealed from the government and the episcopate. The fact that Walsingham's list differs from Knighton's is in itself a welcome sign of their independence. And for what it is worth, both imply that what they were retailing all the world knew. It is the Leicester annalist, within easy reach of the Latimer country, who says that the knights imposed the Lollard preachers on their tenants and maintained them by force. That is not the way to escape notice, and as we have seen Latimer's going-on attracted it. But Walsingham also tells us that they were generally known as the 'hooded knights' because they stood with heads covered in the presence of the Host:[1] precisely what Henry IV's courtiers were rebuked for doing, again according to Walsingham, in 1404.[2] Whether or not they were Lollards or merely the protectors of Lollards, their being so was notorious. And they did not hesitate to make wills which were so different from the normal run as to be bound to attract notice both by those who executed them and by the episcopal officials who proved them. There is no suggestion of secrecy. Even Clanvow assumes their notoriety and the scorn in which they are held by the worldly wise as these hasten down the

[1] *Chronicon Angliae*, p. 377.

[2] *Johannis de Trokelowe . . . Chronica et Annales*, p. 395.

primrose path to an eternity of hell-fire. Finally it was not only Walsingham and Knighton who believed that the Lollards had influential lay protectors; Pope Boniface IX did so too and said so in the bulls he addressed to Richard II and the English hierarchy in September 1395.[1] And it is assumed in at least one anti-Lollard tractate, that by John Devereux, D.D., of Cambridge, written about 1390 in defence of image-worship.[2] That does not mean that there was no underground of poor preachers, the vulnerable Herefords and Swinderbys seeking to escape notice, receiving protection and being maintained in secret. Their protectors, however, were great men, knights of the Garter, rich, powerful, and prominent at court; their connection with Lollards neither could be nor needed to be, concealed. It must have been a thing well known to their friends and it is difficult to imagine how the princes they served or the bishops sitting with them in Council can have been ignorant of their reputation—or can have failed to witness their irreverent practices and their equally conspicuous devotions.

What has caused historians to miss this point is the freedom that they enjoyed from persecution. They were notorious and conspicuous and yet immune—for rather more than thirty years. For that matter the severity of the persecution meted out to the humbler missionaries can be, generally indeed is, exaggerated. The reluctance of Bishop Trefnant of Hereford to deal severely with Swinderby[3] might be explained as the consequence of the king's unwillingness to provide the episcopate with the backing of the lay arm. But at any rate Swinderby bargained and prevaricated and eventually disappeared to safety over the border. And so did many others even after 1401. Outward or occasional conformity seems to have satisfied not only Repton but most bishops. Ralph Mungin, a former student of St. Edmund Hall who was imprisoned for heresy by Chichele in 1428, had been of

[1] *Cal. Pap. Letts.* iv. 515–16.

[2] Merton College MSS. (Coxe) 68 and 175; cf. Worcester College MS. L.R.A. 6 (formerly Merton MS. (Coxe) 318), fo. 120, and A. B. Emden, *Biographical Register of the Members of the University of Cambridge* (Cambridge, 1963), p. 186.

[3] *Registrum Johannis Trefnant*, ed. W. W. Capes (Canterbury and York Soc., 1916), pp. 280–358.

ill fame for twenty years and more.[1] There were only two known cases of the extreme penalty being paid by a heretic between 1401 and 1413: the famous martyrdoms of Sawtry and Badby.[2] The bishops shrank from stern measures; almost any sort of outward conformity satisfied them and like Repton they treated their duties in this respect perfunctorily; having excommunicated a man for not appearing they tried to forget all about him if he allowed them to. Not even Bishop Henry Despenser seems to deserve his reputation as a hammer of heretics, partly perhaps because there were hardly any in the diocese in his day; they got their hold on East Anglia later. But his correspondence shows him to have been an urbane and broadminded prelate.[3]

Sawtry and Badby may have lacked aristocratic protectors; certainly none came forward or was in any way involved in their stories. The lay sympathizers themselves provided no trial between *De Heretico Comburendo* and Oldcastle's in March 1413. This failure to slake Foxe's thirst for the blood of the martyrs helps to explain why in the end Waugh could doubt the reality of their Lollard sympathies. When Oldcastle was brought to trial his Lollardy was clear enough. But his encounter with Arundel in 1413 was the first occasion on which a Lollard knight was made to answer for his opinion before an ecclesiastical judge and then it was only by the new king's express consent.[4] Neither Richard II's nor Henry IV's orthodoxy required that such men should be touched; and therefore many of the preachers they befriended also escaped. The two laymen who were put down in those early years, Thomas Compworth[5] and Walter Brute,[6] were of humble stock; their claims to be called esquires rested upon very little land.

[1] A. B. Emden, *Biographical Register of the University of Oxford to A.D. 1500* (Oxford, 1958), ii. 1329.

[2] K. B. McFarlane, *Wycliffe*, pp. 150–2, 154–5.

[3] Cf. letter no. 34 in W. A. Pantin, 'Medieval Treatise on Letter-writing', *Bulletin of the John Rylands Library*, 13 (1929), 359–64; *Anglo-Norman Letters and Petitions*, ed. M. Dominica Legge (Anglo-Norman Text Soc., 1941), nos. 44, 55, 58, 62, 64, 297, 298(?), and 318.

[4] McFarlane, *Wycliffe*, pp. 164–5.

[5] An esquire of Kidlington, near Oxford (ibid., p. 143).

[6] His property seems to have consisted of one-third of three messuages, 120 acres of land and 5 acres of meadow in Lyde Priour, Lyde Sausy, and Lyde Godfrey, Herefordshire: cf. *Cal. Close Rolls, Henry IV*, iii. 169, 272.

Oldcastle's defiance where a nominal conformity would have freed him, and still more his resulting treason, brought this long period of immunity to an end. 1382 was not as significant a date as is generally implied though it saw the disciplining and the scattering of the university Lollards. But the obscurity that followed was not at first the obscurity of the hunted and concealed; it was still largely the obscurity of the tolerated and ignored; the turning-point came slowly between 1401 and 1413.

The reason for this tolerance, I believe, was not merely respect for the persons of noble and knightly class and its protégés. It was a compound of this with two other elements: one reason was that the knights' views found more than an echo in many hearts, even those of some of the higher clergy; the other was the temper of those educated and politic administrators who held the higher offices in the Church; this was too sceptical and too humane for them to become all at once effective persecutors, especially of their own class. As we have seen also, the knights were literate and civilized as well as well connected.

Each of these two reasons needs some expansion. The chief characteristic of English religious life in the fourteenth century is the growth of moral fervour among the laity. It was inspired and whipped up by the sermons and discourses of mendicants and other poor preachers and it infected the clergy also, but its strength was derived from its success among laymen. It expressed itself in the familiar denunciations of provisors and of the traffic flowing to and from the sinful city of the popes; in the enormous popularity of the sermon—and we know from Owst what kind of sermon,[1] violently puritanical in tone; in the growing demand for devotional and mystical literature by a laity proud of its literacy; and even in the production by laymen of that literature itself. It was one of the most distinguished captains of that age, Henry, Duke of Lancaster, the last of the old Lancastrian line, who wrote and signed a typical example of it.[2] For such men to

[1] G. R. Owst, *Preaching in Medieval England* (Cambridge, 1926), cap. 6; *Literature and Pulpit in Medieval England*, 2nd edn. (Oxford, 1961), cap. 6.

[2] *Le Livre de Seyntz Medicines*, ed. E. J. Arnould (Anglo-Norman Text Soc., 1940).

read their Bibles for themselves it was unnecessary to wait for the Wycliffite translations; they had French translations already and it was in French that Lancaster wrote. But it was the spread of lay literacy (the English form of *Devotio Moderna*) which led in the second half of the century to the wider and wider use of the vernacular. The period was one by the way much given to private devotions, to private chapels in the houses of the laity, the privilege of appointing one's own confessor with a portable altar and no parochial responsibility—and hence independence of episcopal surveillance. This is the background of the Lollard movement and it merges with its background. That a group of retired army officers should have adopted a slightly eccentric or extreme form of the prevailing fashion is understandable; it was not the last time that the soldiers were to prove the best independents. The contemporary spirit in religion was puritan, biblical, evangelical, anarchic, anti-sacerdotal, hostile to the established order in the Church. Hence there was widespread sympathy with at least the moral content of the Lollard teaching. And it is doubtful how far the knights accepted or even grasped the theological implications of their views. Theirs was a moral revolt by the laity against the visible Church, a rejection of sacerdotalism in favour of the personal, immediate contact between the believer and his Creator. They protected the revivalist missionaries, studied their Bibles and homilies, and believed that Holy Writ rather than the tradition of the Church was the measure of truth. Many who went less far were in full sympathy with most of their prejudices.

As for the reluctance of the hierarchy, that too is intelligible. There was no tradition of heresy, and therefore no tradition of persecution, in England. The majority of the higher appointments in the Church were in fact made by the king; erastian notions were widespread among the lay nobility and the court and were accepted in practice by the bishops; ecclesiastical thunders were not treated very seriously, episcopal discipline lacked teeth, the rights of lay patrons had to be left severely alone. It took time and thought to rouse bishops, only too much a part of the landed governing class, to the point of trying to force those who enjoyed wordly honour and position—and with whom they were accustomed to co-operate in government—to come to heel. And since patronage was the essence of the social order, those whom the knights protected were in no danger either. And after all the real drive against the heretics did not begin until the heretics under Oldcastle's irresponsible leadership had also become traitors; Chichele and the episcopal persecutors of the next period were assisting the state to suppress the preachers of sedition and rebellion. After Oldcastle the governing class, apart from a few of his surviving connections (e.g. the Brokes and Cheynes), produced no more Lollard knights.

That is my reading of the facts. In such matters and with such evidence it is as well to be tentative. But the facts need reconciling and that is the only explanation I can see which makes sense.

APPENDIX A

Sir William Trussell

SIR WILLIAM TRUSSELL of Peatling, Fleckney, and Thorpe by Narborough, Leicestershire, of Flore, Northamptonshire, and of Nuthurst in the county of Warwick (the manors listed are those of the demesnes of which Sir William was granted free warren, 19 May 1330 [*Cal. Charter Rolls*, iv. 172 and 214]) was by 1310 one of the knights of Thomas of Lancaster's retinue and remained closely associated with his lord's service right down to the battle of Boroughbridge (*Parliamentary Writs*, ed. F. Palgrave, ii, pt. i, p. 406; pt. ii, div. ii, p. 182–3; and pt. iii, p. 1528). The date of his birth can be deduced from the fact that his son and namesake was old enough to be one of Lancaster's adherents by 1 November 1318 (ibid., pt. ii, div. ii, p. 128 and pt. iii, p. 1529). For his presence at Burton, 10 March 1322 and Boroughbridge see ibid., pt. ii, div. ii, p. 201; *Collections for a History of Staffordshire*, William Salt Arch. Soc., orig. ser. 10, pt. i (1889), 48 (*Cal. Close Rolls, 1318–23*, pp. 463, 580, and 586); he was an adherent of Queen Isabella in 1326 (*Chronicles of the Reigns of Edward I and Edward II*, ed. W. Stubbs (R.S., London, 1882–3), i. 314 and ii. 86; J. S. Roskell, *The Commons and their Speakers*, pp. 5–6). The fragment of a chronicle printed by M. V. Clarke at the end of her paper, 'Committees of Estates and the Deposition of Edward II', in *Historical Essays in Honour of James Tait*, ed. J. G. Edwards, V. H. Galbraith, and E. F. Jacob (Manchester, 1933), p. 45, conclusively identifies him as of Peatling. It was he who as Proctor of the Whole Realm of England informed the captive Edward II at Kenilworth that magnates and commons alike renounced their allegiance (cf. Ibid. and *Knighton*, i. 441–2). Always extreme in his partisanship, it was not long before his acts had caused him to become once more an exile overseas. For he was one of those who in the autumn of 1328 joined Henry of Lancaster, Earl Thomas's brother and heir, in his rising against Mortimer and Queen Isabella. When the attempt petered out at Bedford, Trussell was excluded along with three other prominent Lancastrians from pardon (*Knighton*, i. 451). See *Calendar of Plea and Memoranda Rolls of the City of London, 1323–1364*, ed. A. H. Thomas (London, 1926), pp. 83–4 and 85–6;

Calendar of Letter Books . . . of the City of London, Letter Book E (London, 1903), ed. R. R. Sharpe, p. 229; *Cal. Fine Rolls*, iv. 116–17, 118, 119, 120, 125, and 154; *Cal. Close Rolls, 1327–30*, p. 425; *Cal. Pat. Rolls, 1327–30*, pp. 357, 360, and 392.

When Henry of Lancaster returned in 1330 he was reappointed escheator south of Trent (on 17 January 1331: *Cal. Fine Rolls*, iv. 222). His first appointment had been dated 26 February 1327 (ibid., p. 22). He continued in office from 1327 until 23 Oct. 1330 (ibid., p. 193); see S. T. Gibson, 'The Escheatries 1327–1341', *E.H.R.* 35 (1921), 219; and E. R. Stevenson, 'The Escheator', *The English Government at Work, 1327–1336*, ii, ed. W. A. Morris and J. R. Strayer (Med. Acad. of America, 1947), especially pp. 126–66. For a forfeited wardship see *Cal. Pat. Rolls, 1330–4*, p. 365. From 1330 until his death in or soon after 1346 he was much engaged, as the king's 'secretary' (that is, confidential messenger) and later councillor, in diplomatic and other business. (His first diplomatic mission had been to the papal court to procure Thomas of Lancaster's canonization, 28 February 1327 [T. Rymer, *Foedera*, ii, pt. ii, p. 695). Since Chancery enrolments do not in every case distinguish the knight from William Trussell of Kibbelstone, Edward III's yeoman, it is not always possible to be sure which was the ambassador. But since when any attempt is made to particularize him he is given the rank of knight, it seems probable that Sir William of Flore was the man employed in diplomacy. This is confirmed by the award of 50 marks p.a. to the yeoman 'for dwelling continually by the king's side', in 1331–5 (*Cal. Pat. Rolls, 1330–4*, p. 233; *1334–8*, pp. 176 and 181). Sir William's second mission, the first since his return, was to the Kings of Aragon, Portugal, Majorca, and Castile, 5 May 1330 (*Cal. Close Rolls, 1330–3*, p. 137; *Foedera*, ii, pt. ii, p. 790). For the numerous later missions see ibid., pp. 821–2, 854, 880–2, 891, 903, 915, 941, 966–7, 1144, 1156, 1224, 1227; iii, pt. i, pp. 21–2, 27, and 46. For his appointment to the Council of Regency 1 July 1345, ibid., p. 50; he received (as of Flore) £40 p.a. at the Exchequer for the duration of his attendance (*Cal. Pat. Rolls, 1343–5*, p. 527). Evidently his long periods of residence abroad had equipped him to become a knowledgeable ambassador. It is probable that he had made good use of his first exile to commend himself to the future Edward III and of both to extend his acquaintance with foreign courts. A series of land purchases and royal grants in the 1330s and 1340s indicated his growing prosperity. (Before the rebellion he had acquired the reversion of the manor of Gayton, Northamptonshire [Baker, *Hist. and Antiquities of*

. . . *Northants.* ii. 274–5]; free warren in the manors of Flore, Nuthurst, Peatling Magna, Little Thorpe, and Fleckney, 19 May 1330 [*Cal. Chart. Rolls*, iv. 172 and 214]; licence to empark his wood at Nuthurst, 8 October 1331 [*Cal. Pat. Rolls, 1330–4*, p. 174]; a grant in fee-tail for his services to the king's progenitors, and for his arduous and costly labours in the king's service, of the whole land of 'Berges' [?Bruges—if so, very much a castle in Spain] in Flanders, its lordships, demesnes, services, homages, etc., 18 October 1331 [ibid., p. 214]; and a gift of £1000 for services beyond the seas and within, 10 July 1337 [ibid., *1334–8*, p. 466]). As an envoy he seems to have received 13*s.* 4*d.* a day and expenses [e.g. *Cal. Close Rolls, 1333–7*, pp. 561 and 621]. By 1 July 1343 he had acquired lands in Solihull and Tamworth, Warwickshire [ibid., *1343–6*, pp. 104 and 126]. In addition to diplomatic work Sir William [also] served as Admiral to the West [*Cal. Pat. Rolls, 1338–40*, p. 215] and to the North [ibid., *1343–5*, p. 258]. Although probably not a member of the Commons, he declared their views to the king and lords in the Parliament of 1343 [*Rotuli Parliamentorum* (collected by R. Blythe and others, ed. J. Strachey (1767–1832)], ii. 136; J. S. Roskell, op. cit., pp. 7–8).

APPENDIX B

Sir John Clanvow

SIR JOHN CLANVOW (?1341–91) of Michaelchurch-on-Arrow, co. Radnor, Ocle Pychard, Lyde Bevis, and Hergest, Herefordshire, and perhaps of Yazor, Herefordshire, and Gladestry co. Radnor, was perhaps the son and heir of John Clanvow, son of Philip Clanvow. Philip Clanvow had been M.P. for Herefordshire in March 1340 (*Members of Parliament, Returns*, pt. i, 130). On 27 January 1336 he had been granted free warren in Ocle Pychard, King's Pyon, Yazor, and Cusop, Herefordshire, and Michaelchurch, co. Radnor. An inquisition taken at Weobley, Herefordshire, 10 June 1339, found that Philip Clanvow and his ancestors were tenants in Gladestry of lands held of the Mortimer manor of Radnor, taking 7 ells of cloth price 5 marks the cloth, p.a. by hereditary right 'racione prepositure predicte'—(were they hereditary reeves?) . . . 'They say that Philip ap Hywel, Philip's uncle whose heir he is, had them from Edmund Mortimer and Maud, Edmund's mother. They say that Hywel ap Meurig, father of Philip ap Hywel and grandfather of Philip Clanvow, whose heir he is, had them from Maud Mortimer and that Meurig ap Philip, Hywel's father, had them of William Braose. Margaret Mortimer was dowager 1304–34; her mother-in-law Maud died in 1301, having held the Braose lands since her marriage in 1247 to Roger Mortimer (d. 1282). Her husband Edmund, Maud's son and heir, held them 1301–4 (*Complete Peerage*, ix. 278–84). This dates the generations of Philip Clanvow's ancestry and shows that he had succeeded his uncle before 1334 (*Scrope* v. *Grosvenor*, ii. 436 n). Philip was on commissions of peace for Herefordshire, 6 July 1338 (*Cal. Pat. Rolls, 1338–40*, p. 135) and 20 July 1344 (ibid., *1343–5*, p. 395), and 7 February 1347 (ibid., *1345–8*, p. 301). A commission was there 1 April 1339 (ibid., *1338–40*, p. 279); 30 May 1339 (ibid., p. 284); 20 April 1340 (ibid., p. 502); and 15 March 1341 (ibid., *1340–3*, p. 155). He held half a knight's fee in Hergest and West Hergest extended at £10 p.a., part of the Badlesmere inheritance, 10 November 1339 (*Cal. Close Rolls, 1339–41*, p. 282). A commissioner for Gilbert Talbot's castles 8 December 1339 (ibid., pp. 316–17) and for the Ninth, 15 July 1340 (ibid., p. 436). He owed Ralph Linger

£220 in Herefordshire 15 July 1340 (ibid., p. 490). He was collector of taxes for Herefordshire 1 October 1344 (*Cal. Fine Rolls*, v. 391), but too busy on the king's other business 4 November 1344 (ibid., p. 394); again on 8 March 1347 (ibid. vi. 4). On 20 October 1347, at Thomas, Lord Bradston's request, he got a licence to mortmain 5 marks p.a. of land and rent not held in chief for a chantry in St. Mary's chapel, Yazor (*Cal. Pat. Rolls, 1345–8*, p. 418). He may have died soon after his son's return to the Parliament of January 1347/8; this would seem to be his last mention.

By a fortunate chance the M.P. for Herefordshire in January 1347/8 is described as John, son of Philip Clanvow (*Members of Parliament Returns*, pt. i, p. 143). On 15 July 1354 John Clanvow, donsel, and Maud, his wife, of the diocese of Hereford were granted indults to choose their own confessors and plenary remission in the hour of death (*Cal. Pap. Letts.* iii. 533) so it is likely that he had succeeded his father by that date. In 1349 John was an esquire of the king's household (Waugh, op. cit., p. 75). From *Calendar of Papal Petitions, 1342–1419*, ed. W. H. Bliss (1896), i. 261, we learn that he was nephew of Sir Richard Talbot of Mar (*c.* 1305–56), whose widow married Sir John Bromwich (*Complete Peerage*, xii, pt. i. 612–14); it looks as if Philip Clanvow married Richard Talbot's sister. This is supported by the fact that Philip Clanvow was deputy to Gilbert Talbot, Richard's father, as Justice of South Wales, on 24 September 1344 (*Cal. Pat. Rolls, 1331–8*, p. 20).

On 13 December 1361 the king presented to the church of Gladestry, co. Radnor, by reason of the nonage of John Clanvow's heir, tenant of Roger, Earl of March, (being) a minor in the king's ward (*Cal. Pat. Rolls, 1361–4*, p. 123). On 11 August 1362 John Clanvow, apparently not a knight, with five others, including Walter Huwet, entered into recognizances towards the king for £1000, levied in Herefordshire by instalments (*Cal. Close Rolls, 1360–4*, p. 421). This would suggest that our John Clanvow born *c.* 1341, was son and heir of another John Clanvow, dead by 1361. The minor in 1361, however, is not named and nowhere is Sir John called John's son. On the other hand he held some at least of Philip Clanvow's lands. Unfortunately the history of Yazor after Philip Clanvow's death until it is found in Sir Thomas Clanvow's possession, is blank. So is that of Michaelchurch, though in 1426 John Clanvow's name was still given as tenant in Michaelchurch and Lyde Bevis in a Mortimer inquisition (*Cal. Close Rolls, Henry VI*, i. 253). And in 1384 he held Hergest (*Cal. Close Rolls,*

1381–5, p. 512). Thomas Clanvow, the husband of Perrin, clearly held most of Philip Clanvow's lands after 1391. But there is a blank 1347–91. Sir Thomas did not marry until the 1390s so his youth may be presumed. It is therefore highly probable, though unproved, that the succession was father to son; Philip–John–Sir John–Sir Thomas. But if Sir John never married (and no wife is recorded), Sir Thomas must be regarded as his nephew; brother is unlikely.

APPENDIX C

Henry V's Books

THE list of Henry V's books referred to above on page 117 can be identified as that in P.R.O., Exchequer K.R., Various Accounts, E 101/335/17, which also survives in an eighteenth-century copy among the papers of Thomas Rymer in British Museum MS. Add. 4603 ff. 134–7. It appears from the heading that these books were captured after the siege of the Market of Meaux which surrendered on 10 May 1422, and they evidently formed the collection of one or more of the religious houses of the town.[1] It is likely that Henry V took possession of them with the intention of giving them to one of his own foundations, for he had already made such a gift to the monastery at Sheen in November 1418; it is possible, however, that this was the collection which the University of Oxford claimed under the bequest of Henry's last will.[2] Following the king's death four months later his personal effects were gathered together by the new Treasurer, John Stafford, who on 23 August 1423 delivered the king's jewels, tapestries and other treasures, valued at 40,000 marks, to his executors.[3] However this collection of books, which Stafford seems to have received about this time from the king's almoner, John Snell,[4] remained in his own possession for as long as he was Treasurer, and only on 6 October 1427 did he deliver them into the custody of the Treasury, the indenture recording this being preserved in the Hanaper. The collection remained in the Treasury until July 1435 when first two chronicles and then 'divers books of

[1] These are listed in Dom L. H. Cottineau, *Répertoire Topobibliographique des abbayes et prieurés*, ii (Mâcon, 1937), 1802–3.

[2] F. Palgrave, *The Antient Kalendars and Inventories of the Treasury of the Exchequer*, ii (London, 1836), p. 97; *Epistolae Academicae Oxon.*, ed. H. Anstey, i (Oxford, 1898), p. 151.

[3] *Rot. Parl.* iv. 213 ff. John Stafford, Bishop of Bath and Wells 1424–43, was Treasurer of England 18 December 1422–16 March 1426.

[4] John Snell is mentioned as King's Almoner in May 1421 and was still holding this office in January 1425 (*Cal. Pat. Rolls, 1416–1422*, pp. 362, 390, 414; ibid., *1422–1429*, pp. 47, 266). He was probably dead by 1431 (J. Le Neve, *Fasti Ecclesiae Anglicanae, 1300–1541*, v. (1963) *St. Paul's London* (compiled by Joyce M. Horn), pp. 8, 67.)

civil law and other books' were delivered to Master Richard Caudrey, Warden of King's Hall, Cambridge, to be kept in the college during the king's pleasure. Finally by a writ of privy seal of 2 July 1440 these books were given to the college in perpetuity.[1] The survival of the indenture listing the books received by King's Hall in 1440 confirms that this gift was part of the collection (77 volumes out of 110) obtained from Meaux.[2] What happened to the remaining books is not known.[3]

The list of 1427 is printed here for the first time. The books marked with an asterisk are those which passed to King's Hall in 1435. Where the word at the commencement of the second folio is given only in part I have, where possible, supplied the remainder either from the text, or from the King's Hall list, placing this in square brackets.

(G. L. H.)

Haec indentura facta sexto die Octobris Anno Regni Regis Henrici Sexti post conquestum Anglie sexto testatur quod venerabilis in Christo pater Johannes Bathoniensis et Wellensis episcopus nuper Thesaurarius Anglie deliberavit Thesaurario et Camerariis de Scaccario ad usum Domini Regis videlicet apud Westmonasterium diversos libros et mitram ac alia bona et jocalia de Capella nuper capta in Marcheio de Meux que fuerunt domini Henrici Quinti nuper Regis Anglie patris domini Regis nunc supradicti quae quidem libri, mitra, bona et jocalia supradicta praedictus venerabilis in Christo pater recepit apud London' de Johanne Snell Clerico et Elemosinario dicti domini Regis ut patet inferius.

1. *In primis liber decretorum ij° fo. Patriarcharum
2. *Item liber Clementinarum ij° fo. Refittari
3. *Item liber Decretalium ij° fo. [per]ficiend[um]

[1] Palgrave, op. cit. ii. 155.

[2] This is printed by C. E. Sayle, 'King's Hall Library', *Cambridge Antiquarian Society Proceedings*, 24 (1923), pp. 71–2. See also *Medieval Libraries of Great Britain*, ed. N. R. Ker, 2nd ed. (London, 1964), p. 26; Alan B. Cobban, *The King's Hall within the University of Cambridge in the Later Middle Ages* (Cambridge, 1969), pp. 254–8.

[3] The twenty-seven books delivered from the Treasury of the Exchequer to All Souls College, Oxford, in 1440 evidently came from another collection. See *Proc. and Ord.*, v. 117–19; R. Weiss, 'Henry VI and the Library of All Souls College', *E.H.R.*, 57 (1942), pp. 102–5.

1. Decretum Gratiani.
2. Clementis Papae Quinti Constitutiones.
3. Gregorii Papae Noni Decretales.

4. *Item liber inforciati ij° fo. errogat[ur]
5. Item liber digesti novi ij° fo. ad ipsius
6. *Item Innocentius super decretales ij° fo. constitutionem
7. *Item Augustinus de Civitate Dei ij° fo. perficiend'
8. *Item Innocentius super Decretales ij° fo. procur'
9. *Item liber Cronicum Helinand' de creatione mundi ij° fo. peritos esse
10. *Item liber sententiarum Petris Lumbardi ij° fo. sub[stanti]am dicatur
11. *Item Thomas super quartum ij° fo. ergo dicend[um]
12. *Item Augustinus de Verbis Domini ij° fo. moribus
13. *Item Hillarius Pittavensis de Trinitate ij° fo. Et successionis
14. *Item Pollicronicon in papiro ij° fo. post tabulam pelle
15. *Item Augustinus contra quinque hereses ij° fo. [volun]tas quomodo
16. *Item parvum Psalterium glossatum ij° fo. secundum hoc
17. Item Solinus de mirabilibus mundi ij° fo. cum et aureum
18. *Item Cassianus de Institutis Senobiorum ij° fo. possunt
19. *Item Petrus Blesensis ij° fo. quia inter
20. *Item Epistolae Senece ij° fo. [ad me] perferre[ndas]
21. *Item Gregorius in pastoralibus ij° fo. post tabulam quisque
22. *Item Concordantie parve super Bibliam ij° fo. Johannis
23. Item liber de ludo Scaccorum in papiro ij° fo. Solacii

4. The Inforciatum was the part of the Digest comprising Book 24, 3 to Book 38.
5. The Digestum Novum comprised Books 39–50.
6. Apparatus Decretalium Domini Innocentii Papae Quarti.
7. This is an error. The King's Hall list reads 'Augustinus de Trinitate . . . proficiend', the second folio coming at 'inquisitione proficiente nectuntur' (J. P. Migne, *Patrologia Latina*, xlii, p. 818).
9. This volume is now London, British Museum, Cotton Claudius B. ix, fos. 2–263. See N. R. Ker, *Medieval Libraries of Great Britain*, p. 26.
11. St. Thomas Aquinas, Super Quartum Librum Sententiarum.
12. St. Augustine, De Sermone in Monte, I, i, i–2 'cum autem minora minoribus maiora maioribus dantur' (Migne, *P.L.*, xxxiv, p. 1231).
14. The King's Hall list reads 'Policraticon . . . pelle, C in textu; vicinam in papiro'. The work referred to is the Polycraticus by John of Salisbury.
15. St. Augustine, Tractatus Adversus Quinque Haereses (Migne, *P.L.*, xlii, p. 1102).
20. Lucius Annaeus Seneca, ad Lucilium Epistulae. The commencement of the second folio comes in Epistola III.
21. St Gregory the Great, Regulae Pastoralis Liber.
23. By Jacobus de Cessolis.

24. *Item liber Cronicorum Helinandi Monachi unus ij° fo. Annus qui et alius humane
25. *Item Thullius in Rothorica ij° fo. neque amicitia
26. *Item liber Cronicorum ij° fo. et excessus
27. Item Pontificale in papiro ij° fo. ut hoc
28. Item Historia Egesippi ij° fo. [cum filiis] suis
29. *Item liber Decretalium ij° fo. co[mmun]em essentiam
30. *Item epistole Pauli glossate ij° fo. sumus
31. *Item sermones Bernardi super diversos versus versus Psalterii ij° fo. qui peccat [in spe]
32. *Item parvum volumen ij° fo. depositum
33. Item Pontificale ij° fo. tequam veniat
34. *Item Archidiaconus super Sextum ij° fo. [specia]lit[er] non est
35. Item liber Decretorum ij° fo. Ysidorus
36. Item liber Decretalium ij° fo. verus homo
37. *Item Apparatus Innocentii super Decretales ij° fo. proposuisti
38. *Item Judiciale Durandi ij° fo. sit moribus
39. *Item Archidiaconus super Sextum ij° fo. sponcione
40. *Item duo Codices unus ij° fo. codicis alius ij° fo. divine memorie
41. *Item duo parva volumina ij° fo. desuetudine et aliud Sci[enti]a est [divinarum]
42. *Item duo digesta vetera unum ij° fo. Istorum et aliud Scientie
43. *Item duo digesta nova unum ij° fo. opera et aliud presenti
44. *Item unum digestum inforciatum ij° fo. [qui de]ducta [impensa]
45. *Item lectura Johannis Fabri super Instituta ij° fo. et qui

25. Marcus Tullius Cicero, De Inventione.
28. Hegesippus, Historia de Bello Judaico.
31. St. Bernard, Sermo de Psalmo Qui Habitat (sermo prius, pars secunda).
32. The 'Parvum Volumen' of the Corpus Iuris Civilis comprised the Instituta, Tres Libri, Autenticum and Usus Feodorum.
34. The 'Archdeacon' is a common reference to Guido de Baysio.
38. Gulielmus Durandus, Speculum Judiciale.
40. Codex Justiniani.
42. The Digestum Vetus comprised Books 1–24, 2.
45. Johannes Fabre, In Quatuor Libros Institutionum Justiniani Lectura.

46. *Item parvum volumen ij° fo. solum humani
47. *Item ff. novum ij° fo. edificare
48. Item ff. novum ij° fo. renunciare
49. *Item ff. novum ij° fo. puelle
50. *Item Mandagod ij° fo. [in] quolibet [ecclesia]
51. *Item liber Sextus cum glosa Jo an ij° fo. multa
52. *Item ff. inforciatum ij° fo. est
53. *Item Codex ij° fo. [cum dei auxi]lio ad prosperum
54. *Item Decretale ij° fo. nec procedens
55. *Item ff. novum ij° fo. renunciare possit
56. *Item liber Sextus cum glosa Cardinalis ij° fo. Episcopum
57. Item parvum volumen ij° fo. liberorum procreatio
58. *Item Will[elm]us super Cle[mentinas] ij° fo. de q. d. a.
59. Item Codex ij° fo. pretorio
60. *Item ff. vetus ij° fo. [ex his dere]licto
61. Item ff. novum ij° fo. et ideo
62. *Item parvum volumen ij° fo. quia in terra
63. *Item Raymundus ij° fo. q. i. latorem
64. *Item ff. vetus ij° fo. et dilucide
65. Item Codex ij° fo. Augustus
66. *Item apparatus libri sexti ij° fo. Re periculoso
67. *Item Godefridus in Summa ij° fo. Romanus
68. *Item Rofridus ij° fo. si non distinctione
69. *Item Clementinii apparatu Jo an ij° fo. Apostolica
70. *Item Codex ij° fo. fori tue sublimitatis
71. Item ff. vetus ij° fo. ex primordiis
72. *Item ff. inforciatum ij° fo. ex mercede
73. *Item parvum volumen ij° fo. ex scripto
74. *Item ff. novum ij° fo. omnibus
75. Item Codex ij° fo. generalium
76. *Item Bartholus in papiro ij° fo. innominata [lectura]

50. Gulielmus de Mandagoto, Tractatus de Electione Novorum Praelatorum.
51. The glossator is Johannes Andreae.
56. The glossator, 'Cardinalis', is Johannes Monachus, Episcopus Meldensis.
58. Gulielmus de Monte Lauduno, Glosa super Clementinas. See the King's Hall list which gives the second folio as 'de q.d. prima (?)'. Could this refer in the text to 'dicere quod ars sum conceptus'?
63. Raymundus de Pennaforte, Summa.
66. By Gulielmus de Monte Lauduno: see King's Hall list.
67. Godefridus de Trano, Summa.
68. Rofredus Beneventani, Tractatus super Utraque Censura.
76. Bartholus de Saxoferrato.

77. *Item ff. inforciatum ijº fo. supprema [die]
78. Item liber decretalium ijº fo. sub[stanti]a
79. *Item Codex ijº fo. stent commissa
80. Item ff. novum ijº fo. noceret
81. *Item Instituta ijº fo. Jus civile
82. Item Codex ijº fo. ff
83. Item Decretales ijº fo. solum autem
84. Item Codex ijº fo. vir illustris
85. Item liber Sextus cum glosa Cardinalis ijº fo. scionibus
86. Item Cle[mentinae] ijº fo. ab aliquibus
87. Item Codex ijº fo. [Hermoge]niani atque [Theodosiani]
88. *Item ff. vetus ijº fo. quas diximus
89. Item Decretales ijº fo. nos autem
90. Item liber de observantiis Papae ijº fo. Cardinal'
91. Item ff. vetus ijº fo. temporis
92. Item Johannes de Blancisto ijº fo. nunciatorem
93. Item Repertorium Juris Civilis in papiro ijº fo. [?di]vino testatore
94. Item antiqua compilacio Decretalium ijº fo. ne pro defectu
95. *Item Repertorium super libello Institut' in papiro ijº fo. omnes homines
96. Item libellus Institut' ijº fo. conjunctio
97. *Item Repertorium super Codicem ijº fo. sonarum
98. *Item Valerius Maximus ijº fo. profecti salverunt
99. *Item Repertorium super ff. veterum et inforciatum ijº fo. poterit fieri
100. Item Quaestiones Bartholomei Brixeniensis ijº fo. primo dicuntur (et caret primo quaterno)
101. *Item Summa Raymundi ijº fo. consuetudine
102. *Item liber Tophicorum ijº fo. quia admirationes
103. *Item Magister Historiarum ijº fo. fieret
104. Item Catholican in papiro ijº fo. et Ysiderus

(There follows a list of jewels and vestments.)

92. Johannes de Blanasco, Super Titulum de Actionibus in Institutis, sect. quinto.
98. Valerius Maximus, Dictorum et Factorum Memorabilium libri novem.
102. Aristotle, Liber Topicorum.
103. That is, Petrus Comestor. The King's Hall list reads 'Historia Scolastica'.
104. Johannes Balbus, Summa quae vocantur Catholicon.

List of Works Cited

A. ORIGINAL AUTHORITIES

(i) *Unprinted. Manuscript and Record Sources*

British Museum:

MS. Cotton, Cleopatra E. II

Egerton Rolls, 8746, 8769, 8770

Lambeth Palace Library:

Register of Thomas Arundel, Archbishop of Canterbury, 1396–7, 1399–1414, 2 vols.

Lincoln Diocesan Register Office:

Register vii, Thomas Bek, Bishop of Lincoln, 1342–7

Registers xii and xiiB, John Buckingham, Bishop of Lincoln, 1363–98

Oxford University:

Magdalen College, Muniments, Hickling 81, 98, 105

Merton College, MSS. Coxe 68, 175

University College MS. Coxe 97

Worcester College MS. L.R.A. 6 (formerly Merton MS. Coxe 318)

Northamptonshire Record Office:

Griffin Cartulary I (uu)

Public Record Office:

C. 1 Early Chancery Proceedings

C. 81 Chancery Warrants

DL. Duchy of Lancaster

E. 28 Exchequer, Council and Privy Seal File

E. 101 King's Remembrancer, Various Accounts

E. 364 Lord Treasurer's Remembrancer, Enrolled Accounts

E. 403 Issue Rolls

SC. Special Collections

Somerset House:

Prerogative Court of Canterbury, Registers, Rouse; Marche; Luffenam

(ii) *Printed. Chronicles, Records, Contemporary Prose and Verse*

Abstract of Inquisitiones post mortem . . . Nottinghamshire 1350–1436, ed. K. S. S. Train (Thoroton Society Record ser., vol. xii, 1952)

Anglia Sacra, ed. H. Wharton, 2 vols. (London, 1691)

Anglo-Norman Letters and Petitions, ed. M. Dominica Legge (Anglo-Norman Text Soc., 1941)

Annales Ricardi Secundi et Henrici Quarti (1392–1406), ed. H. T. Riley in *Johannis de Trokelowe et Henrici de Blaneford Chronica et Annales* (R.S., 1866), pp. 155–424

The Anonimalle Chronicle, ed. V. H. Galbraith (Manchester, 1927)

The Antient Kalendars and Inventories of the Treasury of the Exchequer, ed. F. Palgrave, 3 vols. (London, 1836)

BAKER, GEOFFREY LE, *Chronicon (1303–1356)*, ed. E. M. Thompson (Oxford, 1889)

BEKYNTON, THOMAS, *Official Correspondence*, ed. G. Williams 2 vols. (R.S., 1872)

A Book of London English, 1384–1425, ed. R. W. Chambers and Marjorie Daunt (Oxford, 1931)

The Brut, ed. F. Brie, 2 vols. (E.E.T.S., 1908)

Calendar of Close Rolls, Edward III (14 vols.); Richard II (6 vols.); Henry IV (4 vols.); Henry V (2 vols.) (London, 1896–1932)

Calendar of Fine Rolls, vols. iv–viii (Edward III); ix–xi (Richard II) (London, 1913–29)

Calendar of Inquisitions Post Mortem, vol. xiii (London, 1954)

Calendar of Letter Books of the City of London, Letter Book E, ed. R. R. Sharpe (London, 1903)

Calendar of Papal Letters, ed. W. H. Bliss and J. A. Twemlow, vol. iv (London, 1902)

Calendar of Papal Petitions, 1342–1419, ed. W. H. Bliss, vol. i (London, 1896)

Calendar of Patent Rolls, Edward III (16 vols.); Richard II (6 vols.); Henry IV (4 vols.); Henry V (2 vols.) (London, 1891–1910)

Calendar of Plea and Memoranda Rolls of the City of London, 1323–1364, ed. A. H. Thomas (London, 1926)

Calendar of Select Pleas and Memoranda of the City of London . . ., 1381–1412, ed. A. H. Thomas (London, 1932)

Calendar of State Papers, Milan, 1385–1618, ed. A. B. Hinds (London, 1912)

Calendar of State Papers, Venetian, ed. Rawdon Brown, vol. i, (London, 1864)

Calendar of Wills proved and enrolled in the Court of Husting, London, pt. ii 1358–1688, ed. R. R. Sharpe (London, 1890)

CAPGRAVE, JOHN, *Liber de Illustribus Henricis*, trans. F. C. Hingeston (R.S., 1858)

—— *Chronicle of England*, ed. F. C. Hingeston (R.S., 1858)

Catalogue des rolles gascons, ed. T. Carte, vol. ii (London and Paris, 1743)

CHAUCER, G., *Canterbury Tales*, ed. J. M. Manly (London, 1929)

—— *Works*, ed. W. W. Skeat, 7 vols. (Oxford, 1894–7)

Chronicle of London, 1089–1483, ed. E. Tyrell and N. H. Nicolas (London, 1827)

Chronicles of the Reigns of Edward I and Edward II, ed. W. Stubbs, 2 vols. (R.S., 1882–3)

Chronicon Adae de Usk, ed. E. M. Thompson (London, 1904)

Chronicon Angliae (1328–88), ed. E. M. Thompson (R.S., 1874)

La Chronique d'Enguerrand de Monstrelet . . . 1400–1440, ed. L. Douët d'Arcq, 6 vols. (Société de l'histoire de France, 1857–62)

Chronique du religieux de Saint Denys, ed. M. L. Bellaguet (Paris, 1839)

CRETON, JEHAN, *Histoire du roy d'Angleterre Richard*, ed. J. Webb (London, 1819)

DESCHAMPS, EUSTACHE, *Œuvres complètes*, vol. iii, ed. Marquis de Queux de Saint-Hilaire and G. Raynaud (Paris, 1878–1903)

The Diplomatic Correspondence of Richard II, ed. E. Perroy (Roy. Hist. Soc., Camden, 3rd ser., xlviii, 1933)

DYMMOK, ROGER, *Liber*, ed. H. S. Cronin (London, 1922)

ELMHAM, THOMAS (Pseudo Elmham), *Vita et Gesta Henrici Quinti*, ed. T. Hearne (Oxford, 1727)

Epistolae Academicae Oxonienses, ed. H. Anstey (Oxford Historical Society, 1898)

Eulogium Historiarum sive Temporis Chronicon . . ., ed. F. S. Haydon, 3 vols. (R.S., 1858–63)

Expeditions to Prussia and the Holy Land made by Henry, Earl of Derby (afterwards King Henry IV) in 1390–1 and 1392–3 . . ., ed. L. Toulmin Smith (Camden Soc., new ser. lii, 1894)

'Extracts from the plea rolls of the reign of Edward II, A.D. 1307 to A.D. 1327', ed. Hon. G. Wrottesley in *Collections for a History of Staffordshire* (William Salt Arch. Soc., orig. ser., vol. x part i, 1889)

Feudal Aids, Inquisitions and Assessments relating to 1284–1431, 6 vols. (London, 1899–1920)

The Fifty earliest English Wills in the Court of Probate, 1387–1439, ed. F. J. Furnivall (Early Eng. Text Soc., lxxviii, 1882)

The First English Life of King Henry V, ed. C. L. Kingsford (Oxford, 1911)

FROISSART, JEAN, *Chroniques*, ed. K. de Lettenhove, 25 vols. in 26 (Brussels, 1867–77)

GASCOIGNE, THOMAS, *Loci e Libro Veritatum*, ed. J. E. T. Rogers (Oxford, 1881)

GIBBONS, A., *Early Lincoln Wills, 1280–1547* (Lincoln, 1888)

The Great Chronicle, ed. A. H. Thomas and I. D. Thornley (London, 1938)

HENRY, DUKE OF LANCASTER, *Le Livre de seyntz medicines*, ed. É. J. Arnould (Anglo-Norman Text Soc., 1940)

HIGDEN, RANULF, *Polychronicon* (to 1352, with a continuation to 1394), ed. J. R. Lumby, vols. viii, ix (R.S., 1882, 1886)

The Historical Collections of a Citizen of London, ed. J. Gairdner (Camden Soc., new ser., xvii, 1876)

HOCCLEVE, T., *Minor Poems*, ed. F. J. Furnivall and I. Gollancz, 2 vols. (E.E.T.S., extra ser., lxi, lxxiii, 1892, 1925)

Incerti Scriptoris Chronicon Angliae, ed. J. A. Giles (London, 1848)

Issues of the Exchequer (Henry III–Henry VI), ed. F. Devon (London, 1837)

John of Gaunt's Register (1372–76), ed. S. Armitage-Smith, 2 vols. (Roy. Hist. Soc., Camden 3rd ser., xx, xxi, 1911)

John of Gaunt's Register (1379–1383), ed. E. C. Lodge and R. Somerville, 2 vols. (Roy. Hist. Soc., Camden 3rd ser., lvi, lvii, 1937)

Joutes de saint Ingelbert, ed. J. Pichon (Paris, 1863)

KNIGHTON, HENRY, *Chronicon* (959–1366, with a continuation 1377–95), ed. J. R. Lumby, 2 vols. (R.S., 1889, 1895)

Monk of Evesham, *Vita Regis Ricardi II*, ed. T. Hearne (Oxford, 1729)

MURATORI, L. A., *Rerum Italicarum Scriptores*, 25 vols. (Milan, 1723–51)

NICHOLS, J., *Collections of all the Wills . . . of the Kings and Queens of England* (London, 1780)

Original Letters Illustrative of English History, ed. H. Ellis, 2nd ser., 4 vols. (London, 1827)

OTTERBOURNE, THOMAS, *Chronica Regum Angliae*, ed. T. Hearne (Oxford, 1732)

Parliamentary Writs, ed. F. Palgrave, vol. ii (1827–34)

Proceedings and Ordinances of the Privy Council of England, ed. Sir N. H. Nicolas, 7 vols. (London, 1834–7)

Register of Edward the Black Prince, ed. M. C. B. Dawes and H. C. Johnson, 4 vols. (London, 1930–3)

The Register of Henry Chichele, Archbishop of Canterbury, 1414–1443, ed. E. F. Jacob, 4 vols. (Oxford, 1943–7)

Registrum Johannis Trefnant, ed. W. W. Cape (Canterbury and York Soc., 1916)

Rotuli Parliamentorum, ed. J. Strachey and others, vol. ii, iii (London, 1767); *Index* (R.C., 1832)

Royal and Historical Letters, ed. F. C. Hingeston, vol. i (R.S., 1860)

RYMER, T., *Foedera*, 20 vols. (London, 1704, etc.); New Edn. (*1069–1383*) by A. Clarke, F. Holbrooke and J. Caley, 4 vols. in 7 pts. (R.C., 1816–69)

The St. Albans Chronicle, 1406–1420, ed. V. H. Galbraith (Oxford, 1937)

Sede Vacante Wills, ed. C. E. Woodruff (Kent Arch. Soc. records, vol. iii, 1914)

Select Documents of English Constitutional History, 1307–1485, ed. S. B. Chrimes and A. L. Brown (London, 1961)

Testamenta Eboracensia, ed. J. Raine, vol. i (Surtees Soc., 1836), iii (1864)

Testamenta Vetusta, ed. N. H. Nicolas (London, 1826)

Traison et mort de Richard II, ed. B. Williams (London, 1846)

WALSINGHAM, THOMAS, *Historia Anglicana (1272–1422)*, ed. H. T. Riley, 2 vols. (R.S., 1863–4)

Wills and Inventories, ed. J. Raine (Surtees Soc., (2) i, 1835)

WYCLIFFE, JOHN, *De Dominio Divino*, ed. R. L. Poole (London, 1890)

B. SECONDARY AUTHORITIES

ARMITAGE SMITH, S., *John of Gaunt* (London, 1904)

ASTON, MARGARET, *Thomas Arundel* (Oxford, 1967)

BAKER, G., *History and Antiquities of the County of Northampton*, 2 vols. (London, 1822–41)

BALDWIN, J. F., *The King's Council in England during the Middle Ages* (Oxford, 1913)

BARBER, M., 'John Norbury, *c.* 1350–1414, an Esquire of Henry IV', *E.H.R.*, 68 (1953), pp. 66–76

BARRON, C. M., 'The Tyranny of Richard II', *Bull. Inst. Hist. Res.*, 41 (1968), pp. 1–18

BEAN, J. M. W., 'Henry IV and the Percies', *History*, 44 (1959), pp. 212–27

BELLAMY, J. G., 'Appeal and Impeachment in the Good Parliament', *Bull. Inst. Hist. Res.*, 39 (1966), pp. 35–46

—— 'The Northern Rebellions in the Later Years of Richard II', *Bull. of the John Rylands Lib.*, 47 (1965), pp. 254–71

BELTZ, G. F., *Memorials of the Order of the Garter* (London, 1841)

BRIDGES, J., *History and Antiquities of Northamptonshire*, 2 vols. (Oxford, 1791)

British Museum, *Catalogue of MSS. Old, Royal and King's Collections*, ed. Sir G. F. Warner and H. R. Gilson, vol. ii (London, 1921)

BROWN, A. L., 'The Authorization of Letters under the Great Seal', *Bull. Inst. Hist. Res.*, 37 (1964), pp. 125–56

—— 'The Commons and the Council in the Reign of Henry IV', *E.H.R.*, 79 (1964), pp. 1–31

—— 'King's Councillors in Fifteenth Century England', *T.R.H.S.*, 5th ser., 19 (1969), pp. 95–118

—— *The Early History of the Clerkship of the Council* (Glasgow, 1969)

BRUSENDORFF, A., *The Chaucer Tradition* (Copenhagen, 1925)

CLARKE, M. V., 'Committees of Estates and the Deposition of Edward II', in *Historical Essays in Honour of James Tait*, ed. J. G. Edwards, V. H. Galbraith and E. F. Jacob (Manchester, 1933), pp. 27–45

—— *Fourteenth Century Studies*, edited by L. S. Sutherland and M. McKisack (Oxford, 1937)

COBBAN, ALAN B., *The King's Hall within the University of Cambridge in the Later Middle Ages* (Cambridge, 1969)

Complete Peerage, 2nd edition, ed. V. Gibbs and others, 12 vols. (London, 1910–59)

COOKE, A. H., *The Early History of Mapledurham* (Oxford, 1925)

COTTINEAU, L. H., *Répertoire topobibliographique des abbayes et prieurés*, 2 vols. (Mâcon, 1937)

COXE, H. O., *Catalogus Codicum MSS. qui in Collegiis . . . Oxoniensibus adservantur*, vol. i (Oxford, 1852)

DUGDALE, SIR W., *The Antiquities of Warwickshire* (London, 1730)

—— *The Baronage of England* (London, 1675–6)

EDWARDS, J. G., 'The Parliamentary Committee of 1398', *E.H.R.*, 40 (1925), pp. 321–33

EMDEN, A. B., *Biographical Register of the Members of the University of Cambridge to 1500* (Cambridge, 1963)

—— *Biographical Register of the University of Oxford to A.D. 1500*, 3 vols. (Oxford, 1957–9)

FARNHAM, G. E., and HAMILTON THOMPSON, A., 'The Manor, House and Chapel of Holt', *Trans. Leics. Arch. Soc.*, 13 pts. ii (1924), pp. 199–244

—— —— 'History of the Manor of Withcote', *Associated Architectural Socs. Reports and Papers*, 36 (1921), pp. 127–81

GIBSON, S. T., 'The Escheatries 1327–1341', *E.H.R.*, 35 (1921), pp. 218–25

GWYNN, A., *The English Austin Friars in the time of Wyclif* (Oxford, 1940)

HARRISS, G. L., 'Aids, Loans and Benevolences', *Historical Journal*, 6 (1963), pp. 3–19

HILL, J. H., *The History of Market Harborough* (Leicester, 1875)

JACOB, E. F., *The Fifteenth Century* (Oxford, 1961)

JONES, R. H., *The Royal Policy of Richard II* (Oxford, 1968)

KINGSFORD, C. L., *English Historical Literature in the Fifteenth Century* (Oxford, 1913)

—— *Henry V* (London, 1901)

KIRBY, J. L., 'Councils and Councillors of Henry IV, 1399–1413', *T.R.H.S.*, 5th series, 14 (1964), pp. 35–66

—— *Henry IV, King of England* (London, 1970)

KNOWLES, M. D., *The Religious Orders in England*, 2 vols. (Cambridge, 1948, 55)

—— and HADCOCK, R. N., *Medieval Religious Houses* (London, 1953)

LAPSLEY, G. T., *Crown, Community and Parliament*, ed. H. M. Cam and G. Barraclough (Oxford, 1951)

LE NEVE, J., *Fasti Ecclesiae Anglicanae*, new edn. Lincoln Diocese, ed. H. P. F. King (1962)

—— —— Northern Province, ed. B. Jones (1963)

—— —— St. Paul's, London, ed. Joyce M. Horn (1963)

Lewis, N. B., 'The "Continual Council" in the Early Years of Richard II, 1377–80', *E.H.R.*, 41 (1926), pp. 246–51

Lowes, J. L., 'The Prologue to the *Legend of Good Women* Considered in its Chronological Relations', *Publications of the Modern Language Association of America*, 20 (1905), pp. 749–864

Lyndwood, William, *Provinciale seu Constitutiones Angliae* (Oxford, 1679)

McFarlane, K. B., 'The Lancastrian Kings' in *The Cambridge Medieval History* vol. viii (Cambridge, 1936)

—— 'Bastard Feudalism' *Bull. Inst. Hist. Res.*, 20 (1945), pp. 161–80

—— 'Loans to the Lancastrian Kings: the Problem of Inducement', *Cambridge Historical Journal*, 9 (1947), pp. 51–68

—— *John Wycliffe and the Beginning of English Nonconformity* (London, 1953)

McKisack, M., *The Fourteenth Century, 1307–1399* (Oxford, 1959)

Madox, T., *Formulare Anglicanum* (London, 1702)

Matthew, D. J. A., *Norman Monasteries and their English Possessions* (Oxford, 1962)

Maxwell Lyte, H., *Historical Notes on the Use of the Great Seal in England* (London, 1926)

Medieval Libraries of Great Britain, ed. N. R. Ker, 2nd edition (London, 1964)

Members of Parliament, Returns, pt. 1 (Parliaments of England, 1213–1702) (London, 1878)

Mirot, L. and Déprez, E., 'Les Ambassades anglaises pendant la guerre de Cent Ans', *Bibl. de l'École des chartes*, 60 (1899), pp. 177–314

Moranvillé, H., 'Conférences entre la France et l'Angleterre 1388–93', *Bibl. de l'École des chartes*, 50 (1889), pp. 355–80

Myres, J. N. L., 'The Campaign of Radcot Bridge in December 1387', *E.H.R.*, 42 (1927), pp. 20–33

Nash, T., *Collections for the History of Worcestershire*, 2 vols. (London, 1781–2, 1799)

Nicolas, Sir N. H., *The Controversy between Sir Richard Scrope and Sir Robert Grosvenor*, 2 vols. (London, 1832)

Owst, G. R., *Preaching in Medieval England* (Cambridge, 1926)

—— *Literature and Pulpit in Medieval England*, 2nd edn. (Oxford, 1961)

Pantin, W. A., 'Medieval Treatise on Letter-Writing', *Bulletin of the John Rylands Library*, 13 (1929), pp. 359–64

Parliamentary Representation of the County of York 1258–1832, ed. A. Gooder, 2 vols. (Yorks. Arch. Soc. Record Ser. 91)

PERROY, É., *L'Angleterre et le grand schisme* (Paris, 1933)

—— *The Hundred Years War* (trans. D. C. Douglas, London, 1965)

PLUCKNETT, T. F. T., 'Chaucer's Escapade', *Law Quarterly Review*, 64 (1948), pp. 33–6

—— 'State Trials under Richard II', *T.R.H.S.*, 5th Series, 2 (1952), pp. 159–66

—— 'Impeachment and Attainder', *T.R.H.S.*, 5th Series, 3 (1953), pp. 145–60

POULSON, G., *History and Antiquities of the Seignory of Holderness*, 2 vols. (Hull, 1840–1)

POWELL, J. E. and WALLIS, K., *The House of Lords in the Middle Ages* (London, 1968)

Public Record Office Museum Catalogue (London, 1948)

Report . . . touching the Dignity of a Peer of the Realm, 5 vols. (London, 1820–9)

RICHARDSON, H. G., 'Heresy and the Lay Power under Richard II', *E.H.R.*, 51 (1936), pp. 1–28

RICKERT, E. ed., *Chaucer's World* (Oxford, 1948)

RICKERT, M., 'Thou Vache', *Modern Philology*, 11 (1913–14), pp. 209–25

ROGERS, A., 'Parliamentary Appeals of Treason in the Reign of Richard II', *American Journal of Legal History*, 8 (1964), pp. 95–124

—— 'The Political Crisis of 1401', *Nottingham Medieval Studies*, 12 (1968), pp. 85–96

—— 'Henry IV, the Commons and Taxation', *Medieval Studies*, 31 (1969), pp. 44–70

ROSKELL, J. S., 'William Stourton of Stourton', *Proc. Dorset Nat. Hist. and Arch. Soc.*, 82 (1960), pp. 155–66

RUSSELL, P. E., *The English Intervention in Spain and Portugal in the Time of Richard II* (Oxford, 1955)

SAYLE, C. E., 'King's Hall Library', *Cambridge Antiquarian Society Proceedings*, 24 (1923), pp. 54–76

SOMERVILLE, R., *Duchy of Lancaster*, vol. i (London, 1953)

STEEL, A., *Richard II* (Cambridge, 1941)

—— *The Receipt of the Exchequer, 1377–1485* (Cambridge, 1954)

STEVENSON, E. R., 'The Escheator', in *The English Government at Work, 1327–1336*, vol. ii, ed. W. A. Morris and J. R. Strayer (Med. Academy of America, 1947)

STOREY, R. L., 'The Wardens of the Marches towards Scotland, 1377–1489', *E.H.R.*, 72 (1957), pp. 594–603

STOW, J., *The Annales of England*, continued by E. Howes (London, 1631)

STUBBS, W., *Constitutional History of England*, 4th edn. (Oxford, 1890)

TAIT, J., 'Did Richard II murder the Duke of Gloucester?' in *Historical Essays by Members of Owen's College Manchester*, ed. T. F. Tout and James Tait (Manchester, 1907), pp. 193–216

TILLYARD, E. M. W., *Shakespeare's History Plays* (London, 1944)

TOUT, T. F., *Chapters in Medieval Administrative History*, 6 vols. (Manchester, 1920–1933)

TUCK, J. A., 'Richard II and the Border Magnates', *Northern History*, 3 (1968), pp. 27–52

TYLER, J. E., *Memoirs of the Life and Character of Henry V*, 2 vols. (London, 1838)

VALOIS, N., *La France et le grand schisme d'Occident*, vol. iii (Paris, 1896–1902)

WATTS, P. R., 'The Strange case of Geoffrey Chaucer and Cecilia Chaumpaigne', *Law Quarterly Review*, 63 (1947), pp. 491–515

WAUGH, W. T., 'The Lollard Knights', *Scottish Historical Review*, 11 (1913–14), pp. 55–92

WEDGWOOD, J. C., *History of Parliament, Biographies, 1439–1509* (London, 1936)

WEISS, R., 'Henry VI and the Library of All Souls College', *E.H.R.*, 57 (1942), pp. 102–5

WILKINS, H. J., *Was John Wycliffe a Negligent Pluralist?* (London, 1915)

WILKINSON, B., *Constitutional History of Medieval England*, ii (London, 1952)

—— 'The Deposition of Richard II and the Accession of Henry IV', *E.H.R.*, 54 (1939), pp. 215–39

WOLFFE, B. P., 'Acts of Resumption in Lancastrian Parliaments', *E.H.R.*, 73 (1958), pp. 584–93

WROTTESLEY, HON. G., *Crecy and Calais* (London, 1898)

—— 'Military Service performed by Staffordshire Tenants', *Collections for a History of Staffordshire* (William Salt Arch. Soc., orig. ser., vol. viii, part i, 1887)

WYLIE, J. H., *History of England under Henry the Fourth*, 4 vols. (London, 1884–98)

—— and WAUGH, W. T., *The Reign of Henry V*, 3 vols. (Cambridge, 1914–29)

Index